Arabs at Home and in the World

This volume brings together an interdisciplinary group of scholars from the United States, the Middle East, and North Africa, to discuss and critically analyze the intersection of gender and human rights laws as applied to individuals of Arab descent. It seeks to raise consciousness at the intersection of gender, identity, and human rights as it relates to Arabs at home and throughout the diaspora. The context of revolution and the destabilizing impact of armed conflicts in the region are used to critique and examine the utility of human rights law to address contemporary human rights issues through extralegal strategies. To this end, the volume seeks to inform, educate, persuade, and facilitate newer or less-heard perspectives related to gender and masculinities theories. It will provide readers with new ways of understanding gender and human rights and proposes forward-looking solutions to implementing human rights norms.

The goal of this book is to use the context of Arabs at home and throughout the diaspora to critique and examine the utility of human rights norms and laws to diminish human suffering with the goal of transforming the structural, social, and cultural conditions that impede access to human rights. This book will be of interest to a diverse audience of scholars, students, public policy researchers, lawyers, and the educated public interested in the fields of human rights law, international studies, gender politics, migration and diaspora, and Middle East politics.

Karla M. McKanders is a Clinical Professor at Vanderbilt University, School of Law in Nashville, Tennessee, USA.

Routledge Research in Human Rights Law

Comparative Executive Clemency
The Prerogative of Mercy in the Commonwealth
Andrew Novak

Social and Economic Rights in Theory and Practice
A Critical Assessment
Helena Alviar Garcia, Karl Klare, and Lucy A. Williams

Challenging Territoriality in Human Rights Law
Building Blocks for a Plural and Diverse Duty-Bearer Regime
Wouter Vandenhole

Care, Migration and Human Rights
Law and Practice
Siobhán Mullally

China's Human Rights Lawyers
Advocacy and Resistance
Eva Pils

Indigenous Peoples, Title to Territory, Rights and Resources
The Transformative Role of Free Prior and Informed Consent
Cathal M. Doyle

Arabs at Home and in the World
Human Rights, Gender Politics, and Identity
Edited by Karla M. McKanders

For more information about this series, please visit: www.routledge.com/Routledge-Research-in-Human-Rights-Law/book-series/HUMRIGHTSLAW

Arabs at Home and in the World

Human Rights, Gender Politics, and Identity

Edited by
Karla M. McKanders

Routledge
Taylor & Francis Group
LONDON AND NEW YORK

First published 2019
by Routledge

2 Park Square, Milton Park, Abingdon, Oxfordshire OX14 4RN
52 Vanderbilt Avenue, New York, NY 10017

Routledge is an imprint of the Taylor & Francis Group, an informa business

First issued in paperback 2020

British Library Cataloguing-in-Publication Data
A catalogue record for this book is available from the British Library

Library of Congress Cataloging-in-Publication Data
A catalog record has been requested for this book

ISBN: 978-1-138-57885-2 (hbk)
ISBN: 978-0-367-66262-2 (pbk)

Typeset in Galliard
by codeMantra

Contents

Foreword vii
ADRIEN K. WING

Introduction xi
KARLA M. McKANDERS

Acknowledgments xvii
List of contributors xix

PART I
Defining gender and human rights for Arabs at home and throughout the diaspora 1

1 **Hegemonic femininity and hijab as a human right** 3
LOUISE CAINKAR

2 **Palestine's accession to CEDAW: one step of the thousand-mile journey** 25
MUTAZ M. QAFISHEH

PART II
At home: Arab Spring, gender, and human rights 55

3 **The sources of public patriarchal authority in Morocco** 57
FATIMA SADIQI

4 **Media representations of Palestinian women: post-Arab Uprisings** 91
HALLA SHOAIBI

PART III
The Arab diaspora: gender, human rights, and migration 109

5 Theorizing sexual violence against men in the Middle East and North African region as gender-related persecution under refugee and asylum law 111
VALORIE K. VOJDIK

6 Gender, Islamophobia, and refugee exceptionalism 126
KARLA M. McKANDERS

7 Moroccan women migrants in Europe: a transformative experience 158
MOHA ENNAJI

Bibliography 179
Index 181

Foreword

Adrien K. Wing

I got involved in the Arab world because of love. It was not love of the region, an academic subject, or the Arabic language. I did not know anything about these things. It was love of a man, my then-boyfriend Enrico, that motivated me. In 1982, he was a brand-new doctor who volunteered to go into a war zone in Beirut, Lebanon. We were young and in love, and so I went with him. While he was busy treating patients, I assisted the overworked staff in many areas. While I was mainly an administrator, I did hands-on work as well. We were very short of nurses. So one of the tasks I ended up doing was helping out in the burn unit. Patients had been hit by phosphorous bombs, leading to very nasty burrowing injuries, including second- and third-degree burns. I will never forget holding on to a young boy as staff ripped dried gauze from his wounds. He writhed and screamed in horrific pain, "Mama, mama," and leaned into me for comfort. On that day, I became an Arab mother.

I often wonder what happened to that boy, especially since immediately after Rico and I left the area, a terrible massacre took place right where we had been working and living—the Sabra and Shatila Palestinian refugee camps of West Beirut. Countless men, women, and children were killed, including patients at our hospital.

My life changed forever as a result of that summer. Partly in memory of those whose fate I will never know, I was determined to rectify my ignorance and help educate others. For more than thirty-five years since then, as an international law professor, I have specialized in the Middle East and North Africa (MENA) region, including teaching a course I created entitled "Law in the Muslim World." I have conducted research, presented lectures, and authored dozens of publications. I have led many delegations and visited countries including Egypt, Israel, Indonesia, Jordan, Kuwait, Lebanon, Morocco, Palestine, Qatar, Sudan, Turkey, Tunisia, United Arab Emirates, Bosnia, and Kosovo. I have had the privilege of advising the founding fathers and mothers of three constitutions, including one in the MENA area—the Palestinian Basic Law. As a women's rights scholar, I have placed a special emphasis on Arab women's rights. In particular, as a critical race feminist scholar, I have been most interested in the intersections of gender, race/ethnicity, discrimination, and human rights focusing on law in the Muslim world.

On a personal level, one of my surrogate daughters is a Muslim who wears a hijab. In particular and in part because of my daughter's situation confronting Islamophobia, I have also always been involved in advocating for improving the treatment of Muslim women within the United States as well.

Given my long-term interests, I attended a relevant panel presentation at the Law and Society Conference in Mexico City during spring 2017. The event was entitled *The Impact of Gender, Identity, and Human Rights in Times of Conflict and Revolution for Arabs throughout the Diaspora*. The speakers were all notable scholars in the field of gender and human rights from the MENA as well as from the United States. They included Mutaz M. Qafisheh (Hebron University); Louise Cainkar (Marquette University); Karla McKanders (Vanderbilt University); Fatima Sadiqi (University of Fez); Halla Shoaibi (Birzeit University); Valorie K. Vojdik (University of Tennessee College of Law); and Moha Ennaji (Sidi Mohamed Ben Abdellah University). In particular, I had known one of the panelists, Dr. Cainkar, since 1982, and have read and admired her work throughout her career. The scholars came together in an International Research Collaborative to explore the impact of conflict upon gender inequalities and the limitations of, and possibilities for, enforcement of international human rights in the region and globally. The quality of their collective voices was very impressive.

I was subsequently delighted when the Law and Society Association panel chair and discussant, Professor Karla McKanders, whom I have known for a number of years, asked if I would do the foreword to the volume associated with the panel. As editor, McKanders has produced a highly significant and timely volume. Globally, we are at a potentially critical moment regarding the treatment of individuals of Arab descent. Many years past the broken promise of the Arab Spring, we are mired in the intersection of ongoing armed conflicts, dictatorial regimes, underemployed frustrated youth, and overwhelming migrations from some Muslim-majority countries. Women remain at the bottom in all the societies—educationally, economically, politically, legally, and culturally, while gay men continue to experience discrimination at the intersection of their religion and nationality in obtaining basic human rights and equality.

This volume utilizes diverse interdisciplinary perspectives of scholars whose work is grounded as academics with an activist perspective and connection with their communities of concern. The authors in this volume focus on the interconnections in the research in the following areas: (1) legal strategies to address the gendered impact of conflict and uprisings throughout the region; (2) the role of gender in secular and religious interpretations of the law in Islamic contexts in Morocco; (3) gender and inward and outward migration in the MENA region focusing on Morocco and the United States; (4) the discriminatory application of the Refugee Convention against male refugees in conceptualizing persecution and vulnerability; (5) women's role in the MENA revolution and gendered conceptions of justice; and (6) gender, family, and domestic violence laws in Morocco and Palestine.

The volume is particularly useful in utilizing examples that critique and examine the utility of human rights law to address contemporary issues through legal and extralegal strategies aimed at diminishing human suffering and helping to transform the structural, social, and cultural conditions that impede women's access to human rights. Each chapter is focused on examining the challenges in utilizing international law and human rights to advance human rights in the MENA region. The volume engages in activist- and solution-oriented discussion, which seeks to not only describe and analyze but also contemplate how systemic change in conflict and postconflict systems can protect and promote gender and human rights.

This anthology makes a powerful contribution to existing literature in several fields. It is wonderful for those who are like I was thirty-five years ago, lacking any knowledge of the issues in the MENA region. It is equally useful for those wanting more specialized information.

Introduction

Karla M. McKanders

The complexities of the uprisings, political conflicts, and wars in the Middle East and North Africa (MENA) have had a resounding impact on human rights on individuals of Arab descent:

> Much of the news reporting and analysis of the Middle East seems to lurch from one crisis to another on the basis of whatever crisis has the most visibility on a given day. Sometimes the focus is Yemen, other times it is ISIS, Assad, or terrorism outside the region.[1]

These events caused the world to experience an unprecedented increase in migration and refugee flows from the MENA region.[2] The increase was a result of the height of the Civil War in Syria and the proliferation of the Islamic State of Iraq and the Levant (ISIL or, in Arabic, *Daesh*). While the international community fixates on Arabs in the region and in the world, MENA scholars have been evaluating the challenges in governance, demographics, economics, religion, and social change and their impact on gender politics, human rights, and identity.

The primary purpose of this book is to present scholarship that sheds light on how gender and human rights are conceptualized in relation to individuals of Arab descent in contemporary national and international contexts. The authors' chapters explore three main areas of inquiry: how individuals of Arab descent's human rights are experienced based on their gender in relation to the implementation of human rights norms within a particular country and internationally, how the recent uprisings in the MENA affect the conceptualization of gender and human rights, and how gender affects migrants of Arab descent's experience of human rights in the Western countries to which they migrate and the reception of refugees from the region. The main theme connecting each of the chapters is how gender at the intersection of politics, legal systems, and institutions affects the application of human rights norms. Each author utilizes different forms of analysis from ethnographic studies to detailed analysis of existing legal norms to extract common themes.

This edited volume approaches gender, identity, and human rights as the orientation and policy strategy for diagnosing, countering, and preventing dehumanization and for promoting human dignity and justice. It is unique in that it utilizes both hegemonic femininity and masculinity and intersectionality frames to analyze and find solutions for sexual- and gender-based violence, as scholarly discussions often remain on women alone. "Gendered inequalities are also often not analyzed in relation to other social, economic and political inequalities, and the categories of 'men' and 'women' are often dealt with as if they were static and homogenous."[3] This volume provides a contemporary analysis at the intersection of gender, identity, and social structure, utilizing both feminist and masculinities theories to analyze how international human rights norms are applied.

This book utilizes contemporary issues of revolution, war, and violence in the MENA region as the context to assess the impact of these destabilizing factors on gender and human rights discourses. It builds upon existing international human rights frameworks and gender theories to discuss the intersection of religion, gender, and migration status, for individuals of Arab descent. The goal is to challenge gender hegemonies and binaries through critically engaging the relationship between gendered assaults and Islamophobia. This collection of scholarly research provides readers with new ways of understanding gender and human rights, and proposes forward-looking solutions to implementing human rights norms.

Gender politics and identity

The central theme of this book is how gender politics and identity interface to affect the realization of human rights broadly for individuals of Arab descent. Gender is a social construct, a process, and even a social institution that "creates and maintains socially significant differences between men and women, differences that naturalize social inequality between men and women."[4] The scholars utilize different frames to theorize how gender affects the implementation and enforcement of human rights. While most scholarship has focused on utilizing feminist theories to examine how men, patriarchy, and masculine characteristics define sources of power, domination, inequality, and subordination,[5] the authors of this book frame their analysis utilizing hegemonic theory to understanding cultural dominance as it operates in the particular cultural and societal context in which the implementation of human rights is understood[6] for Arabs in the diaspora and in countries throughout the MENA. Each chapter is distinct in that each author reflects on how maleness is "currently accepted" within the specific context in which they are writing.[7] This is important because while gender influences how human rights are recognized, this notion is highly contextual and cultural which is reflected in each author's analysis on how individuals of Arab descent are often afforded particular human rights based on their conformance to hegemonic notions of masculinity and femininity.

In this book, how individuals of Arab descent experience the implementation and realization of human rights is also the centering theme that is considered in relation to gender. The authors pay close attention to the multidimensional aspects that affect the realization of human rights, which requires simultaneously taking into account the interface between gender, sex, race, migration status, and national origin. This book is timely because international nongovernmental organizations, such as the United Nations (UN), have just begun recognizing the import of the intersectionality theory as an instrument to understand how human rights norms are implemented or rejected around the world. The UN recently addressed gender and peacekeeping on national and international levels, and Security Council Resolution 2106 included reference to male gender-based violence survivors.[8] Notably, the UN adopted intersectionality theory as a lens for analyzing the administration of human rights. International and human rights laws have been criticized for not incorporating an intersectionality framework into their policies. Intersectionality theory rejects the notion that issues surrounding discrimination should be categorized as singular issues.[9] The theory requires individuals to view issues through a multidimensional lens, simultaneously taking into account multiple identities.[10] The UN began incorporating intersectional discrimination into resolutions and "acknowledged that discrimination is understood as having multiple forms that combine to heighten the vulnerability of some women and girls to violence."[11] Education level, marital status, economic status, access to justice, race, religion, education level, social status, and sexual orientation present differences among women, and these differences will make some women more likely to be subjected to discrimination and/or violence.

Overview of book contents

Part I provides the context within which gendered norms operate in the realization of human rights for Arab individuals at home and throughout the diaspora. These chapters explore various intersectional and gender theoretical and analytical frameworks and place them in the context of family law in Palestine and the legal restrictions against and harassment of women wearing hijab in public spaces in the United States. The chapters in Part I explore human rights abuses against women of Arab descent utilizing the analytic lenses of hegemonic femininity, masculinity, and intersectionality. *Hegemonic Femininity and Hijab as a Human Right* (Chapter 1) analyzes the impact of wearing the hijab on the treatment of Muslim women. This chapter examines culturally specific social constructions of the feminine ideal in the United States in relation to the hegemonic masculinity to scrutinize what drives people to render women in hijabs as social deviants deserving of outcasting. The author posits that gender and sexuality theories help explain why women might attack other women, even, or maybe especially, if they consider themselves feminists, by demonstrating convincingly that persons who pose threats to dominant notions of heteronormative masculinity and femininity have historically faced verbal and physical sanctions from men and women who uphold them.

Palestine's Accession to CEDAW: One Step of the Thousand-Mile Journey (Chapter 2) examines the application of the primary human rights convention for the protection of women globally in Palestine—the Convention on the Elimination of All Forms of Discrimination against Women (CEDAW). This chapter looks at the application of CEDAW in Palestine and how it interfaces with family law (marriage age, divorce, alimony, polygamy, and inheritance), labor law and social security, criminal law, and political participation. Theoretically, this chapter relies on comparative jurisprudence and cases that exist in the Middle East region as it scrutinizes the legal apertures that comprise the main bodies charged with administering and applying CEDAW—the parliament, judiciary, the police, relevant ministries, and municipalities. Both chapters take into account the political, social, cultural, and religious contexts within the United States and Palestine that affect Arab women's human rights.

Part II focuses on gender and human rights in recent politically charged uprisings and revolutions. Specifically, this part addresses whether human rights laws are equipped to handle contemporary iterations of gender within the context of hegemonic gender norms. *The Sources of Public Patriarchal Authority in Morocco* (Chapter 3) conceptualizes patriarchy in North Africa as both private and public, with the latter regulating social change and law. This conceptualization is framed in the context of transformative events, such as the so-called Arab Uprisings and the rise to power of Islamists, and how these events have slowed down the implementation of the new Personal Status Codes or family laws. This chapter is juxtaposed to "Media Representations of Palestinian Women" which also places the Arab Uprisings at the center of its analysis on how the foreign media's fixation on Palestinian women's images in popular resistance and protests resulted in creating a distorted image of the reality of women's involvement. Similar to Chapter 3, *Media Representations of Palestinian Women: Post-Arab Uprisings* (Chapter 4) situates its legal analysis within the Palestinian context of the Post-Oslo Peace Accords to examine the following key questions: (1) Whether the distorted portrayal is new to the Palestinian context, or is it one that has been repeated within the Palestinian history at different times of the struggle? (2) Whether the backlash against these women Post-Oslo Accords different from previous historical moments, such as the First Intifada and the rise of Islamic Parties? (3) Whether the existence of social media create new "spaces" in which the impacts of the images were more profound? and (4) Whether the backlash (or the improvement?) was more significant or at least "felt" by the women. Both Chapters 3 and 4 in Part II enable the reader to understand country-specific contexts and examples in which gender and human rights affect societal change.

Part III addresses gender, migration, and human rights for Arabs globally. Current instabilities in the region have led to a surge in migration to the West, where emigrants face a tough transition on resettlement. It examines the application of human rights norms at the intersections of gender, race, nationality, religion, and culture for individuals of Arab descent. It contains three chapters that analyze the impact of destabilization in the MENA region, the resulting migration to countries outside the region, and legal responses to increased MENA migration in the West. Both *Theorizing Sexual Violence against Men in the Middle East and North African Region as Gender-Related Persecution Under*

Refugee and Asylum Law and *Gender, Islamophobia, and Refugee Exceptionalism* (Chapters 5 and 6) critically analyze the failure of human rights instruments to recognize violence against male refugees from the MENA region as it relates to gender-related persecution in the United States and in Western refugee resettlement programs. These chapters engage the reader in analyzing the invisibility of men and boys as victims of gender persecution by drawing on the experiences of men and boys in the MENA region.

These chapters uniquely contribute to a growing body of literature examining the effectiveness of the 1951 Refugee Convention in light of contemporary refugee flows, and broaden the legal and theoretical framework of refugee law to recognize the gendered nature of particular types of violence and persecution and exceptionalism directed at men and boys. These chapters analyze the relevant laws (of the UN and Western nations) and the interpretive guidelines, and relevant judicial opinions concerning claims for refugee protections for men from Muslim-majority countries. Drawing on masculinities theory, in Chapter 6, the author demonstrates how feminists and human rights advocates could conceptualize claims of male refugees as gender-based persecution. Furthermore, Chapter 6 engages in a comparative analysis of the gendered norms that pervade Western countries' refugee resettlement programs which exclude males from Muslim-majority countries. This chapter interrogates the increasing norm of stereotyping males from Muslim-majority countries as threatening terrorists from whom countries need protection rather than as refugees. This chapter examines how legal categories of vulnerability have been formulated in a manner to facilitate this population's exclusion from protection.

Contrastingly, *Moroccan Women Migration in Europe: A Transformative Experience* (Chapter 7) analyzes how the migration of Moroccan women to Europe is an experience that affects women's participation in economic development and, in turn, transmutes conventional family relations, gender roles, and rejection of restrictive social environment of their native land. In Part III, the authors focus on intersectionality theory, which underscores the interconnection of fields of domination—social class, political power, gender, religion, language, ethnicity, and education, and the resulting impact on migration and integration into countries to which migrants from the MENA are moving.

This edited volume is a forward-looking interdisciplinary and international book geared toward various audiences to engage readers in much-needed conversations regarding contemporary gender and human rights issues facing individuals of Arab descent. The authors hope that this book will catalyze more work as interdisciplinary scholars reconceptualize gender and identity in a manner that facilitates transformation of the structural, social, and cultural conditions that impede access to human rights. This book has used the context of Arabs at home and throughout the diaspora to critique and examine the utility of human rights norms and laws to diminish human suffering with the goal of transforming the structural, social, and cultural conditions that impede access to human rights.

Notes

1 Anthony H. Cordesman, "The [New-Old] Crises and Instability in the Middle East and North Africa in 2016," January 4, 2016, www.csis.org/analysis/new-old-crises-and-instability-middle-east-and-north-africa-2016.
2 Lucy Rodgers et al., "Syria: The Story of the Conflict," BBC News, March 11, 2016, www.bbc.com/news/world-middle-east-26116868.
3 Walter Korpi, "Faces of Inequality: Gender, Class, and Patterns of Inequalities in Different Types of Welfare States," *Journal of Social Politics Oxford* 7, no. 2 (July 1, 2000): 163, https://medicine.gu.se/digitalAssets/1453/1453386_127.full.pdf.
4 Valorie K. Vojdik, "Gender Outlaws: Challenging Masculinity in Traditionally Male Institutions," *Berkeley Journal of Gender, Law & Justice* 17 (2002): 68–120 [citing Cynthia Fuchs Epstein, "The Difference Model: Enforcement and Reinforcement of Women's Roles in the Law," in *Social Roles and Societal Institutions*, edited by Judith R. Blau and Norman Goodman (New Brunswick, NJ: Transaction Publishers, 1995), 53, 58–59 (1995)].
5 Nancy E. Dowd, "Masculinities and Feminist Legal Theory," *Masculinities and the Law* 1, no. 1 (2009).
6 R.W. Connell, Masculinities 78 (1995).
7 *Ibid.*, 77.
8 United Nations Security Council Resolution 2106, Adopted by the Security Council at its 6984th meeting, on 24 June 2013 available at http://undocs.org/en/S/RES/2106 (2013).
9 See generally, Kimberlé W. Crenshaw, "Demarginalizing the Intersection of Race and Sex: A Black Feminist Critique of Antidiscrimination Doctrine, Feminist Theory and Antiracist Politics," *University of Chicago Legal Forum* 1989, no. 1 (1989); Kimberlé W. Crenshaw, "Mapping the Margins: Intersectionality, Identity Politics, and Violence against Women of Color," *Stanford Law Review* 43 (1991): 1241.
10 *Ibid.*
11 Rashida Manjoo, Report of the Special Rapporteur on Violence against Women, Its Causes and Consequences, United Nations, General Assembly, Human Rights Council, May 2, 2011, http://undocs.org/en/S/RES/2106 (2013).

Acknowledgments

This volume was first conceived with the creation of an International Research Collaborative (IRC) on "The Politics of Gender, Identity, and Human Rights for Arabs at Home and in Diaspora" in conjunction with the Law and Society Association—an interdisciplinary scholarly organization committed to social, scientific, interpretive, and historical analyses of law across multiple social contexts. The Law and Society Association, along with the National Science Foundation, funded the IRC to bring together a collaborative group of international, multinational, and multidisciplinary scholars. Our IRC brought together international scholars from the Middle East and North Africa (MENA) and the United States to explore struggles at the intersection of gender and human rights for Arabs at home and around the world. The IRC collaboration focused on

- the impact of state patriarchal structures on women's human rights;
- the impact of media representations of women on political resistance movements;
- the effect of gendered representations on the experiences of migrants and refugees and on their legal protections;
- the commodification of vulnerable populations as vehicles to political ends.

The research collaborative first met at the 2016 Law and Society conference in New Orleans, Louisiana, where the authors presented on a panel titled "Gender Inequalities and Enforcement of Human Rights in the MENA Region." In May 2017, the following year, the IRC met at the International Law and Society conference in Mexico City, Mexico, where the authors participated in a roundtable discussion engaging the audience on the intersection of gender and human rights in the MENA region.

The roundtable discussions ultimately led to this edited volume where we critically analyze the politics of representation and how human rights discourse can capitalize on or challenge gender-based categorizations. While we started out as conference copresenters, in the process of working on this volume, we have created an edited volume that will make a significant contribution to existing law and society scholarship on gender and human rights for individuals of Arab descent.

During this project, it is evident that we share a passion for rigorous, engaged research that elevates international human rights instruments to live up to their promise of gender equality; to improve the legal institutions enforcing human rights norms; and to raise consciousness at the intersection of gender, identity, and human rights as it relates to Arabs at home and internationally.

I am indebted to friends and colleagues who have provided valuable insights along the way. Destiny Birdsong was very helpful in her editing since several of the authors are not native English speakers. Birdsong made many suggestions for clarity and coherent structure of the chapters. I would like to thank my research assistants Samuel Jolly and Jasmine Johnson for the countless hours verifying and formatting endnotes and the bibliography.

Most of all, I want to thank all of my family and friends who have provided me with endless support.

List of contributors

Dr. Louise Cainkar is a sociologist and Associate Professor of Social Welfare and Justice at Marquette University in Milwaukee. She has published dozens of articles and book chapters on Arab Americans and Muslim Americans. In 2004, she won a Carnegie Scholar Award for her work on the reinvigoration of Islamic practices among second-generation Muslim Americans. Her 2009 book, *Homeland Insecurity: The Arab American and Muslim American Experience after 9/11* (Russell Sage Foundation) was honored as Outstanding Adult Non-Fiction by the Arab American National Museum. She has also published on the impact of economic sanctions on women and children in Iraq and the forced migration of Palestinians and Jordanians from Kuwait. In addition to academic research and teaching, she was the founding director of the Palestine Human Rights Information Center. She was the past President of the Arab American Studies Association and treasurer of the Association for Middle East Women's Studies and is a founding board member of the Chicago-based Arab American Action Network.

Dr. Moha Ennaji is a Moroccan linguist, author, political critic, and civil society activist. He is a university professor in the Department of English Language and Literature at Sidi Mohamed Ben Abdellah University at Fes, where he has worked for over thirty years. In addition to his publications in linguistics, he has written on language, education, migration, politics, and gender, and is the author or editor of more than twenty books.

Karla M. McKanders is a Clinical Professor of Law and Director of the Immigration Practice Clinic at Vanderbilt University Law School where she also teaches immigration and refugee law. Her scholarship focuses on immigration federalism and international systems for processing refugees. Prior to joining Vanderbilt, she was an Associate Professor of Law at the University of Tennessee. From 2016 to 2017, she was visiting professor and supervising attorney at Howard University School of Law in the Civil Rights Clinic where she wrote Supreme Court amicus briefs on contemporary civil rights issues with her students and colleagues at the Law School. Her work has taken her around the country and abroad researching the efficacy of legal institutions charged with processing migrants and refugees. In 2011, she received a Fulbright

Award to lecture at the Mohammed V University in Rabat, Morocco. After her Fulbright, she played an instrumental role in establishing Morocco's first *pro bono* Refugee Legal Aid Clinic. She continues to collaborate with law professors and civil society in the Middle East and North Africa to address implementing clinical legal education and disparities in access to justice for immigrants and refugees. Her articles have been published in the *Harvard Journal on Racial and Ethnic Justice*, *University of Iowa's Gender Race and Social Justice Law Journal*, and *Catholic Law Review*, among other law journals. She has also been cited as an authority on immigration and refugee law in *Reuters*, *ABC News*, and *Al-Jazeera*.

Dr. Mutaz M. Qafisheh is the founding Dean and Associate Professor of International Law, College of Law and Political Science, Hebron University, Palestine. He received a PhD in International Relations and International Law from the Graduate Institute of International and Development Studies in Geneva, LLM from Birzeit University in Palestine, and BA in Law and Sharia from the University of Qatar. He previously worked at the United Nations Office of the High Commissioner for Human Rights in Geneva, Beirut, and Ramallah; served as legal advisor to Palestinian parliament; worked as regional director of Penal Reform International in the Middle East and North Africa region; and taught at Birzeit and Al-Quds universities. His academic expertise focuses on public international law, human rights, refugees, migration, citizenship, international criminal law, United Nations system, legislative drafting, women rights, juvenile justice, Islamic law, institutional and security reform, and clinical legal education (he has founded thirteen legal clinics). He advises a number of organizations, including Office of the United Nations High Commissioner for Human Rights, United Nations Development Programme, United States Agency for International Development, European Union, Palestine Liberation Organization, and international nongovernmental organizations. He is an attorney-at-law, and he has been a licensed member of the Palestine Bar Association since 2000. He has published six books and more than fifty peer-reviewed articles published in Oxford, Cambridge, The Hague, London, New York, and elsewhere.

Dr. Fatima Sadiqi is Professor of Linguistics and Gender Studies (University of Fez, Morocco). She has recently been elected President of the Association for Middle East Women's Studies. Her work focuses on women's issues in modern North Africa, the Middle East, and the Mediterranean world. She is the author and editor of numerous volumes and journal issues, including *Women, Gender and Language* (Brill 2003), "Women's Activism and the Public Sphere: Local/Global Linkages" (*Journal of Middle East Women's Studies* 2006), *Women and Knowledge in the Mediterranean* (Routledge 2013), *Moroccan Feminist Discourses* (Palgrave Macmillan 2014), and *Women's Movements in the Post-"Arab Spring" North Africa* (2016). She is also a public speaker in many languages and a member of many national and international scholarly and policy-making boards. She served as Director

General of the Fez Festival of Sacred Music and an Administrative Board Member of the Royal Institute of the Amazigh Language and Culture. Her work has been supported by numerous prestigious awards and fellowships from Harvard University, the Woodrow Wilson Center, the Rockefeller Foundation's Bellagio Center, and Fulbright. She currently serves on the Editorial Board of the *Oxford Encyclopedia of African Women's History.*

Dr. Halla Shoaibi teaches at Birzeit University. She received her S.J.D. at American University Washington College of Law, where she completed her dissertation on "Pregnant Women's Access to Health Care in the Occupied Palestinian Territory: Application under the Rome Statute of the International Criminal Court." Prior to joining Washington College of Law's S.J.D. program, she finished her LLM from the University of Michigan, Ann Arbor, and served as an Associate at Kamal & Associates—Attorneys and Counselors-at-Law in Ramallah, Palestine. Her LLM focused on the interaction of international criminal law and women's rights.

Valorie K. Vojdik is the Waller Landsen Distinguished Professor of Law at the University of Tennessee, College of Law, where she teaches gender and the law, federal courts, civil rights, and civil procedure. She served as Director of Clinical Programs from 2011 to 2015. She has also taught in the Advocacy and Appellate Clinics. Her teaching and research focuses on gender and the law, civil and human rights, and social institutions. Her recent scholarship addresses masculinities theory, international women's rights, and sexual violence against men and women in war. She has worked twice as a consultant to the European Union's Seyada Project to empower the Palestinian judicial system. She has also taught for the Open Society Foundation in its Network Scholarship Program since 2007.

Adrien K. Wing is Associate Dean for International and Comparative Law Programs and Bessie Dutton Murray Professor of Law at the University of Iowa College of Law, where she has worked since 1987. Additionally, she is Director of the University of Iowa Center for Human Rights. She presently teaches International Human Rights, Law in the Muslim World, Sex Discrimination Law, and Critical Race Theory. She also serves as the Director of the Law School's summer abroad program in France and is the former on-site Director for the London Law Consortium semester abroad program. She is, in addition, a member of the University of Iowa's interdisciplinary African studies faculty and North Africa/Middle East faculty groups. Author of more than 130 publications, she has placed a particular emphasis on women's rights in the Middle East, Africa, and the United States. She advised the founding mothers and fathers of the South African, Rwandan, and Palestinian constitutions.

Part I

Defining gender and human rights for Arabs at home and throughout the diaspora

1 Hegemonic femininity and hijab as a human right

Louise Cainkar

Bodies are never naked; they are always clothed with meaning. But the meanings may be reconstructed by imperialism and globalization.[1]

Introduction

Few body-covering (or uncovering) behaviors have brought on more debate, legal restrictions, court cases, harassment, and assaults in the West over the past twenty years than the act of women covering their bodies.[2] The scholarly literature on women's right (or non-right) to freely wear *hijab* (Muslim hair covering and modest clothing) tends to focus on nation-states, laws, and court cases in which her right to do so has been denied (e.g., France, Turkey, and Switzerland). Such bans are defended mainly on the premise that hijab violates national commitments to liberal secularism, although Christian rhythms and modes of comportment are the presumed norms hidden beneath this legislation.[3] This chapter analyzes Western responses to hijab from a wholly different, human rights approach. By examining social practices in a country, the United States, where the right to wear hijab is not legally denied, it locates public actions that seek to discipline, demonize, discriminate against, harass, or otherwise harm women wearing hijab as human rights abuses. Similar to legal bans, these social control actions block the full equality of Muslim women; deny them equal protection, freedom of movement, and human dignity; and deter their social advancement.

Utilizing the lens of the scholarly literature on hegemonic masculinity, femininity, and gender-based violence, this chapter argues that public attacks on women in hijab should be seen as acts of gender policing. Women in hijab defy dominant notions of femininity and suppress hegemonic heterosexual male access to their bodies. Furthermore, as is the case with Lesbian, Gay, Bisexual, Transgender, and Queer ("LGBTQ") persons, their gender nonconformity is challenged and policed by dominant groups—in many cases, white women. Citing intersectionality studies, this chapter argues that Western interpretations of hijab as an inferior practice that embodies women's submission rather than their agency are not objective but rather laden with white supremacy. This chapter further maintains that the disciplining of Muslim women in hijab enforces global hierarchies of power.

Data to support my arguments are drawn from two sociological studies I conducted over the past fifteen years. One study was conducted between 2003 and 2006, and includes interviews with more than one hundred adult Arab and Muslim women and men living across the Chicago metropolitan area, as well as secondary data from across the United States. In that study, I found that Muslim women reported being harassed, followed, or assaulted at more than twice the rate of men and that nearly all of the female victims wore hijab. I also found that a woman in hijab was present in more than half of the cases where men reported hate acts. These findings were surprising, given that the dominant narratives of the day were of the relationship between Islam, terrorism, and *male* bodies, and because male subject were often the focus of state antiterror policies. Additionally, I found that the majority of perpetrators were white women, which signaled to me that matters of culture and gender hegemonies, not terrorism, played key roles in these attacks.

The second study was conducted in 2011 and was composed of interviews with ninety-three Arab American teenagers living transnationally in Palestine, Jordan, and Yemen. When describing their younger years in the United States, I found more accounts of verbal and physical assaults on women in hijab—this time, observed by children and, once again, mainly perpetrated by white women.[4] In sum, these studies demonstrate that attacks on women in hijab must be explained intersectionally, at the juncture of anti-Muslim sentiments and intra-gender policing.

This chapter contains five sections. Section "Gender policing, gender-based violence, and hegemonic masculinity" reviews the literature on gender policing, gender-based violence, and hegemonic masculinity, and finds that the literature supports the proposition that Muslim women who cover their hair and bodies stand as affronts to hegemonic masculinity and femininity. Section "Race and women of color critique of dominant feminism's erasures" examines hijab through the lens of intersectionality theory and shows that from the standpoint of white supremacy, hijab is interpreted as being representative of an inferior religion and way of life. Section "Cartographies of gender performance" discusses how the hijab can racialize women's bodies and act as a form of cultural racism, as well as the ways in which attacks on women in hijab in changing social contexts are related to global hierarchies of masculinities. Section "Changes in domestic climate: 2008 to present" examines the experiences of women wearing hijab in the United States who were subject to hate incidents between 2001 and the present. This section focuses on two sociological studies I conducted over the past fifteen years and on more recent media stories related to hate crimes perpetrated against Muslim women, noting similarities and differences between post 9/11 hate acts and more recent ones. Section "International human rights and its instrument's failure to address attacks on Muslim women in hijab as gender-based violence" analyzes how international human rights and its instrumentalities have failed to recognize and address attacks on Muslim women in hijab as gender-based violence.

Whether through law or acts of social control, Muslim women who wear hijab are placed into socially subordinate and vulnerable positions. In the context of the United States, known to be a highly religious nation,[5] which is significantly different from Europe, hostile actions against women in hijab are viewed as violations of religious freedom; when recorded as hate crimes, they are labeled anti-Muslim attacks. However, when viewed from the perspective of "gender policing" and gender-based violence, the difference between legal bans and social control through harassment, disciplining, and violence withers away, taking on a symmetry in meaning and outcome; as such, the secular versus religious context loses some of its meaning. In both contexts, women who do not conform to grounded notions of hegemonic femininity—gender performances that satisfy the desires and gaze of hegemonic masculinity or, in the case of the gender-based hate crimes I outline here, hegemonic femininity—they are disciplined: one legally and one extralegally.

Gender policing, gender-based violence, and hegemonic masculinity

According to anthropologist Sally Merry, gender policing is accomplished through narratives and actions that stigmatize and punish "people who fail to conform to normative expectations of male or female appearance."[6] Such persons face an "environment of danger and threat" and "high levels of violence," usually delivered by strangers.[7] In Merry's treatment of the topic, discussions of gender policing center on performances of gender that do not conform to heteronormativity, thereby posing a threat to hegemonic masculinity, "the culturally idealized form of masculine character (in a given historical setting)."[8] The foundation of hegemonic masculinity is the taken-for-granted right to experience heterosexual desire, which is built upon binary notions of male–female difference and the complementary character of femininity and masculinity.[9] Assaults on persons who defy these norms are considered acts of gender-based violence.[10] Muslim women who cover their hair and bodies stand as affronts to hegemonic masculinity and femininity. Their gender embodiment practices physically and symbolically refuse hegemonic men their claimed right to heterosexual desire by denying them gazing rights and their sense of free access to women. Therefore, it seems logical to consider the impediments placed upon, the harassment of, and the assaults perpetrated on women who cover their bodies and hair as punishments for gender nonconformity, in the same light as gender practices that violate heteronormativity.

As expressed in hegemonic femininity, the feminine ideal is a culturally specific social construction produced in relation to the hegemonic masculine. In American culture, this ideal is racialized as white, sexualized as heteronormative, aged as young, and tempered as submissive to male desires. Female compliance with this hegemonic masculinity is demonstrated through the embodiment of "emphasized femininity"[11]: desired body shapes that are tightly or scantily clad, thus emphasizing biologically female body parts, fair skin, made-up faces, long and visibly straight hair, and the appearance of active hormones. The high social importance of these bodily traits cannot be denied; there is a vast, multibillion dollar industry geared toward helping women and girls attain them. Indeed, when not naturally bequeathed, these physical traits can be realized through a range of commercial products and services, including weight loss and weight gain products, health club memberships, plastic surgery, liposuction, Botox, wigs, hair pieces, hair straighteners, wrinkle removers, concealer creams, push-up bras, and butt pads. Interestingly, Octavio Romero has called these bodily enhancements the "American woman's burqa."[12] Similarly, there is a vast conforming clothing market for female sizes 2–14 (with less availability for larger sizes) and a complimentary market of shoes designed with emphasized femininity in mind.

By refusing to "embody the relationship between masculinity and femininity demanded by gender hegemony," self-covering women in hijab are practicing a form of "pariah femininity."[13] They contaminate the accepted relationship between masculinity and femininity, and challenge hegemonic male dominance as it is understood in the United States and much of the West. The historical record is clear: persons who challenge hegemonic gender constructions are vulnerable to harassment, bullying, social ostracization, and physical attacks by those who conform to them. Merry argues, "From a performative perspective, doing violence is a way of doing gender."[14] As noted above, this sanctioning is usually demonstrated in the literature by the ways in which persons posing threats to heteronormativity have been harassed, faced discrimination, and been subjected to physical violence.[15] The narratives I present below demonstrate that such actions have also been taken against Muslim women in hijab. They are harassed, spat on, followed, and called "aliens" who need to leave the United States. The American Civil Liberties Union (ACLU), a U.S. organization that defends individual rights under the Constitution, reports that women in hijab have been "fired from jobs, denied access to public places, and otherwise discriminated against because they wear hijab."[16] Both Muslim men and women understand that wearing hijab is an act that places women at risk of assault and even murder.

I propose that these experiences of Muslim women in hijab are mainly about performing gender and not backlash for acts of terrorism, and while racialized bodies and anti-Muslim sentiments clearly play a role, as I discuss below, they take place at the intersection with hegemonic femininity, which is already constituted to render them inferior. I argue that these hostilities are about gender performance, not only because it makes sense theoretically but also because of what my study data say when the contexts of harassment and the deployed narratives are analyzed. First, the data illustrate that women in hijab were not random victims of persons with anti-Muslim sentiments; women were specifically targeted, since these encounters largely occurred in places with plenty of visible Muslim men to target. Second, most of the perpetrators were white women, the women with the most to gain from defending the feminine ideal. Third, most of the harassment occurred in majority-white areas, where whites are culturally hegemonic. Finally, Muslim women and men recognized that hijab made women vulnerable in public spaces and that surrendering hijab offered freedom of movement, even if their raced bodies were still visibly recognizable as brown-skinned, presumed Muslim

Arab women. These actions were largely women-on-women encounters—more precisely, encounters between white women and Muslim women who cover their bodies and hair. Race or religion alone mattered less than the fact of the material cover—that is, the clothing that violates hegemonic femininity.

Race and women of color critique of dominant feminism's erasures

Dominant Western feminist discourses have emerged from the position of white privilege and centered patriarchy as the primary obstacle to women's freedom. These Western feminist discourses infer that "all women suffer the same oppression simply because we are women."[17] Critiques of this approach's reduction of all women's experiences to those of white middle-class women, and its obliviousness to the ways in which patriarchy intersects with racism—from Sojourner Truth's "Ain't I a Woman" through the Combahee River Collective's "A Black Feminist Statement"; Angela Davis' *Women, Race and Class*; Moraga and Anzaldúa's *This Bridge Called My Back*; Hazel Carby's "White Women, Listen! Black Feminism and the Boundaries of Sisterhood"; and bell hooks' *Feminist Theory: From Margin to Center*—eventually broke through into mainstream gender theory in the form of intersectionality, a theoretical framework stipulating that gender, race, and class oppression should be understood as multiple and simultaneous. These feminist women of color pointed out that patriarchy is not their sole struggle; that racism is violent; that women of color experience racism differently than men of color; and, most critical to this argument, that their womanhood has been cast as inferior by white women. As scholar Hazel V. Carby wrote, "History has constructed our sexuality and our femininity as deviating from those qualities with which white women, as the prize objects of the Western world, have been endowed."[18] It took another decade for "gender and all forms of discrimination, particularly racism, racial discrimination, xenophobia, and related intolerance" to be elevated to a main conference theme at the United Nations (U.N.) Commission on the Status of Women (Commission), despite its being a global forum.[19] At this meeting, the Commission recognized "the crucial importance of taking account of the intersectionality of gender-based and other forms of discrimination."[20]

Submission to patriarchy is precisely how wearing hijab is interpreted, whether by proponents of legal hijab bans or by assailants on women who wear it.[21] The hijab-clothed body is interpreted in only one way: as a symbol of subservience to men that is symptomatic of an inferior culture—for example, Islamic gender oppression. As Razack's analysis of the cultural policing of Muslim communities in Europe under the guise of gender equality finds, "the Muslim woman's body is used to articulate European superiority."[22] Noticeably, absent from these framings of hijab by external onlookers are the voices of Muslim women, as well as any notion that they make their own decisions and possess their own agency.[23]

The meanings of hijab to the women who deploy it are irrelevant in these constructions, because its role as a "material prison" is understood to be totally disabling to women: physically, affectively, psychically, and intellectually.[24] The veiled body, according to Al-Saji, is "over-determined as an 'oppressed' body [...] Oppression is taken to belong to the materiality of the veil itself, molding the veiled body in ways that exclude its subjectivity or agency."[25] Ali-Saji argues that this overdetermination simultaneously casts veiling as static, essentialized, and homogeneous, just as Islam is represented as stagnant and inferior compared to the dynamic and diverse formations of modernity. In this way, she argues, veiled women are racialized, with the veil taking the place of skin color as the site of difference and determinism. This racialization not only imagines Muslim women in hijab as passive victims but "de-subjectifies" them; it "excludes their multiple subjectivities, reducing the complex meanings and enactments of their veiling to Islamic oppression."[26] From this perspective, unveiling is "the sole means not only to freedom but to subject-formation."[27]

Audre Lorde's spirited rebuke to white radical lesbian feminist Mary Daly's 1973 book *Gyn/ecology* charged Daly with "dismissing the heritage" of non-European women and "denying the real connections that exist between all of us."[28] According to Lorde, Daly's mentioning of "non-white women and our herstories [...] only as decorations, or examples of female victimization" denies "the fountain of non-European female strength and power," and ignores "how the tools of patriarchy are used by women without awareness against each other."[29] When we are dismissed, argues Lorde, "it encourages our murderers."[30] More than forty years have passed since Lorde spoke those words, yet little has changed. Today, Muslim women are among the main casualties of both terrorism and the war on terror, dying at rates far greater than any women living in the West.[31] Yet their lives and deaths remain invisible to persons whose thinking is impaired by racial privilege and whose feminism acts like imperialism.[32] For example, the invisibilities and rendered silence of Muslim women gave traction to the Bush Administration's call for the invasion of Afghanistan in order to save them, with total disregard for the devastating impacts of war on women. How does one account for these layers upon layers of silencing and ignorance?

Cartographies of gender performance

While we should not assume that racialization of the hijab works in the same way for Black, Brown, East Asian, Latino, and White women,[33] as Al-Saji argues, hijab does racialize women's bodies, and opposition to women in hijab is a form of cultural racism.[34] Indeed, most of the perpetrators of attacks on them in the United States have been white, and so too are most of those who defend hijab banning in Europe. Cultural racism is a compelling explanation; yet an analysis of the narratives cast upon Muslim women in hijab suggests that a larger global dimension is also at play. As Connell notes, "The racial hierarchies of colonialism have been reasserted in new contexts, including the politics of the metropole."[35] In the United States, the narratives shouted at Muslim women are those of ostracization. As demonstrated below, they suggest that Muslim women should not be permitted to perform gender in the ways they choose "here" in the United States. Instead, they should "go back to where they came from." There is no intention to save or civilize them; there is no humanitarian mission lurking in the background. Such comments, made to both U.S.- and foreign-born Muslim women, indicate that hijab codes the covered body as foreign and out of place. In essence, if Muslim women want to perform gender in a covered way, they should do it over *there*, paired up with Muslim masculinities, in their lower position on the global "hierarchy of masculinities."[36] By doing so, they take their rightful place in the imperial world order, in locations where both men and women are subordinated to Western hegemony, dying in large numbers in its wake. Connecting the subordination of Muslim women who cover to the concept of empire squares with the racialization of Arabs and Muslims in the United States, which emerged not from classical white supremacy or settler colonialism but from essentializing narratives deployed to support U.S. global military policies.[37] This difference in genesis may explain why, rather than cultural assimilation, expulsion to places "where war, assassination through drone strikes, extensive surveillance, indefinite detention, and other such practices are presented as the only means by which to keep the 'barbarians' at bay" is the stated goal.[38] These ostracizing messages are not those of feminist solidarity but those of undisguised imperial feminism.[39] Race, class, and global relationships such as colonialism and imperialism—as well as a host of other human inequalities—matter to gender policing because they intersect in particular ways with gender hegemonies. It is not possible to understand the subordination of Muslim women in hijab outside of these hierarchies of power.

Attacks on women in hijab in changing social contexts

If we look closely at the five or so years that followed the 9/11 attacks, we find an immediate period of intensified hate crimes across the nation, contextualized within a much longer period of government national security policy implementation that targeted Arab and Muslim men.[40] My post-9/11 study of the Chicago metropolitan area found that area-wide acts of hate diminished after about six months, became concentrated in white neighborhoods with large Arab Muslim populations, and mainly focused on women in hijab. A gendered pattern emerged, in which the government's focus was on Arab and Muslim men as "potential terrorists," while public harassment, largely perpetrated by white women, targeted Muslim women in hijab. To this day, women in hijab remain vulnerable to harassment, assault, and even murder; yet it is important to recognize that the social context for all Muslims in the United States has changed and worsened over the past ten years. While many scholars refer to the intervening years since 9/11 as the "post-9/11 era," such a broad characterization of this time span is somewhat messy; it attributes blame for everything harmful that has occurred to Muslims since 9/11 on Muslims and the 9/11 attacks. Rather, it is important to recognize that Arabs and Muslims were held collectively responsible for the 9/11 attacks due to preexisting racism, not due to the attacks alone,[41] as well as the more recent harmful contributions of the financially endowed and highly organized domestic Islamophobia movement.

This movement, which began to gain wide social traction around 2008, during the presidential campaign of Barack Obama, casts Islam and Muslims as threats to American culture and democracy.[42] Proponents of the movement asserted that Muslims are engaging in a "civilization jihad" that needs to be taken seriously. During the 2008 election cycle, the movement actively demonized presidential candidate Obama as a closet Muslim, and even sent the anti-Islam DVD *Obsession* to voters in swing districts.[43] During the 2010 election cycle, the movement was even more visible, with nationwide anti-Sharia campaigns, the "Ground Zero mosque" protest, "Stop Islamization of America" bus ads, and Florida preacher Terry Jones' threat to burn the Qur'an on camera.[44] These activities were all given extensive coverage in mainstream media and significantly worsened conditions for Muslims in the United States. A study by the Institute for Social Policy and Understanding reported spikes in Islamophobic sentiments in 2008 and 2012, showing that upsurges were connected to election campaigns and had "nothing to do with terror."[45] A 2012 report in *Mother Jones* documented a "sharp uptick in anti-Islamic sentiment" during the 2010 midterm elections.[46] The Council on American-Islamic Relations and the University of California, Berkeley, reported that between 2008 and 2013, "more than $200 million was spent towards promoting fear and hatred of Muslims in the United States."[47] These Islamophobic trends in U.S. society were leveraged by the 2015–2016 presidential campaign of Donald Trump, who repeatedly demeaned Muslims, among other subordinate groups.[48] According to the Southern Poverty Law Center (SPLC), a U.S.-based organization specializing in civil rights and public interest litigation, in its hate monitor report, the number of anti-Muslim hate groups rose from 5 in 2010 to 34 in 2015 and 101 in 2016. As a result, hate crimes against all groups increased by 7% in 2015 but by 67% for Muslims during the same time period.[49] In sum, the Islamophobia movement, its adoption by the Trump campaign, and its institutionalization by his administration has rendered American Muslim public safety even more tenuous than in the years immediately after 9/11. These changes have little to do with the 9/11 attacks, except when they are cited to justify anti-Muslim activities.

Cultural sniping against Muslim women in hijab

In my post-9/11 study, women reported experiencing hate acts at a rate more than double that of men. Sixty-five percent (30/46) of women interviewed in the study reported personally experiencing physical or verbal hate acts, compared to 30% of men (17/56). A majority of these experiences occurred in the majority-white southwestern suburbs, where Arabs and Muslims comprised a rapidly increasing population. Arab Muslim women were also much more likely than Arab Muslim men to say they felt unsafe in certain places: 83% of women and 45% of men said that there were certain places they felt unsafe. When men and women described these threatening places, another gender difference appeared.

Women mentioned places in more local spaces, such as their own neighborhoods, ethnic shopping districts, mosques, parks, and suburban shopping malls. Men, on the other hand, mentioned these places as well as airports and rural areas—places connected to travel.

A woman wearing hijab was present in more than 90% of the hate incidents reported by Arab Muslim women, signaling its key role in these incidents. Sixty percent of women who reported experiencing hate acts were wearing hijab when the incidents occurred, and an additional 30% were in the company of women wearing hijab.[50] In addition, more than half of the men who reported experiencing hate acts were in the company of women wearing hijab when the incidents occurred. Furthermore, 55% of study respondents identified women wearing hijab as the most affected (in any way) by post-9/11 events. Women wearing hijab were more likely than other women and men to be spat at, experience road rage, have items thrown at their cars, be followed by strangers, be subjected to hateful language, and report home vandalism and sieges. Below, I provide a sample of interview quotes to describe conditions experienced by women in hijab, as well as the ways in which the women deployed U.S. American flags in an attempt to preempt hate incidents.

While Arabs, Muslims, and women in hijab had hateful experiences before the 9/11 attacks, their safety significantly declined after 9/11 with women in hijab as the main targets. One Arab American woman, who says she has chosen not to wear hijab for now, described it as follows:

> I was insulted even before 9/11. They used to call us "camel jockeys" or the "hijab" and make fun of us. After 9/11, it got worse and it's still going on. It's mostly women with the hijab who are being attacked verbally.

Hate incidents initially occurred across the Chicago metropolitan area.[51] The following incident took place within weeks of the 9/11 attacks near a university campus just west of downtown Chicago. One Arab Muslim woman, who experienced the threat of vehicular assault, reported a new sense of fear attached to wearing hijab. Prior to the attacks, she had not experienced this fear. She relayed,

> Literally, I could not leave my apartment because I was scared to leave and lived in fear. For the first time in my life, I was fearful for my life. When I did go out, I would have things thrown at my car, remarks made. People who used to be friendly with me were not so friendly. Some of them may not have said anything directly to me but were standoffish now. And I understand, because I think I'm a reminder of what happened that day. Before, I would walk around and nobody ever said anything to me, but, immediately thereafter, especially the couple of days after 9/11, I would be screamed at, yelled at, "go back to your country." It was just a very scary time in my life. I actually had a bottle thrown at my car [...] One time, I was crossing the street here at Paulina and a man who was driving came to a stop sign and was slowing down. Then I started crossing because I thought he was coming to a full stop. He pressed on the accelerator and I retracted from

> crossing the street. He yelled out of his car, "you terrorist" [...] To be honest, I have friends who have considered and have actually taken off their hijab just because they were fearful of their lives. I didn't come to that point where I would consider ripping it off, but I can see why some women did.

The relationship between public safety (or lack thereof) and wearing hijab was so highly interconnected that Arab Muslim women who did not wear hijab believed that their lack of hijab was the source of their safety. I asked one woman, "Do you feel safe shopping?" to which she responded, "Because I don't wear hijab, yes."

Inside the city of Chicago, where Arabs, Latinos, and African Americans share public space, Muslim women in hijab were not assaulted and felt safer overall. As one woman noted,

> Actually I feel safer in this community than going to 87th and Roberts Road (southwest suburbs) where it's all Arab. Actually, I don't at all feel safe there. It's such a target place. Here I feel comfortable when I was up 64th Street. It's a mixed neighborhood and it's kind of like my own place.

Her observations point toward a safe space in connection with other groups subjected to subordination in the United States.

Contrastingly, white majority southwest suburban malls and supermarkets were places where Muslim women's rights to walk freely were challenged, often accompanied by narratives of outcasting. Muslim women in hijab were cast as foreign and told to go home, even though a large proportion of them were born in the United States. The southwest suburban Arab Muslim woman quoted below reveals her understanding of how many white American women interpret the relationship between being American and wearing hijab, where one negates the other. When a flag, the symbol of being American, was denied to the American-born woman wearing hijab, she removed her hijab and purchased a flag, taking actions that support a specific hegemonic concept of an American woman:

> One of my friends was wearing a scarf, but not anymore. Her neighbor put small flags at all of the houses (on the block) and my friend asked her, "Why you didn't put flags in front of our house?" She said, "Because you are Muslim." My friend said, "No, I was born here, my husband was in the army," and she went out and bought a big flag. A lot of women who wore the scarf stopped. They were afraid someone would attack them.

Other women continued to wear hijab and leave the house, but their husbands took on some of their usual public tasks. As one woman remarked,

> I have another friend who insisted that his wife take off her hijab and she refused. She kept going out but he was worried about her. He would do lots of the errands that she used to do because he was worried.

Aware that they did not have freedom of movement, women in hijab exercised more caution about where they went: "Forest preserves and parks were definitely out," said one woman. "Places where soccer moms go were places I would not go." The perceived danger of moving in public spaces—even those generally presumed safe, such as places "soccer moms" would go—provoked heart-wrenching challenges to women's commitment to their religious beliefs. "We have begun to feel less secure than before," noted one woman. "And because I wear a veil, I have been living in a conflict: I have been confused about what to do. Should I take off the veil? Keep it on? What to do? If I keep it on, I might endanger myself, and if I take it off I would endanger my faith. I have been living in fear and anxiety."

Aware that the hijab was bringing on assaults, some women were encouraged not to wear one: "My husband told me to take it, the hijab, off. I said 'No. I am wearing it for my religion. If I'm not bothering anyone, no one should bother me.'" Women in hijab were clearly central targets of post-9/11 popular backlash. What I argue here, and below, is that by locating the perpetrators and the spaces that characterize these events, we find larger gendered global hierarchies and hegemonies at play, in addition to anti-Muslim sentiments.

Youth observations of harassment of their mothers and sisters

In 2011, I interviewed ninety-three transnational Arab American youth who were attending high school in their parent's homelands: Palestine, Jordan, and Yemen. Among many other questions, I asked about their memories of life in the United States. Some did not have extensive memories because they left the United States at a very young age (between five and seven). Yet, although most of them missed living in the United States (and especially missed the friends and family still living there), slightly more than half of them reported experiencing incidents of hate connected to being Arab or Muslim in the United States. Most of the hate incidents involved encounters at school, where they were bullied and called names by other kids, sometimes got into fights, or were insulted by teachers. However, when the encounters took place outside of school, they were nearly always about subtle and not so subtle hostilities directed toward their hijab-wearing mothers and sisters. Most of the young women interviewed felt that the hate incidents prompted their move to Palestine, Jordan, and Yemen.

As with the study above, these encounters tended to occur in majority-white areas. Below are hate incidents some of the youth recalled during their time in the United States, which further my argument that wearing hijab, while not legally denied, subjects women and their children to discipline, demonization, discrimination, harassment, and other human rights abuses.

Miriam (a pseudonym) who lived in a majority-white neighborhood in Atlanta, Georgia, recalled this experience at a mall:

> Oh, I remember this one time we were at the mall and there was a woman with her little toddler. And so, we were walking past her and I was with

> my mom and sister, both. My sister used to wear the hijab, but she took it off. But back then she was wearing it. So, me and her and my mom were walking and she was coming toward us, and then she literally went to the other side and then went back after she passed us. So, it's kinda like that kind of stuff.

This is one of the subtle forms of bias and discrimination tied to the freedom of wearing hijab which prompted Miriam's sister's decision to move the family to Palestine. Mariam recounted that

> She got kind of really depressed [in Atlanta] because she was wearing hijab and she just did not feel accepted at all in the university; she felt like she was being bullied [... and] she did not feel secure.

Miriam also said that her mother faced stares at her school: "My mom wears the hijab so it's like when she [came] to the parent-teacher meetings, all eyes [were] on us."

Inas, another young Muslim American, lived in a majority-white neighborhood in Boston. She recalled that her mother had repeated bad experiences while working in the neighborhood public school:

> Yeah, at my mom's work. She used to work at this school, and, you know ... the normal stuff [...] "why do you wear the hijab?," "What is Islam?," and, and [...] what else? [...] She used to come every day with her story. (L: Were people trying to learn or were they being nasty?) I: Mm, some were like that, but some didn't want to learn.

In addition to experiencing comments on their family members' decisions to wear a hijab, young girls wearing hijab also faced harassment. Saif from Albuquerque, New Mexico, said, "People would harass my sisters, cause they wear the hijab." Diana, who lived in Ohio, Georgia, and Florida before moving to Palestine, came to understand that if she wore hijab in the United States, she would be made fun of and not fit in. She stated,

> Like if I were in America I would not be able to wear this [hijab]. I will be afraid that I wouldn't fit in. But here I can be who I am and can wear this and no one will make fun of me.

Dalal summed it up another way; people were nice to them in Roanoke because her mom did not wear hijab:

> In Roanoke, we were the only Muslims in my neighborhood. But everybody was very nice to us, and I think because you know when you first see us we don't look like a typical Arab family, you know. My mom, actually, she doesn't wear the scarf.

The interviews with the young women reveal both a derivative bias toward them for their female relative's decisions to wear a hijab and also direct hate incidents evincing an extralegal, societal bias that adversely affected their daily lives and prompted their relocation to Muslim majority countries.

2015–2016: hate crimes perpetrated against Muslim women

The SPLC's hate watch blog further substantiates the interviews conducted in my study. SPLC's hate crimes tracker documents hate incidents broadly across the United States.[52] This section focuses on the more recent hate crimes perpetrated against Muslim women from SPLC hate watch and other incidents compiled through news media outlets. [53]

The SPLC and news information recounted below, while valuable, lacks the rich detail of qualitative research data, including the demographic context in which these attacks are occurring. Without the demographic context, these incidents appear simply as anti-Muslim hate crimes, bearing no relationship to gender policing; in addition, some are not considered hate crimes by the police. The SPLC narratives present the contrasting argument that Muslim women are assaulted because they are more visible than Muslim men, which discounts that gender has meaning—an interpretation I challenge throughout this chapter. In U.S. American society, bodies are raced, and brown male bodies, assumed to be associated with Islam, are also hypervisible. This fact is evident in a wide range of behaviors, such as extra security checks at airports, forced removals from airplanes, and more recent murders of brown-skinned men presumed to be Muslim. The recent uptick in anti-Muslim hate crimes and the expansion of their victims (as discussed above) certainly signal the entrenchment of anti-Muslim attitudes against men and women. However, there still exists a trend of gender policing of Muslim women in hijab performed by white women in public spaces across the country.

Asma Jama was smashed in the face with a beer mug at a Coon Rapids, Minnesota, Applebee's restaurant on October 30, 2015, by a white woman who told her to speak English. The cut required seventeen facial stitches. Jama is "a Muslim woman who forgave her assailant during sentencing. Jama, who wears a hijab and speaks English as well as Swahili, told her attacker that she didn't harbor 'any ill feelings' for the 2015 attack that left her scarred."[54]

Two Muslim-American women in hijab were physically assaulted and harassed on August 11, 2016, in a Chicago neighborhood. Suzanne Damra reported that a (white) woman followed her and her mother as they walked to their car just after daybreak, spitting at them and shouting anti-Muslim slurs. Captured on cellphone video, the assailant tried to open the car's locked doors and then broke the car's side view mirror. The woman can be heard shouting at the women terrified in the car: "You're ISIS [expletive redacted]. You're ISIS [expletive redacted].' Damra said it was at least the fifth time she and her mother had been accosted by the same woman."[55] They blamed the political climate created by Donald Trump for the attack.

Two Muslim women pushing their babies in strollers in Brooklyn, New York, on September 14, 2016, were punched in the face by a (white) woman attacker who also tried to pull their hijabs off. The attacker hurled Islamophobic insults such as "'Get the fuck out of America, bastards.' The perpetrator was charged with a misdemeanor hate crime."[56]

On November 11, 2016, a child left an anonymous hate note for a Gwinnett County high school Muslim teacher, Mairah Teli.[57] The note contained statements telling her that "her Muslim headscarf 'isn't allowed anymore,'" and stating, "Why don't you tie it around your neck & hang yourself with it."[58] The note ended with the word "America" along with a drawing of the American flag.[59] Teli feels that the note was a direct response to Donald Trump's victory in the presidential race. In response to the hate note, Teli stated, "As a Muslim, I wear a headscarf as a practice of my faith. I want to share this to raise awareness about the reality and climate of our community. Spreading hate isn't going to 'make America great again.'"[60] At the time of the incident, the gender, race, and social context of the child who wrote the note was unspecified.[61]

How do we understand these recent attacks on women in hijab? Is the hijab still a central element in them or are they more broadly anti-Muslim attacks? Do they continue to bear the marks of gender policing? Societal changes brought on by the Islamophobia movement have shifted and expanded the patterns of hate attacks, including increased attacks on Muslim institutions and on men, as well as more males perpetrating attacks on Muslim women. Evidence from attacks on men shows that anti-Muslim attacks on men are coded by race thinking: certain types of brown skin mark a man as Muslim. If the same racial thinking is applied to women, we should expect attacks on brown women whether or not they wear hijab, but there is little evidence of that. This chapter argues that hijab marks a woman's body as Muslim and, in doing so, increases her visibility and the certainty, in the eye of the observer, that she is willfully submissive to Muslim men and, therefore, out of place in the West. Yet, because "bodies are always clothed with meaning,"[62] non-hijab wearing brown women must symbolize something else: women who are free from the yoke of supposed Muslim male oppression. This interpretation protects the non-hijab wearing brown woman from anti-Muslim, gender policing attacks, though not from other forms of racialized attack. When the essentialized, de-subjectified, and agency-less Muslim woman is symbolically and discursively cast out, the superiority of white, Western culture and its version of proper womanhood is reinforced. Indeed, an intersection with anti-foreigner nativism is also evidenced in some of these attacks; as noted above, it is not always an either/or.

In sum, the presence or absence of hijab is central to attacks on Muslim women because it defines who she is and which "side" of civilization she is on in the eye of the perpetrator. Assaults and harassment of women in hijab are anti-Muslim acts, but they are also acts of hegemonic gender policing, and gender-based violence. This fact would be clearer if data collectors disaggregated attacks on women from broader anti-Muslim hate crime reporting, just as the International Gay and Lesbian Human Rights Commission has called for not assuming heterosexuality in the reporting of crimes against women.[63]

International human rights and its instruments failure to address attacks on Muslim women in hijabs as gender-based violence

Before concluding, it is important to examine the history of human rights discourse with regard to women in order to understand why it has so far failed to consider attacks on Muslim women in hijab as gender-based violence. Promoting the equality and advancement of women were the primary concerns of the 1979 Convention on the Elimination of All Forms of Discrimination against Women (CEDAW), the international human rights document focused on women's rights.[64] When CEDAW was formulated, gender equity and empowerment were its concerns; however, gender-based violence was never mentioned. Its main thrust was to obligate state signatories to take measures that insured the "equality of men and women, of human rights, and fundamental freedoms in the political, economic, social, cultural, civil or any other field."[65] Specific rights mentioned in CEDAW concern areas such as maternity, child rearing, trafficking and prostitution, nationality, education, public life, work, elections, health care, loans and credit, movement, marriage, the special problems faced by rural women, and "prejudices and customs based on the idea of the inferiority or the superiority of one sex or on stereotyped roles for men and women."[66]

As a remedy to the omission of gender-based violence, the Committee on the Elimination of Discrimination against Women, which was formed in 1981 as the U.N. body that oversees CEDAW, issued a statement in 1992 identifying gender-based violence as a form of discrimination and called upon states to eliminate it in both its governmental and public forms. In addition, the U.N. Commission on the Status of Women, formed in 1946 as part of the Economic and Social Council, issued a Declaration on the Elimination of Violence against Women that was adopted by the U.N. General Assembly in 1993.[67]

This document addressed physical, psychological, and sexual violence perpetrated against women and considered gender-based violence a human rights violation tied to discrimination and inequality that impedes women's advancement. It considered violence against women "a manifestation of *historically unequal power relations between men and women*, which have led to domination over and discrimination against women by men and to the prevention of the full advancement of women."[68] Violence against women, it argues, "is one of the crucial social mechanisms by which women are forced into a subordinate position compared with men." The Preamble to Article 4 specifically states, "States should condemn violence against women and should not invoke any custom, tradition or religious consideration to avoid their obligations with respect to its elimination." In all of these iterations, gender-based hierarchies are the source of concern and oppression, and the male/female binary is central. Yet headscarf bans and attacks on women in hijab are about both racial and gender hierarchies. They flow from ideological constructions that privilege a specific form of femininity and sexuality, a preferred performance of gender, and derive from specific customs, traditions, and religious considerations attached to whiteness and Western Christian culture.

The 2001 meeting of the Commission on the Status of Women elevated "gender and all forms of discrimination, in particular racism, racial discrimination, xenophobia, and related intolerance" to main conference themes.[69] Meeting documents noted "the crucial importance of taking account of the intersectionality of gender-based and other forms of discrimination."[70] Racism not only affects women and men differently, they also experience racism in very different ways.[71] A paper delivered by Philomena Essed at this meeting noted, "European common sense considers African women generally as promiscuous, Asian women as passive and exotic, and women in Islamic cultures as super-exploited. Anti-Islam sentiments are manifest in the demonizing of Islamic cultures as super-sexists ...." Essed also noted, "Ideological constructions of racially specific femininity and sexuality shape the standard of womanhood and female beauty as a measure of (middle class) whiteness."[72]

These statements highlight the racialized perceptions of Muslim and other non-white women by dominant whites, and recognize that ideological constructions shape standards of ideal womanhood and beauty. Their hegemonic status attached to white privilege is what gives them power, for example, the power to enact headscarf and burqa/niqab bans. Missing from the analysis, however, is recognition that *historically unequal power relations between the West and the Global South* are driven by race, and hegemonic notions of femininity and womanhood are products of these relations. Interpretations of the symbols of Muslim womanhood as inferior are authorized and given power in a specific set of global relationships that also authorize their repression.[73]

In sum, racism/racialization, hegemonic notions of femininity, white privilege, and empire are interrelated, and all reveal themselves in attacks on women in hijab. In the United States, attacks on Muslim women in hijab expose these intersections in that they are largely carried out by whites, accompanied by language of casting out, an expression of power and global dominance, and given support through dominant narratives about Muslims as a global threat. The struggle for recognition that attacks on women in hijab are acts of gender policing should be waged in parallel with the struggle for recognition that hegemonic notions of femininity also drive violence against lesbian, bisexual, and transgender women.

Conclusion

In much of the West, women in hijab lack unfettered freedom of movement, face harassment and job discrimination, and must cope with fear. The particular character of their ostracization makes a specific statement: you are not welcome here. In the United States, assaults on women in hijab are not only anti-Muslim but also gender-based acts of cultural sniping taken to shore up the boundaries of American womanhood. Harassments, rude behavior, assaults, vehicular pursuits, and murder are belligerent acts of aggression, asserting that American femininity precludes hijab. Understanding that attacks on women in hijab are motivated solely by religious bias fails to look deeply at the data. If states have an obligation to protect gender nonconforming persons from violence, then this obligation should apply in all of its manifestations.

Notes

1 Robert Connell, "Globalization, Imperialism, and Masculinities," in *Handbook of Studies on Men & Masculinities*, edited by Michael Kimmel, Jeff Hearn, and Robert Connell (Thousand Oaks, CA: Sage, 2004), 82.
2 See the timeline published by the *Guardian*; however, the ban in Turkey, which is not listed here, is the oldest one: see Matthew Weaver, "Burqa Bans, Headscarves and Veils: A Timeline of Legislation in the West," *The Guardian*, March 14, 2017, www.theguardian.com/world/2017/mar/14/headscarves-and-muslim-veil-ban-debate-timeline.
3 Norma Moruzzi, "A Problem with Headscarves," *Political Theory* 22, no. 4 (1994): 653–672.
4 Names used in reporting research data are fictional to respect the privacy of the individuals.
5 Robert Putnam and David E. Campbell, *American Grace: How Religion Divides and Unites Us* (New York: Simon and Schuster, 2010).
6 Sally Merry, *Gender Violence: A Cultural Perspective* (Oxford: John Wiley & Sons, 2009), 7–8.
7 *Ibid.*, 8.
8 Robert Connell, *The Men and the Boys* (Berkeley: University of California, 2000), 69.
9 Robert Connell, *Masculinities* (Berkeley: University of California Press, 1995); Michael Kimmel, Jeff Hearn, and Robert Connell, *Handbook of Studies on Men & Masculinities* (Thousand Oaks, CA: Sage, 2004).
10 Merry, *Gender Violence.*
11 Robert Connell, *Masculinities* (Berkeley: University of California Press, 1995).
12 Octavio Romero, "The American Burqa Industry," *SFGate*, December 30, 2002, www.sfgate.com/opinion/openforum/article/The-American-burqa-industry-2742319.php.
13 Mimi Schippers, "Recovering the Feminine Other: Masculinity, Femininity, and Gender Hegemony," *Theory and Society* 36 (2007): 95, www.doi.org/10.1007/s11186-007-9022-4.
14 Merry, *Gender Violence*, 11.
15 Gregory Herek, Jeanine C. Cogan, and J. Roy Gillis, "Victim Experiences in Hate Crimes Based on Sexual Orientation," *Journal of Social Issues* 58, no. 2 (2002): 319–339; Doug Meyer, "Interpreting and Experiencing Anti-Queer Violence: Race, Class, and Gender Differences among LGBT Hate Crime Victims," *Race, Gender & Class* 15, no. 3–4 (2008): 262–282.
16 See ACLU, "Discrimination against Muslim Women—Fact Sheet," ACLU, www.aclu.org/other/discrimination-against-muslim-women-fact-sheet#9; see also "Types of Workplace Discrimination Experienced by Muslim Women Wearing Hijab," Women Working with Immigrant Women, http://atwork.settlement.org/downloads/atwork/Accommodating_Hijab_Types_Discrimination.pdf.
17 Audre Lorde, "An Open Letter to Mary Daly," in *This Bridge Called My Back: Writings by Radical Women of Color*, edited by Cherrie Moraga and Gloria Anzaldúa (New York: Kitchen Table Press, 1981), 94–97.
18 Hazel Carby, "White Woman Listen! Black Feminism and the Boundaries of Sisterhood," in *The Empire Strikes Back: Race and Racism in 70's Britain*, edited by Center for Contemporary Cultural Studies (London: Hutchinson & Co., 1982), 110.
19 The UN Commission on the Status of Women, Agenda Item 4(b), Forty-Fifth Session (March 6–16, 2001), www.un.org/womenwatch/daw/csw/racesummary.htm.
20 *Ibid.*
21 Lila Abu-Lughod, *Do Muslim Women Need Saving?* (Cambridge, MA: Harvard University Press, 2013); Alia Al-Saji, "The Racialization of Muslim Veils: A Philosophical Analysis," *Philosophy and Social Criticism* 36, no. 8 (October 2010): 875–902, doi:10.1177/0191453710375589; Norma Moruzzi, "A Problem with Headscarves."

22 Sherene H. Razack, "Imperiled Muslim Women, Dangerous Muslim Men and Civilized Europeans: Legal and Social Responses to Forced Marriages," *Feminist Legal Studies* 12 (2004): 168.
23 Al-Saji notes that only two Muslim women were interviewed in Stasi Commission hearings, established to consider the relationship between *laicite'* and *hijab*, and these were conducted near the end of the process when the report had been largely written.
24 Al-Saji, "Racialization of Muslim Veils," 891.
25 *Ibid.*
26 *Ibid.*
27 *Ibid.*, 892.
28 Lorde, "An Open Letter to Mary Daly," 95.
29 *Ibid.*, 95–96.
30 *Ibid.*, 96.
31 See, for example, Physicians for Social Responsibility (U.S. American affiliate), Physicians for Global Survival (Canadian affiliate), and International Physicians for the Prevention of Nuclear War, *Body Count: Casualty Figures after 10 Years of the "War on Terror". Iraq, Afghanistan, Pakistan* (Washington, DC, Berlin, Ottawa, 2015).
32 Chandra Mohanty, "Under Western Eyes: Feminist Scholarship and Colonial Discourses," *Feminist Review* 30, no. 1 (1988): 61–88, doi:10.1057/fr.1988.42.
33 For example, Su'ad Abdul Khabeer, *Muslim Cool* (New York: NYU Press, 2016).
34 Al-Saji, "Racialization of Muslim Veils."
35 Robert Connell, "Globalization, Imperialism, and Masculinities," 82.
36 Connell, *The Men and the Boys*, 48.
37 Louise Cainkar, "Fluid Terror Threat: A Genealogy of the Racialization of Arab, Muslim, and South Asian Americans," *Amerasia Journal* 44, no. 1 (2018): 27–60.
38 Deepa Kumar, "Imperialist Feminism," *International Socialist Review* 102 (Fall 2016), http://isreview.org/issue/102/imperialist-feminism.
39 Mohanty, "Under Western Eyes."
40 Louise Cainkar, *Homeland Insecurity: The Arab American and Muslim American Experience After 9/11* (New York: Russell Sage Foundation Press, 2009).
41 *Ibid.*
42 Wajahat Ali et al., *Fear, Inc.* (Washington, DC: Center for American Progress, 2011).
43 For example, on a Sunday before the 2008 presidential election, every copy of the *Milwaukee Journal Sentinel* contained a copy of this DVD.
44 John Feffer, "Islamophobia and the 2010 Election: Though Obama's Policies on Islam and the Middle East Differ Little from his Republican Challengers, the Right Still Claims He is Pro-Islamic," *Mother Jones*, March 29, 2012, www.motherjones.com/politics/2012/03/republican-obama-is-muslim-islamophobia/2/.
45 Alejandro Beutel and Saeed Khan, "Manufacturing Bigotry: A State-By-State Legislative Effort to Pushback against 2050 by Targeting Muslims and Other Minorities," November 10, 2014, www.ispu.org/manufacturing-bigotry-community-brief/.
46 John Feffer, "Islamophobia and the 2010 Election."
47 Council on American-Islamic Relations and the University of California, Berkeley Center for Race and Gender, "Confronting Fear: Islamophobia and its Impact in the United States," 2016, www.islamophobia.org/images/ConfrontingFear/Final-Report.pdf.
48 Louise Cainkar, "Constructing and Containing the 'Muslim Threat' Through Immigration and Refugee Policies: An Analysis of Donald Trump's Words and Actions," Paper presentation, The Workshop on Religion and Migration, Arizona State University, Center for the Study of Religion and Conflict, April 28, 2017.
49 Azadeh Ansari, "FBI: Hate Crimes Spike, Most Sharply Against Muslims," *CNN*, November 15, 2016, www.cnn.com/2016/11/14/us/fbi-hate-crime-report-muslims/.
50 Women wearing hijab constituted 46% of the female sample.

51 Cainkar, *Homeland Insecurity*.
52 Hate Watch, Southern Poverty Law Center, a blog that monitors and exposes the activities of the American radical right, accessed on May 10, 2018, www.splcenter.org/hatewatch?gclid=Cj0KCQjw28_XBRDhARIsAEk21FgyP6E25ZT0X0atOsWcZqLMHkH51rklyy3gBnVFcubl4NDxKTrIswcaAuvtEALw_wcB (last).
53 Note: In many of these cases, the larger context is unknown; for example, sometimes, the gender or "race" of perpetrators is unknown. These absences make deeper analysis difficult.
54 Watch her forgiveness: www.youtube.com/watch?v=uUt2tK1dSP4&feature=youtu.be; watch her report on the assault: www.youtube.com/watch?v=0jUZaYPzL58; see also, Doualy Xaykaothao, "Woman Who Attacked Somali Agrees to Assault Charge," Minnesota Public Radio, October 17, 2016, www.mprnews.org/story/2016/10/17/asma-jama-applebees-somali-victim-attacker-pleads-guilty.
55 Phil Rogers, "Cellphone Footage Captures Alleged Assault of Chicago Muslim Women," *NBC Chicago*, August 14, 2016, www.nbcchicago.com/news/local/alleged-assault-chicago-muslim-women-hate-crime-390039261.html.
56 *Ibid.*
57 Kristine Phillips, "A Muslim Teacher Receives An Anonymous Note About Her Headscarf: 'Hang yourself with it,'" November 12, 2016, www.washingtonpost.com/news/post-nation/wp/2016/11/12/a-muslim-teacher-receives-an-anonymous-note-about-her-headscarf-hang-yourself-with-it/?noredirect=on&utm_term=.698e10864fa8.
58 *Ibid.*
59 *Ibid.*
60 *Ibid.*
61 *Ibid.*
62 Robert Connell, "Globalization, Imperialism, and Masculinities."
63 Susana T. Fried and Alex Teixeira, "International Gay and Lesbian Human Rights Commission Input Memo to the UN," accessed on April 26, 2018, www.un.org/womenwatch/daw/vaw/ngocontribute/International%20Gay%20and%20Lesbian%20Human%20Rights%20Commission.pdf.
64 "Convention on the Elimination of All Forms of Discrimination against Women," United Nations Entity for Gender Equality and the Empowerment of Women, www.un.org/womenwatch/daw/cedaw/.
65 *Ibid.*
66 *Ibid.*
67 Merry, *Gender Violence*.
68 "Declaration on the Elimination of Violence against Women," United Nations General Assembly, December 20, 1993, www.un.org/documents/ga/res/48/a48r104.htm.
69 The Commission on the Status of Women, Forty-fifth Session (March 6–16, 2001), Agenda Item 4 (b), www.un.org/womenwatch/daw/csw/racesummary.htm.
70 *Ibid.*
71 *Ibid.*
72 *Ibid.*
73 Talal Asad, *Genealogies of Religion: Disciplines and Reasons of Power in Christianity and Islam* (Baltimore, MD: The Johns Hopkins University Press, 1993).

Bibliography

Abdul Khabeer, Su'ad. *Muslim Cool*. New York: NYU Press, 2016.

Abu-Lughod, Lila. *Do Muslim Women Need Saving?* Cambridge, MA: Harvard University Press, 2013.

Al-Saji, Alia. "The Racialization of Muslim Veils: A Philosophical Analysis." *Philosophy and Social Criticism* 36, no. 8 (October 2010): 875–902. doi:10.1177/0191453710375589.

Ali, Wajahat, Eli Clifton, Matthew Duss, Lee Fang, Scott Keyes, and Faiz Shakir. *Fear, Inc.* Washington, DC: Center for American Progress, 2011.

Ansari, Azadeh. "FBI: Hate Crimes Spike, Most Sharply Against Muslims." *CNN*, November 15, 2016. www.cnn.com/2016/11/14/us/fbi-hate-crime-report-muslims/.

Asad, Talal. *Genealogies of Religion: Disciplines and Reasons of Power in Christianity and Islam*. Baltimore, MD: The Johns Hopkins University Press, 1993.

Beutel, Alejandro, and Saeed Khan. "Manufacturing Bigotry: A State-By-State Legislative Effort to Pushback against 2050 by Targeting Muslims and Other Minorities." Institute for Social Policy and Understanding, November 10, 2014. www.ispu.org/manufacturing-bigotry-community-brief/.

Butler, Judith. *Gender Trouble: Feminism and the Subversion of Identity*. New York: Taylor & Francis, 1990.

Cainkar, Louise. "The Arab American Experience: From Invisibility to Heightened Visibility." In *The Routledge Handbook of Asian American Studies*, edited by Cindy I-Fen Cheng. New York: Routledge, 2017.

———. "Constructing and Containing the 'Muslim Threat' Through Immigration and Refugee Policies: An Analysis of Donald Trump's Words and Actions." Paper presented at the Workshop on Religion and Migration, Arizona State University Center for the Study of Religion and Conflict, Tempe, AZ, April 28, 2017.

———. *Homeland Insecurity: The Arab American and Muslim American Experience After 9/11*. New York: Russell Sage Foundation Press, 2009.

———. "Fluid Terror Threat: A Genealogy of the Racialization of Arab, Muslim, and South Asian Americans." *Amerasia Journal* 44, no. 1 (2018): 27–60.

Carby, Hazel. "White Woman Listen! Black Feminism and the Boundaries of Sisterhood." In *The Empire Strikes Back: Race and Racism in 70's Britain*, edited by Center for Contemporary Cultural Studies. London: Hutchinson & Co., 1982.

Cauterucci, Christina. "'It Could Have Been Any One of Us:' Muslim Community Mourns Murdered Teen Nabra Hassanen." *Slate*, June 22, 2017. www.slate.com/blogs/xx_factor/2017/06/22/after_nabra_hassanen_s_murder_virginia_muslims_resolve_to_carry_on_in_spite.html.

Collins, Patricia Hill. *Black Feminist Thought: Knowledge, Consciousness, and the Politics of Empowerment*. New York: Routledge, 1990.

Combahee River Collective. "A Black Feminist Statement." In *This Bridge Called My Back: Writings by Radical Women of Color*, edited by Cherrie Moraga and Gloria Anzaldúa. New York: Kitchen Table Press, 1981.

Connell, Robert. "Globalization, Imperialism, and Masculinities." In *Handbook of Studies on Men & Masculinities*, edited by Michael Kimmel, Jeff Hearn, and Robert Connell. Thousand Oaks, CA: Sage, 2004.

———. *Masculinities*. Berkeley: University of California Press, 1995.

———. *The Men and the Boys*. Berkeley: University of California, 2000.

"Convention on the Elimination of All Forms of Discrimination against Women." United Nations Entity for Gender Equality and the Empowerment of Women. Accessed April 26, 2018. www.un.org/womenwatch/daw/cedaw/.

Council on American-Islamic Relations and the University of California, Berkeley Center for Race and Gender. "Confronting Fear: Islamophobia and its Impact in the United States." July 2016. www.islamophobia.org/images/ConfrontingFear/Final-Report.pdf.

Crenshaw, Kimberlé. "Mapping the Margins: Identity Politics, Intersectionality, and Violence Against Women of Color." *Stanford Law Review* 43 (1993): 1241–1299.

Davis, Angela. *Women, Race, & Class*. New York: Random House, 1981.

Essed, Philomena. "Towards a Methodology to Identify Converging Forms of Everyday Discrimination." 2001. www.un.org/womenwatch/daw/csw/essed45.htm.

Feffer, John. "Islamophobia and the 2010 Election: Though Obama's Policies on Islam and the Middle East Differ Little from his Republican Challengers, the Right Still Claims He is Pro-Islamic." *Mother Jones*, March 29, 2012. www.motherjones.com/politics/2012/03/republican-obama-is-muslim-islamophobia/2/.

Fried, Susana T., and Alex Teixeira. "International Gay and Lesbian Human Rights Commission Input Memo to the UN." Accessed April 26, 2018. www.un.org/womenwatch/daw/vaw/ngocontribute/International%20Gay%20and%20Lesbian%20Human%20Rights%20Commission.pdf.

Herek, Gregory, Jeanine C. Cogan, and J. Roy Gillis. "Victim Experiences in Hate Crimes Based on Sexual Orientation." *Journal of Social Issues* 58, no. 2 (2002): 319–339.

hooks, bell. *Feminist Theory: From Margin to Center*. Cambridge, MA: South End Press, 1984.

Kimmel, Michael, Jeff Hearn, and Robert Connell. *Handbook of Studies on Men & Masculinities*. Thousand Oaks, CA: Sage, 2004.

Kozlov, Dana. "Man Berates Muslim Girls at Suburban Restaurant." *CBS Chicago*, June 6, 2017. http://chicago.cbslocal.com/2017/06/06/muslim-girls-verbally-abused-restaurant/.

Kumar, Deepa. "Imperialist Feminism." *International Socialist Review* 102 (Fall 2016). http://isreview.org/issue/102/imperialist-feminism.

Lorde, Audre. "An Open Letter to Mary Daly." In *This Bridge Called My Back: Writings by Radical Women of Color*, edited by Cherrie Moraga and Gloria Anzaldúa. New York: Kitchen Table Press, 1981.

———. "The Master's Tools Will Never Dismantle the Master's House." In *This Bridge Called My Back: Writings by Radical Women of Color*, edited by Cherrie Moraga and Gloria Anzaldúa. New York: Kitchen Table Press, 1981.

Merry, Sally. *Gender Violence: A Cultural Perspective*. Oxford: John Wiley & Sons, 2009.

Meyer, Doug. "Interpreting and Experiencing Anti-Queer Violence: Race, Class, and Gender Differences among LGBT Hate Crime Victims." *Race, Gender & Class* 15, no. 3–4 (2008): 262–282.

Mohanty, Chandra. "Under Western Eyes: Feminist Scholarship and Colonial Discourses." *Feminist Review* 30, no. 1 (1988): 61–88. doi:10.1057/fr.1988.42.

Moraga, Cherrie, and Gloria Anzaldúa, eds. *This Bridge Called My Back: Writings by Radical Women of Color*. New York: Kitchen Table Press, 1981.

Moruzzi, Norma. "A Problem with Headscarves." *Political Theory* 22, no. 4 (1994): 653–672.

Piggott, Stephen. "Portland Stabbings: Man Arrested for Double Murder After Allegedly Threatening Muslim Women Has Racist Views, Praised Timothy McVeigh." *The Oregonian* (Portland, OR), May 27, 2017.

Philips, Kristine. "A Muslim Teacher Receives an Anonymous Note about Her Headscarf: 'Hang Yourself with It'." *The Washington Post*, November 12, 2016. https://www.washingtonpost.com/.

Physicians for Social Responsibility (US American affiliate), Physicians for Global Survival (Canadian affiliate), and International Physicians for the Prevention of Nuclear War. *Body Count: Casualty Figures after 10 Years of the "War on Terror". Iraq, Afghanistan, Pakistan*. Washington, DC, Berlin, Ottawa, 2015.

Putnam, Robert D. *American Grace: How Religion Divides and Unites Us*. 1st Simon & Schuster hardcover ed. New York, NY: Simon & Schuster, 2010.

Razack, Sherene H. "Imperiled Muslim Women, Dangerous Muslim Men and Civilized Europeans: Legal and Social Responses to Forced Marriages." *Feminist Legal Studies* 12 (2004): 129–174.

Rogers, Phil. "Cellphone Footage Captures Alleged Assault of Chicago Muslim Women." *NBC Chicago*, August 14, 2016. www.nbcchicago.com/news/local/alleged-assault-chicago-muslim-women-hate-crime-390039261.html.

Romero, Octavio. "The American Burqa Industry." *SFGate*, December 30, 2002. www.sfgate.com/opinion/openforum/article/The-American-burqa-industry-2742319.php.

Schippers, Mimi. "Recovering the Feminine Other: Masculinity, Femininity, and Gender Hegemony." *Theory and Society* 36 (2007): 85–102. www.doi.org/10.1007/s11186-007-9022-4.

Selvam, Ashok. "White Man Harasses Muslim Teens at Suburban Chicago Mexican Restaurant." *Eater*, June 7, 2017. https://chicago.eater.com/2017/6/7/15754568/anti-muslim-incident-teen-girls-video-chicago-suburb-hickory-hills-pepes-mexican-restaurant.

Sharpe, Joshua. "Muslim Gwinnett Teacher Told to 'Hang Yourself' with Her Headscarf." *The Atlanta Journal-Constitution*, November 11, 2016. www.ajc.com/news/local/muslim-gwinnett-teacher-told-hang-yourself-with-her-headscarf/XVrOecQFQRbKc7SuggJMtI/.

Southern Poverty Law Center. "Experts Seeing Spike in Possible Anti-Muslim Hate Crimes." September 13, 2016. www.splcenter.org/hatewatch/2016/09/13/experts-seeing-spike-possible-anti-muslim-hate-crimes.

———. "National Day of Healing Necessary for Nation to Move Forward." January 17, 2017. www.splcenter.org/news/2017/01/17/national-day-healing-necessary-nation-move-forward.

———. "Update: More Than 400 Incidents of Hateful Harassment and Intimidation since the Election." November 15, 2016. www.splcenter.org/hatewatch/2016/11/15/update-more-400-incidents-hateful-harassment-and-intimidation-election.

Stewart, Abigail, and Christa McDermott. "Gender in Psychology." *Annual Review of Psychology* 55 (2004): 519–544.

Suerth, Jessica. "Nabra Hassanen's Murder Highlights the Challenges of Designating a Crime a Hate Crime." *CNN*, June 21, 2017. www.cnn.com/2017/06/21/us/nabra-hassenen-hate-crime-designation-challenge-trnd/index.html.

Talbot, Margaret. "The Story of a Hate Crime: What Led to the Murder of Three Muslim Students in Chapel Hill?" *The New Yorker* (New York), June 22, 2015.

The UN Commission on the Status of Women. "Agenda Item 4(b)." Forty-Fifth Session: March 6–16, 2001. www.un.org/press/en/2001/wom1264.doc.htm.

Wang, Amy. "'Final Act of Bravery': Men Who Were Fatally Stabbed Trying to Stop Anti-Muslim Rants Identified." *Washington Post*, May 27, 2017. www.washingtonpost.com/news/post-nation/wp/2017/05/27/man-fatally-stabs-2-on-portland-ore-train-after-they-interrupted-his-anti-muslim-rants-police-say/?utm_term=.0febd79c3159.

Weaver, Matthew. "Burqa Bans, Headscarves and Veils: A Timeline of Legislation in the West." *The Guardian*, May 31, 2018, sec. World news. https://www.theguardian.com/world/2017/mar/14/headscarves-and-muslim-veil-ban-debate-timeline.

2 Palestine's accession to CEDAW

One step of the thousand-mile journey

Mutaz M. Qafisheh

Introduction

Can the State of Palestine's accession to the Convention on the Elimination of All Forms of Discrimination against Women (CEDAW)[1] be considered a turning point with regard to women's rights? Women's rights are violated not only as a result of the orthodox interpretation of religious texts but also due to local traditions that governments in recent history were either unable or unwilling to confront. However, while declaring its commitment to women's rights in the 2002 Basic Law (as amended in 2003), and by acceding to a number of human rights treaties, Palestine has come a long way toward reforming its legal system, policies, and practices that relate to gender equality and the established traditions thereof.

The State of Palestine acceded to CEDAW on April 1, 2014.[2] By reviewing the list of state parties to CEDAW on the United Nations Treaty System,[3] one finds that Palestine is the only Arab state that joined this treaty without reservation.[4] What does that mean? *Is* Palestine willing to apply CEDAW domestically and to ensure equality between genders? If so, *can* Palestine enforce this treaty, taking into account centuries-long traditions that discriminate against women, the persistent conservative nature of local communities, and the rise of an Islamist renaissance across the Middle East?

This chapter attempts to answer these questions by exploring the legal reform challenges and prospects in Palestine, and focusing on applicable legislative instruments related to women, including family law (e.g., age of marriage, guardian approval of a woman's marriage, interreligious marriages, polygamy, divorce, and inheritance), as well other selected legislation (e.g., penal law, labor law and social security, travel, citizenship, and residence). After a thorough examination, this chapter proposes that some legislative reforms would be easy to bring Palestine in compliance with CEDAW. Others, however, would be more difficult to change.

To explore this question, this chapter relies on both primary and secondary data to examine, from a legal perspective, gaps in the rights of Palestinian women. Sources of data include the provisions of CEDAW and the existing and proposed legislation that affects Palestinian women, including family laws, personal status law, criminal law, labor law, and so forth. This chapter also utilizes data from interviews that the researcher conducted in the city of Hebron, Palestine, in 2017. These interviews were conducted with more than thirty individuals, including Shariah judges, tribal leaders, women's rights activists, nongovernmental organization (NGO) officials, government officials, and both law and Shariah scholars.

This chapter also addresses key legislation (laws, bylaws, decrees, decisions, and instructions) that act to promulgate discrimination against women. While not claiming to be conclusive in reviewing women-related legislation, this chapter examines legislative texts that should be amended in order for Palestine to meet its commitments under CEDAW. To accomplish this goal, this chapter proceeds in three sections. Section "Gender and the Palestinian legal system" provides a historical overview of Palestinian justice and categorizes three major areas of Palestinian laws affecting women: (1) legislation that favors women over men, (2) legislation that provides equality between men and women, and (3) legislation that discriminates against women. The history of Palestine's justice system is important in relation to women's rights, as the current system is a product of various historical regimes that have ruled the country over the past century. Section "Family laws and the prospects of reform" focuses on evaluating selected substantive issues related to the application of family laws (including those concerning the age of marriage, a guardian's approval of a woman's marriage, interreligious marriages, polygamy, divorce, and inheritance), in relation to CEDAW's provisions. Section "Selected discriminatory laws" apprises other legislation: penal law, labor law, social security, travel, citizenship, and residence in relation to CEDAW's provisions. In conclusion, this chapter argues that most legislative instruments affecting women's rights in Palestine were drafted well before the evolution of human rights law at the global stage; therefore, reform should be carried out by adjusting domestic law to be consistent with international law as well as with Palestine's obligations thereof.

Gender and the Palestinian legal system

Before appraising the legislative instruments related to women's rights in Palestine, one must understand the particular history of its justice system. Each political regime that dominated Palestine since its separation from the Ottoman Empire in December 1917 has influenced applicable law in the West Bank and Gaza Strip. While Ottoman legislation was based on both Islamic and Continental Law, legislation enacted by Britain until May 1948 came as a reflection of common laws enforced across the British Empire. The West Bank and Gaza were once again subjected to the continental-like system from 1948 until 1967. When the West Bank was annexed by Jordan, Jordanian law, which largely derived from the Egyptian/French legal school, was extended therein.

Egypt administrated Gaza without imposing Egyptian law; it retained British-enacted legislation but issued certain laws that were influenced by Egyptian law. After its occupation of the West Bank and Gaza in June 1967, Israel did not extend its law, except in East Jerusalem. Instead, Israel ruled by previous legislation but added a series of military orders (separate orders for Gaza and the West Bank) that amended or replaced existing law.[5]

Before setting foot in Palestinian territory, Yasser Arafat, the former Chairman of the Palestine Liberation Organization (PLO), who had just become President of the Palestinian Authority (PA), enacted Decree No. 1 of May 20, 1994.[6] In this decree, Arafat proclaimed that all laws passed before Israeli occupation of the West Bank and Gaza on June 5, 1967, would remain in force until such enactments were amended or unified. The decree demonstrated a will to legislate for the new Palestinian entity. Without having established institutions that would be charged with legislative power, Arafat had begun to rule the territory through the adoption of various types of legislation until the enactment of the first "law" was adopted by the Palestinian Legislative Council (PLC) on December 16, 1996.[7] The PLC lasted until June 2007, when Hamas took over the Gaza Strip. The Palestinian split led to the creation of two de facto governments centered in the cities of Gaza and Ramallah.[8]

From the election of the first parliament in January 1996 until June 2007 (when parliamentary life was frozen upon the new election that led to the Israeli blockade on Gaza and to the Palestinian split),[9] ninety-seven laws were adopted for both Gaza and the West Bank. Such parliamentary acts have shaped the political, economic, social, juridical, and security life in Palestine. Nonetheless, it is apparent that these enactments were adopted on an ad hoc basis without a strategy for systemic legal reform.[10] Key legislation has yet to be passed, including civil codes, penal codes, family laws, commercial codes, land laws, and corporate laws. There is wide variation between legislation in Gaza and the West Bank.

The legislative process in Palestine suffered a setback with the division between the West Bank and Gaza after the takeover of the Gaza Strip by Hamas in June 2007. Since then, Hamas has been ruling Gaza, while the Fatah-led PA retains its self-rule over the West Bank. Each party claims legitimacy for ruling and legislating. Fatah bases its regime on the presidential elections of 2005, which President Abbas won. Hamas, on the other hand, justifies its regime by its victory in the 2006 parliamentary elections.

As the PLC has been unable to meet since 2006, the PA President took over the executive function. Since 2007, the President has begun to use his power under Article 43 of the 2003 Amended Basic Law, which gives him the right to issue "decrees of necessity" that take the effect of law.[11] These decrees are called "decree-law," and the President had issued dozens of decree-laws as of October 25, 2007. While some of these decree-laws meet the emergency requirement found within Article 43, others do not fulfill this emergent criteria. Article 43 itself does not define "the emergency that could not be delayed," which necessitates such laws. However, the fact remains that when the President utilizes this power, he assumes legislative power.[12]

While the President continues to rule the West Bank through presidential decrees, Hamas governs Gaza based on its Prime Minister's enactments, or (as of 2017) a group of entities, including the Gaza Acting Governing Committee, Council of Ministers, other ministers, police, and other various official bodies.[13]

Hamas and Fatah each has its own *Diwan* (legislative bureau) that publishes a distinct official gazette.[14] In Gaza, parliament members hold regular sessions and adopt "laws" that apply in Gaza's local courts. If this situation does not end by reaching national conciliation between rival parties and holding new elections, it seems that two de facto political entities will emerge, each of which encompasses its own state apparatus: one in Gaza and the other in Ramallah.

The aforementioned illustrates that most legislative enactments now applicable in Palestine were brought to the country by foreign powers and not by the Palestinians themselves. These foreigners were, above all, concerned with protecting their interests through legislation. The rights of natives (men and women alike) were not a priority. For this reason, many pieces of legislation contradict modern international human rights standards, and women's rights are no exception. However, after resuming the legislative function during the mid-1990s, Palestinians now have the power to amend applicable legislation to protect the rights of their citizens.

In the vast majority of legislative instruments applicable in Palestine, masculine tenses are used to prescribe legislative regulations for various matters, while feminine tenses are only included by default. The term "man" is often used to mean "person" or "human being."[15] As it is well known, the Arabic language uses two different expressions for males and females. Unfortunately, however, most legislation uses the masculine term only, for example, terms such as *rais* (president or chair*man*),[16] *mudir* (director),[17] *safir* (ambassador),[18] *saik* (driver),[19] *muhami* (lawyer),[20] *tabib* (doctor),[21] *muhandis* (engineer),[22] *mualif* (author),[23] *sabi* (boy),[24] and *shurti* (policeman),[25] provide the most prominent examples of the predominance of masculine terminology.

Such discriminatory expressions within legislation are indicative of the bias toward preferences toward males and are a first step toward legislative equality and reform. Legislative drafters should be more sensitive to gender balance and not take women's rights for granted. Such linguistic usage might create problems of interpretation at the implementation stage. For example, whether the term "young" (*saghir* or *sabi*)—a term that designates who may be allowed to conduct contracts—also includes girls remains unclear within legislation.[26] The gendered terminology evinces an intent, whether intentionally or unintentionally, as if women were never meant to occupy space and place within the law and positions of power within the law.

The Amended Palestinian Basic Law of March 18, 2003,[27] which is the key constitutional instrument of Palestine, states that "Palestinians shall be equal before the law and the judiciary, without distinction based upon race, sex, color, religion, political views or disability."[28] Clearly, this provision recognizes the principle of equality between men and women. However, a survey of applicable Palestinian legislation related to women reveals three legislative positions toward women's rights: (1) legislation that favors women over men, (2) legislation that provides equality between men and women, and (3) legislation that discriminates against women.

Gender bias language within legislation that favors women over men can be found in criminal law, family law, and election law. Criminal law punishes persons who commit particular offences against women, such as forced prostitution,[29] abortion,[30] sexual harassment, and rape.[31] In family law, women have special rights that are not enjoyed by men, including the right of a dowry (*mahr*),[32] housing provisions during the term of marriage,[33] the covering of all other expenses by her father before getting married or by her husband during her marriage (including food, clothing, and medical treatment),[34] alimony,[35] the guardianship of children in cases of divorce or separation or a husband's death,[36] and compensation or a "postponed dowry" after the divorce or upon the husband's death.[37] Legislative and municipal election laws establish a system of quotas for women that guarantees at least 20% of parliamentary or municipal seats.[38] Such provisions are not a subject of concern from the international human rights law viewpoint,[39] as Article 4 of CEDAW does not consider the "special measures aimed at accelerating *de facto* equality between men and women" discriminatory.[40]

The second set of legislation, which guarantees equal treatment for both men and women, can be found in commercial law,[41] public service law,[42] landlord and tenant law,[43] labor law,[44] higher education law,[45] people with disabilities law,[46] public health law,[47] prison law,[48] and professions' laws.[49] These laws are congruent with Decree No. 9 of March 8, 2009,[50] in which the Palestinian President confirmed "the ratification of the Convention on the Elimination of All Forms of Discrimination against Women in accordance with the Palestinian Basic Law."[51] Thus, from the outset, it can be noted that discrimination against women in the applicable legislation in Palestine is the exception, however significant that exception might be.

The third category of legislation, which discriminates against women, is the concern of this chapter and will be referred to in some detail in the following sections. While the mere legislative enactment that adheres to the principle of equality is a relatively easy task given the political will to ensure gender equality, this chapter claims that, due to social and religious attitudes embedded within Palestinian society, the way toward legislative reform that complies with international standards for women's rights will not be an easy journey. A comprehensive reform process on women's rights, in addition to legislative reform, requires socioeconomic, educational, and cultural transformations.

Family laws and the prospects of reform

Family laws in Palestine are inherited from previous periods: predominantly Jordanian law in the West Bank and Egyptian-enacted law in Gaza. These laws, in turn, were influenced by the religions of various communities; chiefly, Muslims and Christians. Although Palestine has acceded to CEDAW without reservations, a note on reservation—particularly in relation to Article 16 of CEDAW, which deals with family law—might be needed.

If Palestine considers maintaining the status quo concerning gender inequality with regard to family law issues such as those discussed in this chapter, it may consider filing a reservation on Article 16 of CEDAW. While such is unfortunate from a progressive global human rights perspective, reservations have been viewed by states to be permissible, and they are widely practiced. Palestine may enter reservations similar to those declared by Algeria, Bahrain, Bangladesh, Israel, Jordan, Libya, Qatar, Saudi Arabia, Syria, and the United Arab Emirates. The latter states, for instance, declared that it "will abide by the provisions of this Article [16] insofar as they are not in conflict with the principles of the Shariah."[52] Algeria declared that "the provisions of Article 16 concerning equal rights for men and women in all matters relating to marriage, both during marriage and at its dissolution, should not contradict the provisions of the Algerian Family Code."[53] Examples of some of the conflicts between Article 16 and Shariah Law relate to any family-relating matters, including marriage, inheritance, divorce, alimony, and abidance. However, filing a reservation might no longer be permissible, as Palestine has lost the opportunity to do so upon its accession, as CEDAW's Article 2(1) requires.[54] Arguably, if a reservation is formally accepted, certain reservations might not be permitted by CEDAW, as they might be considered "incompatible with the object and purpose of the present Convention," based on Article 28(2).

In this regard, the Committee on the Elimination of Discrimination against Women (hereinafter "CEDAW Committee"), the body that monitors the implementation of the Convention by state parties, concluded that "Reservations to Article 16, whether lodged for national, traditional, religious or cultural reasons, are incompatible with the Convention and therefore impermissible and should be reviewed and modified or withdrawn."[55] Hence, the most likely option available for Palestine is to implement CEDAW and change domestic legislation, policies, and practices accordingly.

Age of marriage

The applicable family law in Palestine prescribes different ages of marriage for girls and boys. Under the title "Capacity of Marriage," the Family Law (Order No. 303) of February 10, 1954, which is still applicable for Muslims in the Gaza Strip,[56] fixed the age of marriage at seventeen years for girls and eighteen years for boys (Article 5). This, notwithstanding the different ages between girls and boys, is a fairly reasonable provision.[57] However, the February 10th order forbids "anybody to approve the marriage of boys below twelve years of age or girls under nine" (Article 8). This implies that it is permissible for girls and boys to marry at nine and twelve years of age, respectively. Although it may appear to be an exception, such a stipulation may open the door for forced child marriages. Recent statistics shows that more than 28% of women who got married in the Gaza Strip and more than 21% in the West Bank were under eighteen years of age.[58] Such marriage contradicts not only Article 16 of CEDAW, which requires that women have the "same right [as males] to enter into marriage," but also violates many provisions of the Convention on the Rights of the Child, which was passed on November 20, 1989,[59] and to which Palestine acceded on April 1, 2014. These provisions ban child marriage and establish children's rights to health and education.

Differing ages of marriage or betrothal between males and females also exist in other family laws. In the Personal Status Law No. 61 of December 1, 1976,[60] for Muslims in the West Bank, the age of marriage for boys is sixteen years, while the age for girls is fifteen (Article 5). In the Personal Status Law of the Anglican Arab Christians of 1954,[61] the boy should reach seventeen and the girl sixteen to qualify for engagement (Article 12). The boy should be eighteen and the girl sixteen for marriage (Article 21). The Code of Canon Law of January 25, 1983,[62] which provides the general framework for Catholics worldwide, including in Palestine, fixes the age of marriage at fourteen years for girls and at sixteen for boys (Article 1083).

Article 16(2) of CEDAW prescribes that the "betrothal and the marriage of a child shall have no legal effect." As noted by the CEDAW Committee,

> [s]ome countries provide for different ages for marriage for men and women. As such provisions assume incorrectly that women have a different rate of intellectual development from men, or that their stage of physical and intellectual development at marriage is immaterial, these provisions should be abolished.[63]

Undoubtedly, changing marriage ages would face enforcement challenges, as age is perceived as a customary or religious matter. However, Palestinian legislature might introduce a general provision to forbid child marriage (for example, by amending Palestinian Child Law No. 7 of August 15, 2004,[64] or by adopting a more comprehensive human rights law). The term "child" has already been defined as any person under eighteen by Article 1 of the said Child Law. Alternatively, a provision in the penal code might be introduced to punish any person who facilitates the marriage of children. Penal provisions already punish with up to six months of imprisonment any person who performs the marriage of any girl under fifteen years.[65] Such a provision may simply be replaced to punish any person who conducts the marriage of those younger than eighteen.

Guardian's approval of marriage

In order to marry, a woman must acquire the approval of her guardian regardless of her age, according to various family laws applicable for Muslims and Christians alike in Palestine. Males, on the other hand, do not need guardians. A woman's guardian is always a male person and is normally the bride's father. In the absence of the father for reasons such as death or mental deficiency, the guardian would be the female's paternal grandfather, brother, nephew, uncle, or another man.[66] While it is true that family laws allow females to marry without said approval if the guardian has no legitimate justification for opposing the wedding, the mere principle of requiring a guardian's approval for females and not for males runs counter to Article 16(1) of CEDAW, which guarantees "on a basis of equality of men and women: (a) The same right to enter into marriage."

Such a requirement, which might appear to be for women's protection, implies that women are unable to determine their future partners for themselves. Why is a man, whether a father or an uncle, in a better position to make decisions of marriage for his female relative? Why should a male make such a decision on behalf of his sister or aunt, even if he is younger and less educated?

On the contrary, as it is well known in the Middle East, guardians, particularly fathers, often abuse this power by preventing their daughters from marrying the men they elect—in many instances, for the father's own interests. Indeed, studies prove that more than 50% of underage girls got married based on the decisions of their families, particularly their fathers, against the girls' will.[67] Such a rule should be eliminated from applicable law in Palestine. Women, like men, should determine who they will marry on their own. Indeed, a

> woman's right to choose a spouse and enter freely into marriage is central to her life and to her dignity and equality as a human being .... [A] woman's right to choose when, if, and whom she will marry must be protected and enforced at law.[68]

Interreligion marriages

Marriages between people belonging to different religions are forbidden in family laws. While both the Muslim Family Status Law of 1954[69] and Personal Status Law of 1976[70] make the marriage of Muslim women with non-Muslim men null and void, Muslim men could marry "women of the book,"[71] that is, Christian or Jewish women. In personal status legislation relating to Christians, however, both husband and wife should be from the same religion; namely, no one may have spouses from a different religion.[72]

Prescribing different and discriminatory rules of marriage applicable to women and men violates the principle of equality under CEDAW. In order to meet the requirement of this Convention, the solution for Muslim personal status laws might be found by introducing equal rules that apply to both women and men who marry another from a different religion, similar to the case of family laws relating to Christians. However, this solution would contradict Article 16(1)(b) of CEDAW, which requires states to provide both genders the "same right freely to choose a spouse."

As such, another possible solution for Palestinian legislators is to introduce a civil personal status law under the jurisdiction of civil—not religious—courts. In order to avoid sensitivity and ensure respect for people's religious choices, the proposed civil personal status law could be optional. In other words, those who belong to different religions, or those who have no religion, would have the choice to marry under civil law. This recommendation is consistent with the facts on the ground. The facts are (1) that people from different religions do manipulate religious courts by declaring formal conversion to another religion, solely to acquire a marriage certificate; (2) that no judge or government could control the religious beliefs of others, as religion is a matter of personal conscience; and (3) that people from different religions could marry based on civil marriage rules in other countries that permit secular marriages outside Palestine between individuals who come back to live in the country, while jeopardizing the consequence of nonrecognition from religious institutions and compromising some of their rights such as inheritance, recognition of children, and alimony. In such cases, people create their own rules by sharing property or making wills to each other. By this solution, the legislative body would be true to itself by avoiding anomalous situations and denying existing facts, conforming to international human rights law, and protecting the rights of families that have mixed marriages.

Polygamy

It is common to notice references to polygamy in various pieces of legislation applicable in Palestine. The Personal Status Law of 1976 in the West Bank, for example, states that "it is forbidden for any man who has four wives to enter into a new marriage contract with extra women before divorcing at least one."[73] The same law added that "any man who marries more than one wife should treat them equally. It is prohibited to accommodate more than one wife at the same home without the approval of all wives."[74] The 1954 Family Law of Gaza states that "it is forbidden for a man who has four wives to marry another woman,"[75] and "a man who marries more than one woman shall treat them equally and fairly."[76] Polygamy has been similarly implied in the Compilation of Oriental Churches Laws of 1990,[77] which applies to the entire Middle Eastern Church, including in Palestine.

This established system, which is derived from religious interpretations, prompted the creation of a set of rules governing its legal consequences. Terms such as "wives" and "widows" can be found in legislation relating to, for instance, inheritance and pension. Such legislation includes statements such as "eligible persons are the widow or widows"[78] and "beneficiaries from the fund are ... the lawyer's wife or wives."[79]

Through instructions issued by the Head of the High Shariah Judicial Council on April 24, 2011,[80] The PA tried to restrict polygamy by requiring men who wish to marry a new woman to notify his earlier wife or wives and requiring him to inform his new fiancé that her future husband is a married man. Despite being useful in removing runaway weddings and fraud, this weak attempt is not enough from an international human rights point of view.[81] It is often abused, and earlier wives are often not notified of the corruption that exists among court staff. It has been reported by some men who married without informing existing wives that family court notaries public often accepted bribes and refrained from informing earlier wives but reported to the court that they had indeed notified them.[82] Shariah judges also often tolerate new marriages without notifying earlier wives, as many of them believe that polygamy should be the man's free choice without restrictions.

As noted by the CEDAW Committee, "polygamous marriage contravenes a woman's right to equality with men, and can have such serious emotional and financial consequences for her and her dependents that such marriages ought to be discouraged and prohibited."[83] Hence, in a number of its concluding observations on the reports of state parties, "the Committee has pointed to the grave ramifications of polygamy for the human rights and economic well-being of women and their children, and has consistently called for its abolition."[84] Thus, Palestine, as is the case of other states in which polygamy is still practiced, "should take all legislative and policy measures needed to abolish polygamous marriages."[85]

Gradually, however, the practice of polygamy could be restricted to the point of making it very difficult to practice. Genuine reform measures in this respect may include, for example, (1) restricting new marriages to exceptional circumstances enumerated exclusively in the law and endorsed by a judge with proper monitoring mechanisms; (2) requiring the "approval," not the mere "notification" of previous wives, which would be officially filed at the family court; and (3) giving earlier wives the right to request divorce with the preservation of all rights if a husband decides to enter a new marriage. At the same time, "with regard to women in existing polygamous marriages,"[86] Palestine "should take the necessary measures to ensure the protection of the economic rights of women."[87]

The Personal Status Law of 1976 offers a practical solution that can be activated to restrict or eradicate polygamy.[88] That solution can be found under the provision relating to conditions that may be made by the husband and wife before signing the marriage contract. Under this provision, the wife may request the husband "not to marry another woman." If the man does not respect this condition, "the wife would have the right to end the marriage while retaining all her rights."

Unfortunately, however, this solution is not working effectively in practice, because officials who are normally traditional and religious men in charge of conducting contract marriages do not stress this possibility or even refer to it during the contractual procedure. Marriage contracts often take a few minutes to sign, and the bride is often absent from the room due to local customs that restrict women from interacting in such ways with men, especially in conservative communities. Additionally, the bride's father or guardian, who acts on her behalf, does not request the inclusion of such conditions in the marriage contract, usually in an effort to convey to the future groom and his family signals of trust and respect.

Palestinian legislators or marriage officials may, in the absence of the complete abolishment of polygamy by law, activate the said provision by instructing officials who process marriage contracts to acquire the wife's approval—either in the contract itself or in a separate form—to allow her future husband to marry again. Or, preferably, and in order to remove embarrassment while celebrating marriage, the condition "not to marry another wife" could be inserted in the form of the marriage contract, and the choice could be given to the wife to remove this condition.

With such provisions, it is quite certain that only a small number of women would give such consent. Polygamy is an unwelcome practice for the vast majority of women. Indeed, polygamy's influence is not limited to the mere emotional and sexual sharing of the husband, or to the social marginalization of the wife, all of which are relevant; it virtually affects the wife's rights of inheritance and other financial commitments that are due from the husband. Polygamy even threatens financial assets that the wife might have accumulated for years within the family, such as her salary, a family house purchased from her own savings, or contributions that she might have made from the assets she inherited from her own relatives—assets that, in most cases, would be registered in the husband's name.

Divorce

In Muslim family laws applicable in the Middle East, including in Palestine, the husband unilaterally reserves the right to divorce his wife. This can be directly concluded from the 1954 law applicable in Gaza (Articles 67–111) and the 1976 law applicable in the West Bank (Articles 83–101). Under the law, it is possible for men to divorce orally. With one word, the man can end years of marriage. This creates many hardships for families, particularly for women, as men might choose to divorce with or without reason. Indeed, a man might abuse this possibility, skipping obligations toward his wife for the sake of his own desires.

There are two ways in which women can end marriages. One is by khul', an agreement between husband and wife upon which the wife would pay the husband all expenses he sustained during the marriage. It is a method of compensation for the man. The second way is "separation" by a judicial order, granted at the same footing between husband and wife. Separation may be requested in certain circumstances, such as a spouse's inability to practice sex due to physiological deficiencies, as well as certain types of illness, madness, violence, or improper treatment.[89]

To overcome the problem of men making unilateral decisions to divorce, a provision in personal status law could be adopted to make divorce effective solely before a judge who would determine the rights and obligations of both parties. Marriage is a construct that involves emotions, children, financial arrangements, and future plans that should not be suddenly dissolved. Kuran describes marriage relationships as a "great contract" (methaqan ghlitha).[90] This great contract should not be diminishable by the word of an irresponsible man without a proper monitoring mechanism.

In fact, according to classical Islamic jurisprudence, marriage could be conducted orally, but modern family laws forbid marriage outside the official setting. So, should not the same regulations be used to govern divorce, particularly as divorce might have far-reaching consequences, not only for the couple but also for children and other social relationships?

Women's economic rights in the wake of divorce should not be confined to simply the dowry, as is marked in marriage contracts. Wives often substantially contribute to the economies of their families. At times, they spend their wages, savings, and inheritance rights within the family; however, these expenditures often go undocumented, and most family property is registered in the husband's name, especially as Middle Eastern culture views the man as the head of the household. Women often sacrifice for the family by leaving their careers for the sake of their children's education and their husband's care. Thus, in cases of divorce, wives should be reimbursed for their roles within the family (including lost opportunities) during the course of the marriage. In order to develop such a criteria, husbands and wives should, by law, have shared property after the date of marriage; in other words, any assets or gains that the man or woman make due to commerce, employment, or other effort-generated gain should be divided equally between them upon divorce.

Even when the wife does not work outside the home, she would most likely have lost economic opportunity, spending her emotions, labor, and time on her family, even if her work in the home is less effort-consuming than formal jobs. As indicated by the CEDAW Committee,

> family structures, gendered labour division within the family and family laws affect women's economic well-being no less than labour market .... Indeed, women often do not equally enjoy their family's economic wealth and gains, they usually bear the greater cost of the breakdown of the family.[91]

Indeed, it is unfair that a wife might be left after years of family life with a few thousand dollars in dowry, if any, while the husband harvests the assets to which the wife has contributed. Thus, Palestine, similar to CEDAW's other state parties, is "obligated to provide, upon divorce and/or separation, for equality between the parties in the division of all property accumulated during the marriage."[92] It should "recognize the value of indirect, including nonfinancial, contributions with regard to the acquisition of property acquired during the marriage."[93]

Vesting the primary power of divorce with men and depriving women from it clearly violates a number of CEDAW's stipulations. To be reformed in light of international standards, the law of divorce should be changed. The law should either give equal rights to men and women or limit divorce to decisions that cannot be exercised by the individual will of any spouse but rather through formal court verdicts. The provision of the Personal Status Law of 1976, as it relates to conditions that might be requested by spouses prior to the signing of marriage contracts, offers a practical solution similar to the one presented under "polygamy."[94] This solution can be activated to give the wife (like the husband) the right to divorce by requesting her husband "to divorce whenever she wishes."[95]

Again, as noted above, this type of solution is not working effectively in practice, as officials who conduct marriage contracts do not stress this possibility during the contractual procedure. Palestinian legislators may activate this rule by instructing officials who process marriage contracts to give the wife—either in the contract itself or in a separate paper—the chance to choose the possibility of divorcing her husband with power equal to his. It is likely that most women would choose this possibility. Such a solution might be effectively consistent with CEDAW's provision that requires state parties to take "all appropriate measures to eliminate discrimination against women in all matters relating to marriage and family relations" and to ensure on the basis of equality between men and women the "same rights and responsibilities during marriage and at its dissolution."[96]

Inheritance

In the applicable personal status laws in Palestine, the son, brother, and husband's inheritance shares are twice that of a daughter, sister or wife. These laws do not directly regulate the question of inheritance; laws either refer to the hanafi school of Islamic jurisprudence (one of the major theories of Islamic law)[97] or merely leave the question of inheritance to the general rules of Islam. In both cases, inheritance shares are similar, mostly as fixed by Kuran.[98] This fact leaves it difficult to change the inheritance rules to conform to equality principles under CEDAW.

It should be noted, however, that the law grants equal rights to men and women in certain cases. Fathers and mothers equally succeed their sons or daughters who die without having children.[99] Brothers and sisters inherit siblings from the mother's side with equal power.[100] Certain types of real estate property, particularly endowments and the meri land (i.e., "public" land that is assigned by the state to be used and owned by private individuals), are divided equally between males and females: sons and daughters, brothers and sisters, and husbands and wives. The latter rule can be found in the Law of the Transfer of Immovable Property of March 6, 1913, which was enacted by the Ottoman Empire,[101] and is still applicable in both Gaza and the West Bank. It seems that the Ottomans used discretion to ensure equality between men and women in relation to this type of inheritance, apparently justifying that rule by the fact that the land under consideration is a form of public ownership and therefore the state may determine its legal status despite the fact that this land is virtually used as private property.

Palestinian legislators may use other techniques in order to ensure the equality between men and women with regard to inheritance rights. This would not be an easy task, not only because of the prevailing conservative social attitudes in Palestine that the legislators cannot ignore but also due to the established legal system that distributes rights and obligations within the family construct. It has indeed been argued that men are under more financial obligations within the family. Men's financial obligations include providing dowries, alimonies, and the costs of living (housing, food, clothing, medical treatment, etc.) not only for their wives and children but for all females under their guardianship (sisters, mothers, aunts, nieces, and grandmothers).[102]

Women have no de jure financial obligations toward the family or themselves, even if they work. Nonetheless, most of a man's obligations toward women are increasingly de facto diminishing, and as the numbers of educated and working women rise, women do effectively contribute to the family's economy, including costs of living, housing, and alimony. Following the same logic, if such obligations toward women are not applied in reality, then why should women fail to be compensated through, for example, equality in inheritance rights? When obligations for women's care are lifted or relaxed in a marriage, then the man's share of awards such as inheritances should also be reduced by a decision of the legislature in a way that corresponds to the eased obligations. The division of inheritance shares that includes equality might be gradually applied on a case-by-case basis—namely, depending on the actual division of responsibilities within a given family.[103] It could reach (for the sake of a general legal criteria and consistency in applying the law) the level of full equality over time.

Another preliminary idea toward achieving equality of inheritance between the two genders without contradicting Shariah could also be proposed. There is a consensus within Islamic jurisprudence that heirs can agree among themselves to distribute inheritance assets equally between male and female siblings; in essence, brothers grant their sisters part of the brothers' rights based on the decision of the state. This would be the case if a deceased parent leaves a will asking for equality between his or her male and female children; in such a case, the brothers would have the choice to endorse the will or revoke it—as no will for heirs is allowed in the most common view of Islamic jurisprudence.

In a similar fashion, Palestinian legislators may presume that all heirs are in agreement to equally distribute inheritance assets between male and female siblings. This does not mean that the legislators would change the inheritance provisions of Kuran. On the contrary, it is an application of Kuran made in another way. In this way, by a positive act (equality), the legislature would reinforce the natural principles of justice and equality embodied in the general philosophy underlying Islam by taking into consideration the socioeconomic transformations of modern societies. "It is not denied," as the well-known jurisprudential rule goes, that "rules can be changed when times change."[104]

Currently, brothers by and large no longer contribute to the service of their sisters. Hence, brothers do not make up—and therefore do not deserve—the double inheritance shares assigned to male heirs. If the socioeconomic circumstances would change again (i.e., males assume full responsibility), the rules of inheritance might correspond accordingly. While it can be said that Kuran standards could act as parameters in this connection, such a proposal needs further elaboration that exceeds the scope of this chapter.

The foregoing illustrates that, in order to modify the rules of inheritance by offering equitable rights between men and women, the entire social and family economic system should correspond to such change. This process, if it takes place at all, would require much intellectual, educational, economic, religious, and political reform that would take quite a long time to unfold. If Palestine decides that it is yet unprepared to take on such comprehensive change, it may file a reservation on CEDAW concerning equality on inheritance, as we have noted above. Motivated by conservative religious institutions as well as Islamic fundamentalism, populist attacks on calls for equality in inheritance rights demonstrate that the rules of inheritance are the most challenging aspect of family laws to be reformed.[105] One case in point is the recent August 2017 tensions and politicization in Tunisia following the presidential proposal to Parliament to adopt a draft law on inheritance equality.[106]

Lastly, a word must be said regarding the deprivation of women from their already half-sized inheritance rights in Palestinian society, as is the case in a number of other Middle Eastern countries. In particular, men often prevent their sisters from inheriting from their fathers or mothers. Sisters, in turn, often feel socially reluctant to sue their brothers and, in the end, give up their rights, making takharuj (a procedure by which heirs give up their inheritance rights) in order to maintain good relations with their brothers. This phenomenon is widespread, and the legislature should not remain indifferent.

Palestinian legislators should also intervene to eradicate this practice and protect women from such injustice. There was one attempt to reduce the effect of takharuj by the Islamic High Judicial Council through closely setting up and monitoring its procedures; however, that is not enough.[107] For more credible ways to ensure the application of inheritance shares—especially for women—Palestinian legislators may reactivate the system of kassam that existed at a certain point in the seventeenth century. Kassam is an official who works under the authority of a judge by making an inventory of all the property items owned by the deceased person and distributing shares based on the law without requiring the heirs' intervention.[108]

Selected discriminatory laws

Penal laws

As is the case with other state parties of CEDAW, Palestine is under an Article 2(g) obligation to "repeal all national penal provisions which constitute discrimination against women." Three provisions of the 1960 Penal Code that are applicable in the West Bank relating to "honor" are subjects of concern from CEDAW's standpoint.[109] Fortunately, there is no "honor"-related provision in the 1936 Penal Code Ordinance of Gaza.[110] However, part of the controversy in the former code arises out of the prescription of different or discriminatory penalties for the same crimes committed by men and women. The other is due to the ambiguity of certain provisions of the Penal Code.

For example, under the Penal Code, the "adultery" rule is problematic. Article 282(1) of the 1960 Jordanian-enacted code provides that "she who commits adultery with her consent shall receive a six-month to two-year imprisonment term." In this provision, the code does not define "adultery," leaving the term subject to interpretation. Nor does it provide the same penalty for men in similar circumstances. The punishment of women and men who commit "adultery" with consent constitutes an intervention in one's private life, a right enshrined in the Universal Declaration of Human Rights.[111] And, by adopting stricter penalties for women, this rule runs contrary to CEDAW.

The Penal Code includes another discriminatory contradiction by stating that the "husband who practices adultery at the matrimonial home or who takes a lover in public shall be imprisoned from one month to one year" (Article 283). The code does not impose a similar penalty on the wife under the same circumstance. Another problem relates to the definition of "lover" (the Arabic khalila, which might also be interpreted as "friend" or "girlfriend"). This provision ought to be modified to ensure equal treatment between men and women.

Article 340 of the 1960 Penal Code provides punishment for the most serious "honor" crime. This article was taken verbatim from of the Ottoman Penal Code of 1858.[112] The latter code dates back, in turn, to the French Penal Code of 1810.[113] The 1960 Code's article permits the killing of women by male relatives in the name of so-called honor. According to Paragraph 1 of this article, a man would be exempted from penalty if he "surprisingly found his wife or any of his maharim [i.e., relative females whom a man could not marry] practicing adultery with a man and he kills, injures, or harms one or both of them." Paragraph 2 adds that "the man who kills, injures or harms his wife, daughters, granddaughters, mother, grandmothers or his sisters shall benefit from the reduction of the penalty if he surprisingly found any of them with a man practicing sex without marriage." These provisions clearly discriminate against women.[114] Men are offered the right to take the law in their own hands. This does not only legitimize the killing of women; it, in effect, encourages men to kill, using "honor" as a pretext.[115]

On May 15, 2011, the Palestinian President abolished Article 340 by decree.[116] Although this decree is a step in the right direction, perpetrators of crimes against women in the name of "honor" may still benefit from Article 98 of the code, which gives judges the power to reduce the penalty if the crime is committed under "anger provocation." Shortly after Palestine's accession to CEDAW, President Abbas enacted Decree No. 10 of May 11, 2014, in which he excluded the perpetrator of crimes against women in the name of "honor" from benefiting from the reduction of penalty if he commits the crime under the provocation of anger.[117]

Nevertheless, President Abbas' decree is not enough. The perpetrators of honor killings can still benefit, by judicial interpretations, from other provisions of the code that permit the reduction of penalties in cases where a victim's family chooses to forgive or drop the personal element of crime.[118] Hence, Palestine needs to adopt a provision that removes all stipulations in the Penal Code that open any possibility of reducing the penalty over the killing of women in the name of honor.[119]

The penalty for rape poses another controversy. Article 308 of the 1960 Penal Code exempts the perpetrator of rape and other sexual attacks if the rapist marries his victim. This provision rewards the offender for his crime. At the same time, the victim is victimized twice: first, as a result of the sexual attack, and second, by being forced to live with her foe. Given the conservative nature of Palestinian communities, the victim or her family may agree to let the rapist marry the girl for shame-prevention reasons, especially if she becomes pregnant. Palestine should follow the footsteps of Jordan, who, on August 1, 2017, repealed a provision similar to Palestine's Article 308.[120]

Other problems in the Penal Code can be attributed to the relatively light (or altogether absent) penalties for sexual crimes that target females. The penalty for committing rape is relatively lenient. The Penal Code provides for an imprisonment ranging from five to fifteen years, depending on the victim's age or the relationship between the rapist and victim.[121] Also, the codes prescribe no penalty against a husband who rapes his wife.[122] Furthermore, neither the codes nor other legislative instruments provide clear provisions on the sexual harassment of women, particularly in workplaces.

In short, all provisions of the penal codes that discriminate against women in the West Bank and Gaza must be repealed in future Palestinian penal codes. Meanwhile, in order to comply with CEDAW, the courts must cease in their application of any discriminatory provisions within the Penal Code. Only then would Palestine conform to Article 2(g) of CEDAW, which requires state parties to "repeal all national penal provisions which constitute discrimination against women."

Labor law and social security

Most international labor standards relating to women's rights have been reflected in the 2000 Palestinian Labor Law.[123] According to this law, women have the right to a ten-week maternity leave,[124] a one-hour breastfeeding break each day for one year following the child's delivery,[125] and the right of special leave without pay for one year.[126] The law incorporated considerable rules for the protection of working women, prohibiting gender discrimination regarding work,[127] banning pregnant women from working harmful jobs, forbidding employers from requiring pregnant women to perform extra working hours, and preventing women from working at night except when necessary,[128] such as jobs performed in hospitals, airports, or in the media.[129]

Contrastingly, the law prevents women from working certain jobs, such as mechanical, risky, or difficult-to-perform jobs.[130] Such provisions pose an obstacle toward the freedom of choice for women in this respect.[131] This might contradict Article 11(c) of CEDAW, which guarantees equal rights between men and women regarding the "free choice of profession and employment." Also, the labor law excludes "domestic workers," most of whom are women, from the scope of this law's application (Article 3(2)). The law added that the Minister of Labor shall regulate the status of such workers by issuing a regulation. Seventeen years later, this regulation is yet to be issued, leaving domestic workers without legal protection. This gap in regulating the status of domestic workers is similar to the legislation of other Middle Eastern states, such as Lebanon. This gap has been considered a violation of the right to work by the CEDAW Committee.[132]

The Committee states that it "expresses concern that Article 7 of the [Lebanese] Labor Law excludes domestic workers from its scope of application, thereby depriving them of a range of critical labor protections and making them vulnerable to all forms of exploitation."[133] The Committee required the state to "speedily enact the draft law regulating the employment of domestic workers."[134] The same recommendation, mutatis mutandis, applies to Palestinian labor law.

The applicable law in Palestine gives retirement rights to the widow as a general rule. However, women cannot pass retirement rights to their widower. This rule is drawn from a number of laws relating to retirement. The Law of Insurance and Pensions of the Palestinian Security Forces No. 16 of December 28, 2004,[135] states that the "persons entitled to pension ... shall be 1. The widow or widows of the beneficiary ...."[136] Similar provisions can be found in the General Pension Law of 2005 (with regard to public sector employees) and for members of certain professional associations, such as lawyers (Regulation relating to the Pension of Lawyers No. 1 of January 1, 1998).[137] Such rules imply that women are dependent on men and that it is the man who works, not the woman. This goes against reality, which proves that approximately 20% of the workforce in Palestine is comprised of women.[138] It denies women their retirement rights despite the fact that women are obliged to pay retirement dues at the same rates as men. Such provisions should be changed to guarantee equality concerning retirement—as is the case of the recent Social Security Decree Law No. 19 of September 29, 2016,[139] which governs the pension of the private sector by providing equal pension rights between men and women.

Citizenship, travel, and residence

Citizenship in Palestine is governed by two statutes: the British-enacted Palestinian Citizenship Order of July 24, 1925,[140] applicable in the Gaza Strip, and the Jordanian Nationality Law No. 6 of February 4, 1954, which applies in the West Bank.[141] According to the 1925 Order, a person born to a Palestinian father acquires the father's nationality, wherever the birth may occur. To this effect, the Order considered the following persons as Palestinian citizens:

> (a) Any person born in lawful matrimony within Palestine whose father at the time of such a person's birth was a Palestinian citizen. (b) Any person born in lawful matrimony out of Palestine whose father was a Palestinian citizen at the time of that person's birth.
>
> (Article 3)

A child born to a foreign father is considered a foreigner even if his mother is a Palestinian citizen; as the Order puts it, "minor children shall follow the nationality of their father" (Article 6). As a rule underlying the whole Citizenship Order, "the status of a married woman will be governed by that of her husband."[142] In relation to naturalization in particular, the "wife of a Palestinian citizen shall be deemed to be a Palestinian citizen and the wife of an alien shall be deemed to be an alien."[143]

In one of the most discriminatory provisions against women, the Citizenship Order deems a married woman to be a "disabled person" for all nationality purposes. The term "disability," as defined in the Order, means, inter alia, or "the status of being a married woman" (Article 21(4)). This definition was taken from Article 27(1) of the British Nationality and Status of Aliens Act of August 7, 1914. Thus, a woman was unable on her own account to be naturalized in Palestine;[144] Article 9(3) of the Order stated that "a certificate of naturalization shall not be granted to any person under disability." In other words, a foreign married woman could not acquire Palestinian nationality separately from her husband.[145] She had the right to apply for naturalization only if she was unmarried, widowed, or divorced.[146]

The foregoing laws, however, imply that a foreign man could not be naturalized merely by marrying a Palestinian woman. There is no explicit provision to this effect in the 1925 Order, but the overall dependency of the woman on her husband's nationality indicates that the man is not entitled to be naturalized following his wife's nationality. Such a man could only be naturalized, then, according to the general rules of naturalization applicable to other foreigners. Similar rules can be found in the 1954 Nationality Law: total dependency of the wife on her husband's nationality, children on their father's, and the inability of the woman to pass on her citizenship to her husband or children.

Equality between men and women should underline the new citizenship law of Palestine.[147] Such equality should be particularly envisaged regarding the equality between husband and wife. A Palestinian woman should be empowered to pass on her nationality to her non-Palestinian husband. Children born to at least one Palestinian citizen, mother or father, should get the right to become Palestinians regardless of their place of birth.

By adopting gender equality, the law would be consistent with modern international human rights law and nationality laws of the developed states. Such reform is also needed to satisfy Article 9 of CEDAW, which obliges states to

> grant women equal rights with men to acquire, change or retain their nationality. States shall ensure in particular that neither marriage to an alien nor change of nationality by the husband during marriage shall automatically change the nationality of the wife, render her stateless or force upon her the nationality of the husband.[148]

Women should also get "equal rights with men with respect to the nationality of their children." By such an approach, Palestine would become ready to join other international treaties on nationality, including the Convention on the Nationality of Married Women of January 29, 1957;[149] the Convention on the Reduction of Statelessness of August 30, 1961;[150] and the Convention Relating to the Status of Stateless Persons of July 28, 1951.[151]

Regarding travel, family laws in Palestine restrict a woman who has the custody of children—even if she is the children's mother—from traveling outside the country without a male legal guardian's approval.[152] The guardian is normally the children's father or a grandfather in cases of a father's absence or death. There is no restriction on the travel of men with children in the same situation, and no approval of the mother is required. Furthermore, in most personal status laws for Muslims and Christians alike, the wife is obligated to travel with and join her husband wherever the husband wishes to go. She cannot refuse without express authorization by a court that determines she has a legitimate reason. In the case of refusal, the wife may lose some of her rights, such as alimony.[153] The foregoing runs contrary to Article 15(1) of CEDAW, which requires states to "accord to men and women the same rights with regard to the law relating to the movement of persons and the freedom to choose their residence and domicile." Palestine should change such rules to treat women equal to men in this regard.

Other laws

As mentioned above, there is a minimum 20% representation quota for women in legislative and local elections. This law is intended to promote the principle of equality between men and women in a masculine society. Yet, there is no such quota in the election of other settings, such as Bar Associations, trade unions, and university students' unions. For this reason, most of such institutions lack women representatives. The legislature is called upon to introduce a general rule that guarantees women representation in all professional associations. At that point, Palestine would satisfy the requirement of Article 7(c) of CEDAW, which calls upon states to ensure that women "participate in non-governmental organizations and associations concerned with the public and political life of the country" on equal terms with men.

Other laws give men more rights than women. For example, men reserve an exclusive right to act as arbitrators in cases of conflict between spouses.[154] Witnesses should always be "two men" or "one man and two women," with no possibility of women alone to act as witnesses with regard to marriage contracts,[155] other civil law,[156] or contractual matters.[157] The husband, but not the wife, has the right to divorce a wife who "goes out with other men and gets drunk without her husband's consent."[158] Such provisions are contrary to Article 15(2) of CEDAW, which obligates states to "accord to women, in civil matters, a legal capacity identical to that of men and the same opportunities to exercise that capacity." In particular, states "shall give women equal rights to conclude contracts and to administer property and shall treat them equally in all stages of procedure in courts and tribunals." In order to be compatible with the provisions of CEDAW, Palestinian legislators should adopt provisions in the law: a general rule to the effect that "all contracts and all other private instruments of any kind with a legal effect which is directed at restricting the legal capacity of women shall be deemed null and void," as Article 15(3) of CEDAW stipulates.

Conclusion

Most legislative instruments affecting women's rights in Palestine were drafted well before the evolution of human rights law at the global stage. By this fact alone, one may prima facie predict that the local legislation in that country does not take into consideration international standards as set forth in CEDAW. While declaring its commitment to women's rights by acceding to CEDAW, Palestine has a long way to go toward reforming legislation that undermines women's rights.

Women's rights are violated not only as a result of old implementation of religious laws but also due to the local traditions existing in the entire Middle East region. In fact, using the vehicle of legislation, Palestine could bridge the gap with regard to gender equality in one way or another. What is still missing in this country is the political will to undertake radical legislative reform that eradicates gender discrimination once and for all. The Palestinian legislature needs to survey all legislative instruments that affect women's rights and change them in one way or another. It may alternatively enact human rights laws that clearly repeal any discrimination. Finally, Palestine may adopt CEDAW as a local law.

In parallel to its legislative reform, Palestine needs to adopt comprehensive strategies aimed at raising public awareness of gender equality and removing social stereotyping attitudes toward women. Particular attention should be accorded to the promotion of scientific research on Islamic law with regard to women's rights in order to distinguish religious rules from social traditions. In the view of the present writer, the vast majority—if not all—of discrimination against women stems from social traditions and customs rather than religious beliefs. Once the *ijtihad* (discretion) in Islamic jurisprudence is resumed, there would always be, in the final analysis, approaches from within Islamic law to harmonize local legislation in line with global norms.

Notes

1 Signed on December 18, 1979, and entered into force on September 3, 1981 (1249 U.N.T.S. 13).
2 *Official Initial Report of the State of Palestine on the International Convention on the Elimination of All Forms of Discrimination against Women (CEDAW)*, March 8, 2017, 3.
3 See the list of CEDAW's state parties and the status of reservations at https://treaties.un.org/Pages/ViewDetails.aspx?src=IND&mtdsg_no=IV-8&chapter=4&lang=en#80.
4 *Initial Report of the State of Palestine*, 3.
5 Mutaz Qafisheh, "Legislative Drafting in Transitional States: The Case of Palestine," *International Journal of Legislative Drafting and Law Reform* 2, no. 1 (2013): 26.
6 *Palestine Gazette*, No. 16, November 20, 1994, 10.
7 "Election of Local Government Law No. 5 of 1996," *Palestine Gazette*, No. 16, January 20, 1997, 6.
8 Muwatin (The Palestinian Institute for the Study of Democracy), *Legislation at the Time of Internal Division: Studies on the Legislation Enacted Since 2007* (Ramallah: Muwatin, 2016).

9 Inter-Parliamentary Union, "Statement by the IPU President Concerning the Detention of the Speaker and Other Members of the Palestinian Parliament [Press Release No. 357, Geneva]," January 25, 2012, http://archive.ipu.org/press-e/gen357.htm.
10 Pius Biribonwoha, "The Role of Legislative Drafting in the Law Reform Process," *Commonwealth Law Bulletin* 32, no. 4 (December 2006): 601.
11 Article 43 reads as follows:

The President of the National Authority shall have the right, in cases of necessity that cannot be delayed, and when the Legislative Council is not in session, to issue decrees that have the power of law. These decrees shall be presented to the Legislative Council in the first session convened after their issuance; otherwise, they will cease to have the power of law. If these decrees are presented to the Legislative Council, as mentioned, but are not approved by the Council, then they shall cease to have the power of law.

12 Talal Touqan, *The Necessity Decree-Laws Enacted by the President* (Ramallah: Miftah, 2008).
13 In its press release of July 28, 2009, the Gaza Ministry of Justice stated:

The *Diwan* declares its intention to publish Issue No. 75 [of] *The Palestine Gazette* (the Official Journal of the Palestinian National Authority).... This edition includes several laws that were passed by the [Gaza] Palestinian Legislative Council, the most notable of which are [The] Law Concerning the High Judicial Institute as well as laws amending the Penal Code, Penal Procedures Law, and Reform and Rehabilitation Centers Law. The issue also includes several decisions of the Legislative Council, resolutions of the Council of Ministers for over 25 sessions, Prime Minister's decisions, and a number of ministerial enactments.

Ministry of Justice (Gaza), "Press release," July 28, 2009; see also, Ministry of Justice (Gaza), "The Diwan Publishes Issue No. 75 of *The Palestine Gazette* [press release]," July 28, 2009.

14 Ministry of Justice (Gaza), "The Ministry Publishes New Edition [Extraordinary] of the Palestine Gazette [press release]," August 12, 2012; see also, Ministry of Justice (Gaza), "The Diwan Publishes Issue No. 83 of *The Palestine Gazette* [press release]," August 9, 2012.
15 In the *Majalle*, which is the Ottoman Civil Code of 15 September 1876, which is still applicable in the West Bank, the word "man" was used 75 times, while "woman" was used only 5 times. These five times relate to (1) the possibility for a woman to loan things owned to her husband (Article 822); (2) the possibility for woman to borrow jewels for a specific period of time, as an example of the temporary nature of the loan's contract (Article 826); (3) the necessity to have "two men" or "one man and two women" as witnesses (Article 1030); (4) the donation of money from the husband to the wife (Article 1599); and (5) the possibility for women to serve as witnesses instead of men concerning acts that take place in spaces reserved for the exclusive use of women (Article 1685).
16 "Constitutional Court Law No. 3, Article 5 of February 17, 2006," *Palestine Gazette*, No. 62, March 25, 2006, 93.
17 "The Law of Securities No. 12, Article 55 of December 1, 2004," *Palestine Gazette*, No. 53, February 28, 2005, 10.
18 "The Law of Diplomatic Corps No. 13, Article 6 of September 24, 2005," *Palestine Gazette*, No. 60, November 9, 2005, 5.
19 "Transport Law No. 5, Article 39 of September 17, 2000," *Palestine Gazette*, No. 36, March 19, 2001, 5.
20 "Legal Profession Law No. 3, Article 1 of June 24, 1999," *Palestine Gazette*, No. 30, October 10, 1999, 5.
21 "Public Health Law No. 20, Article 1 of December 27, 2004," *Palestine Gazette*, No. 54, April 23, 2004, 14.
22 "Law on Tenders for Public Works No. 6, Article 19 of 1999," *Palestine Gazette*, No. 32, February 29, 2000, 9.

23 "Press and Publication Law No. 9, Article 30 of June 25, 1995," *Palestine Gazette*, No. 6, August 26, 1995, 11.
24 The *Majalle*, Article 629.
25 Transport Law of 2000, Article 63.
26 The *Majalle*, Articles 776, 970, 976, 977, 1335, 1433, 1457–1458, and 1539; these articles relate to the young *boy* ("sabi") who is permitted by his guardian to conclude various contracts.
27 *Palestine Gazette*, Special Edition, March 19, 2004, 5.
28 Amended Palestinian Basic Law, Article 9 of March 18, 2003 (emphasis added).
29 "Penal Code No. 16, Articles 317–318 of April 10, 1960," *Jordan Official Gazette*, No. 1487, May 1, 1960, 374; "Penal Code Ordinance No. 74, Article 151 of December 14, 1936," *Palestine Gazette*, No. 652, Supplement 1, December 14, 1936, 399.
30 Penal Code of 1960, Article 323; Penal Code of 1936, Articles 175–177.
31 Penal Code of 1960, Article 305(2) (harassment) and Articles 292-295 (rape of women); Penal Code of 1936, Articles 152–153 and 155 (sexual offences).
32 "Personal Status Law No. 61, Article 44 of November 30, 1976," *Jordan Official Gazette*, No. 2668, December 1, 1976, 551.
33 *Ibid.*, Article 36.
34 *Ibid.*, Articles 66–82, 168.
35 *Ibid.*, Article 73; Personal Status Law for Syrian Orthodox, Article 34 of April 3, 2000, enacted in Jerusalem on September 9, 2000; Personal Status Law for Latin Church in Jerusalem, Article 137 of October 31, 1954.
36 Personal Status Law of 1976, Article 154.
37 *Ibid.*, Article 46.
38 "Decree-Law No. 1, Article 5 of September 2, 2007, concerning General Elections," *Palestine Gazette*, No. 72, September 9, 2007, 2; "Local Councils Elections Law No. 10, Article 17 of August 15, 2005, "*Palestine Gazette*, No. 57, August 18, 2005, 79.
39 W. Judah, "Women Political Empowerment: Challenges and Opportunities," *Seyasat*, no. 41, September 2017, 28–53.
40 *Ibid.*; however, such temporary measures "shall be discontinued when the objectives of equality of opportunity and treatment have been achieved."
41 "Trade Law No. 12 of March 8, 1966," *Jordan Official Gazette*, No. 1910, March 30, 1966, 469.
42 "Civil Service Law No. 4, Article 88 of May 28, 1998," *Palestine Gazette*, No. 24, July 1, 1998, 20; this law, however, gave women certain favorable rights: maternity leave and breastfeeding breaks.
43 "Landlord and Tenant Law No. 62 of April 6, 1953," *Jordan Official Gazette*, No. 1140, April 16, 1953, 661.
44 "Labor Law No. 7 of April 30, 2000," *Palestine Gazette*, No. 39, November 25, 2001, 7; Articles 101–106 of this law accorded favorable rights to women, such as protection from dangerous professions, maternity leave, and special leave for mothers.
45 "Higher Education Law No. 11 of November 2, 1998," *Palestine Gazette*, No. 27, December 8, 1998, 28.
46 "Rights of People with Disabilities Law No. 4 of August 9, 1999," *Palestine Gazette*, No. 30, October 10, 1999, 36.
47 Public Health Law 2004; Articles 4–8 assigned particular attention to women's health.
48 "Reformatory and Rehabilitation Centers (Prisons) Law No. 6, Articles 27–29 of May 28, 1998," *Palestine Gazette*, No. 24, July 1, 1998, 87; this law referred to certain special provisions relating to care that should be paid to female prisoners.
49 For example, Legal Profession Law of 1999.
50 *Palestine Gazette*, No. 80, April 27, 2009, 20.
51 Palestinian Basic Law, Article 1.

52 This reservation was made upon the Emirates' accession to CEDAW on October 6, 2004.
53 This reservation was made upon Algeria's accession to CEDAW on May 22, 1996.
54 CEDAW Article 2(1) (providing, "States Parties condemn discrimination against women in all its forms, agree to pursue by all appropriate means and without delay a policy of eliminating discrimination against women").
55 United Nations, *Report of the Committee on the Elimination of Discrimination against Women*, UN doc. A/53/38/Rev.1, 49 (New York, 1998).
56 *Palestine Gazette* (Gaza Strip), No. 35, June 15, 1954, 869.
57 However, Articles 6–7 of this legislation vested the judges of the family (religious) courts with the power to endorse the marriage of the "teenager" (without defining the meaning of this term) even if he or she is under the aforementioned age.
58 Women NGO Coalition on the Implementation of CEDAW in the Occupied State of Palestine, "Report on the Status of Women and Girls in the State of Palestine [submitted to the UN CEDAW Committee in Geneva]," *Seyasat*, No. 41, September 2017, 186.
59 1577 U.N.T.S., 3 (1990).
60 *Jordan Official Gazette*, No. 2668, December 1, 1976, 2756.
61 The Personal Status and Endowments of the Arab Anglican Community Law of 1954 (a scanned copy of this law is available at the Palestinian Legal and Judicial System, "Al-Muqtafi" Institute of Law, Birzeit University, Palestine, without the name, publisher, or the publication date).
62 London: (Collins Liturgical Publishers), September 1983.
63 CEDAW Committee, "General Recommendation No. 21: Equality in Marriage and Family Relations," UN doc. A/49/38, para. 38 (April 12, 1994).
64 *Palestine Gazette*, No. 52, January 18, 2005, 13.
65 Article 279 of the 1960 Penal Code; Article 156 of the Penal Code of 1936 punishes with a two-year imprisonment term any person who marries or facilitates the marriage of any girl under fifteen years of age; however, this article makes exceptions to this rule if the person who marries such a girl proves that she is an "adult," and if he provides a certificate from a physician proving that the marriage would not affect the girl's health. This article clearly contradicts the aforementioned Article 8 of the Personal Status Law of 1954, also applicable in Gaza. As the Penal Code of 1936 was adopted before the Personal Status Law (1954), the latter legislation would prevail based on the logic that the new legislation repeals the former in cases of conflict. This backward situation should be changed.
66 Personal Status Law of 1976 in the West Bank, Article 9; Personal Status Law of 1954 in the Gaza Strip, Article 11; Personal Status Law for Syrian Orthodox of 2000, Article 5.
67 Halawa Niveen, "Early Marriage: Knife in the Side of Palestinian Society," *Seyasat*, No. 41, September 2017, 102–103.
68 General Recommendation No. 21, para. 16.
69 Muslim Family Status Law of 1954, Article 37.
70 Personal Status Law of 1976, Article 33.
71 *Ibid.*, Article 33(2).
72 For instance, the 2000 Personal Status Law for Syrian Orthodox provided that

> if one of the spouses claimed that s/he is Christian and it appeared otherwise, the religious court shall give such a person a period of time to prove his/her Christianity. If s/he refused to become a Christian, the marriage shall be null and void. (Article 28(3))

A similar rule exists in the Personal Status Law for the Anglican Arab Christians of 1954; this law even requires that at least one of the spouses be from the Arab Anglican sect and the other should be "Christian." Personal Status Law for Latin Church in Jerusalem of 1954 prohibits, with certain exceptions, the marriage of Catholics with "non-Catholics" (Article 21).

73 *Ibid.*, Article 28.
74 *Ibid.*, Article 40.
75 *Ibid.*, Article 14.
76 *Ibid.*, Article 42.
77 Article 859 (Beirut: Paulius Library, 1993), 470.
78 "General Pension Law No. 7, Article 32 of April 26, 2005," *Palestine Gazette*, No. 55, June 27, 2005, 16.
79 "Lawyers Solidarity Fund Regulations Amendment No. 4 of April 24, 2009," *Palestine Gazette*, No. 84, December 27, 2009, 60.
80 High *Shariah* Judicial Council, "Press Release" (Ramallah: April 24, 2011).
81 Mutaz Qafisheh, "Notification in Case of Polygamy Is Not Enough," September 16, 2014, www.qanon.ps/news.php?action=view&id=18220.
82 Interviews conducted in Hebron in 2017.
83 General Recommendation No. 21, para. 14.
84 CEDAW Committee, "General Recommendation on Article 16 of the Convention on the Elimination of All Forms of Discrimination Against Women (Economic Consequences of Marriage, Family Relations and their Dissolution)," General Recommendation No. 29, UN doc. CEDAW/C/GC/29, para. 27 (October 30, 2013).
85 *Ibid.*, para. 28.
86 *Ibid.*
87 *Ibid.*
88 Personal Status Law of 1976, Article 19(A).
89 "Separation" in this sense exists in most Christian personal status laws applicable in Palestine: Law of the Personal Status and Endowments of the Arab Anglican Community of 1954, Articles 31–34; Personal Status Law for Latin Church in Jerusalem of 1954, Article 35 (referring to the Code of Canon Law regarding the end of marriage); the Code of Canon Law of 1983, Articles 1141–1155; Personal Status Law for the Syrian Orthodox of 2000, Articles 54–61.
90 *Nisa*, verse 21.
91 General Recommendation No. 29, para. 1.
92 *Ibid.*, para. 46.
93 *Ibid.*
94 Personal Status Law of 1976, Article 19(A).
95 *Ibid.*
96 CEDAW, Article 16(1), item (c).
97 Personal Status Law of 1976, Article 183.
98 *Nisa*, verse 4 (for sons and daughters); *An'am*, verse 6 (for brothers and sisters); *Nisa*, verse 4 (for husband and wife).
99 *Nisa*, verse 4.
100 *Ibid.*, verse 12.
101 Aref Ramadan, ed., *Completion of Laws: Ottoman Laws Valid in Arab States Detached from the Ottoman Government* (Beirut: Science Press, 1928), Vol. 3, 121, Articles 1–7.
102 Yusuf Kardawi, *Introduction to the Study of Islamic Shariah* (Cairo: Wahba Library, 1990), 139–140.
103 And why not? A woman could take more if she proves that she has more obligations.
104 The *Majalle (applicable civil law in Palestine)*, Article 39.
105 This writer was personally attacked, heavily criticized, and had his life threatened over a short article titled "Liberation of Women in Palestine," published in the local media (March 14, 2014), in which he called, among other things, for using discretionary tools available in Islamic jurisprudence to achieve equality between men and women regarding inheritance; see, for example Amira Hass, "Are Sharia and International Law Compatible? [Interview with Mutaz M. Qafisheh]," *Haaretz*, February 7, 2015, http://archive.ipu.org/press-e/gen357.htm; see also Samara Abedlkarim,

"Palestinian Academic is Accused to be Infidel Due to His Courageous Opinions," accessed on May 6, 2014, https://tinyurl.com/yd6xetjz.

106 Iman Zayat, "Tunisian President Triggers Debate after Call for Gender Equality in Inheritance, Marriage," *Arab Weekly*, August 16, 2017, https://thearabweekly.com/tunisian-president-triggers-debate-after-call-gender-equality-inheritance-marriage.

107 *Official Initial Report of the State of Palestine*, 75.

108 Adel Manna, *The District of Jerusalem in the Mid-Ottoman Period: Administration and Society* (Beirut: Institute for Palestine Studies, 2008), 159–160.

109 See Faris Nesheiwat, "Honor Crimes in Jordan: Their Treatment under Islamic and Jordanian Criminal Laws," *Penn State International Law Review* 23, no. 251 (2004): 251–281; more generally, see Anushree Tripathi and Supriya Yadav, "For the Sake of Honour: But Whose Honour? Honour Crimes against Women," *Asia-Pacific Journal on Human Rights and the Law* 5, no. 63 (2004): 63–78.

110 This is probably due to the fact that the main part of this code "follows the English model"; Norman Bentwich, "The New Criminal Code for Palestine," *Journal of Comparative Legislation and International Law* 20, no. 71 (1938): 73.

111 UN Doc. A/811, December 16, 1948, Article 12.

112 Ramadan, Vol. 1, 2, Article 188.

113 Article 324 of the French Penal Code of 1810. This French article reads as "dans le cas d'adultère ... le meurtre commis par l'époux sur son épouse, ainsi que sur le complice, à l'instant où il les surprend en flagrant délit dans la maison conjugale, est excusable" ("In the case of adultery ... husband who kills his wife and her accomplice, at the moment he surprises them in flagrante offense in the matrimonial home, is excusable"); Lama Abu-Odeh, "Honor Killings and the Construction of Gender in Arab Societies," *American Journal of Comparative Law* 58 (2010): 914, referring to E. Garcon, *Code Penal Annoté* (1901), 151; this provision has no relevance to Islamic law; it existed in many Arab and European states, such as France, Spain, Portugal, and Italy; *Ibid.*, 914; *Cf.*, John Cohan, "Honor Killings and the Cultural Defense," *California Western International Law Journal* 40 (2010): 177.

114 For court cases on honor crimes in Jordan, Egypt, and Syria, see Abu-Odeh, "Honor Killings," 924–932.

115 *Ibid.*, 921–923.

116 Decree-Law No. 7 of 2011 Concerning the Amendment of the Penal Code in Northern and Southern Districts, No. 91, October 10, 2011, 17.

117 *Palestine Gazette*, No. 108, July 15, 2014, 6.

118 *Official Initial Report of the State of Palestine*, 11.

119 Danaf Hebatallah, "The Impact of Legal System on Increasing Women Murder in Palestine," *Seyasat*, no. 41, September 2017, 55–75.

120 *Addustour*, no. 17969, August 2, 2017, 1.

121 Articles 292–295 of the 1960 Code; Article 152 of the 1936 Penal Code, applicable in the Gaza Strip, punishes rape more strictly (fourteen years of imprisonment term).

122 Even Article 292(1) of the Penal Code explicitly excludes forced sex with the wife from rape's definition.

123 See generally, Mutaz Qafisheh, "The Interplay between International Human Rights and Labour Rights in Palestine," *Journal of Islamic State Practices in International Law* 9 (2013): 1.

124 Article 103 of the 2000 Palestinian Labor Law; this period is below international standards of the minimum fourteen weeks according to Article 4(1), of the Convention Concerning the Revision of the Maternity Protection Convention of 1952 (Revised), June 15, 2000 (ILO No. 183).

125 Article 104 of 2000 Palestinian Labor Law.

126 *Ibid.*, Article 105.

127 *Ibid.*, Article 100.

128 *Ibid.*, Article 101. *Cf.*, Convention Concerning Employment of Women during the Night, November 28, 1919 (ILO No. 4).
129 "Decision of the Council of Ministers No. 14 of December 22, 2003 concerning the Work of Women Overnight," *Palestine Gazette*, No. 49, June 17, 2004, 152.
130 "Decision No. 2 of the Minister of Labor of May 6, 2004, Concerning Banned Dangerous or Strenuous Works for Women," *Palestine Gazette*, No. 54, April 23, 2005, 145.
131 Official Initial Report of the State of Palestine, 44.
132 *Concluding Comments of the Committee on the Elimination of Discrimination Against Women*, Lebanon: UN Doc. CEDAW/C/LBN/CO/3 (April 8, 2008).
133 *Ibid.*, para. 30.
134 *Ibid.*, para. 31.
135 *Palestine Gazette*, No. 53, February 28, 2005, 94.
136 *Ibid.*, Article 36.
137 *Palestine Gazette*, No. 25, September 24, 1998, 58.
138 Palestinian Central Bureau of Statistics, *Survey of the Workforces in Palestine* (Ramallah: Palestinian Central Bureau of Statistics, 2012), 24.
139 "Articles 65 and 69," *Palestine Gazette*, Special Edition, October 20, 2016, 2.
140 Robert Drayton, ed., *The Laws of Palestine in Force on the 31st Day of December 1933* (London: Waterlow and Sons, 1934), 3404.
141 *Jordan Official Gazette*, No. 1171, February 16, 1954, 105.
142 Palestinian Citizenship Order of 1925, Article 6.
143 Palestinian Citizenship Order 1925, Article 129(1). This provision was taken, *mutatis mutandis*, from the first sentence of Article 10 of the British Nationality Act of August 7, 1914; see J. Mervyn Jones, *British Nationality Law and Practice* (Oxford: Oxford University Press, 1947), 178.
144 Chrystal Macmillan, "Nationality of Married Women: Present Tendencies," *Journal of Comparative Legislation and International Law* 7 (1925): 142.
145 Hence, the female person was either a minor girl who followed the nationality of her father or a "minor woman" who followed the nationality of her husband. A woman was considered to be an adult for nationality purposes only if she was single and eighteen years of age or above.
146 Immigration and Travel Section, *Instructions to Immigration Officers and Deputy and Assistant Superintendents of Police* (Jerusalem: Government of Palestine, 1930), Article 87(i).
147 See generally, Mutaz Qafisheh, "Who Has the Right to Become a Palestinian Citizen? An International Law Analysis," *Yearbook of Islamic and Middle Eastern Law* 2014, 18 (2017): 112.
148 Article 9 of CEDAW.
149 309 U.N.T.S. 65 (1958).
150 989 U.N.T.S. 175 (1975).
151 360 U.N.T.S. 117 (1960).
152 Personal Status Law of 1976, Article 166.
153 Personal Status Law of 1976, Article 37; Personal Status Law for Latin Church in Jerusalem of 1954, Article 157; Personal Status Law for Syrian Orthodox of 2000, Article 33; Personal Status Law for the Catholics of 1929 (Beirut: Lebanese Labour Press, 1929), Article 160.
154 Personal Status Law of 1976, Article 132; Personal Status Law of 1954, Article 56.
155 Personal Status Law of 1976, Article 16.
156 Women NGO Coalition on the Implementation of CEDAW, 189.
157 The *Majalle*, Article 1030; see the exception of Article 1685 of the *Majalle* relating to witnessing by women only in places dedicated for the use of women.
158 Personal Status Law for the Syrian Orthodox of 2000, Article 54(3).

Bibliography

Abu-Odeh, Lama. "Honor Killings and the Construction of Gender in Arab Societies." *American Journal of Comparative Law* 58 (2010): 911–952.

Bentwich, Norman. "The New Criminal Code for Palestine." *Journal of Comparative Legislation and International Law* 20, no. 71 (1938): 71–79.

Biribonwoha, Pius. "The Role of Legislative Drafting in the Law Reform Process." *Commonwealth Law Bulletin* 32, no. 4 (December 2006): 601–608.

Cohan, John. "Honor Killings and the Cultural Defense." *California Western International Law Journal* 40 (2010): 177–252.

Danaf, Hebatallah. "The Impact of Legal System on Increasing Women Murder in Palestine." *Seyasat* no. 41 (September 2017): 55–75.

Drayton, Robert, ed. *The Laws of Palestine in Force on the 31st Day of December 1933.* London: Waterlow and Sons, 1934.

Halawa, Niveen. "Early Marriage: Knife in the Side of Palestinian Society." *Seyasat* no. 41 (September 2017): 100–105.

Hass, Amira. "Are Sharia and International Law Compatible? [Interview with Mutaz M. Qafisheh]." *Haaretz*, February 7, 2015. www.haaretz.com/.premium-are-sharia-and-international-law-compatible-1.5302933.

Inter-Parliamentary Union. "Statement by the IPU President Concerning the Detention of the Speaker and other Members of the Palestinian Parliament [Press Release No. 357, Geneva]." January 25, 2012. http://archive.ipu.org/press-e/gen357.htm.

Jones, J. Mervyn. *British Nationality Law and Practice.* Oxford: Oxford University Press, 1947.

Kardawi, Yusuf. *Introduction to the Study of Islamic Sharia.* Cairo: Wahba Library, 1990.

Macmillan, Chrystal. "Nationality of Married Women: Present Tendencies." *Journal of Comparative Legislation and International Law* 7, no. 4 (1925): 142–154.

Manna, Adel. *The District of Jerusalem in the Mid-Ottoman Period: Administration and Society.* Beirut: Institute for Palestine Studies, 2008.

Muwatin (The Palestinian Institute for the Study of Democracy). *Legislation at the Time of Internal Division: Studies on the Legislation Enacted Since 2007.* Ramallah: Muwatin, 2016.

Nesheiwat, Faris. "Honor Crimes in Jordan: Their Treatment under Islamic and Jordanian Criminal Laws." *Penn State International Law Review* 23, no. 251 (2004): 251–281.

Palestinian Central Bureau of Statistics. *Survey of the Workforces in Palestine.* Ramallah: Palestinian Central Bureau of Statistics, 2012.

Qafisheh, Mutaz. "Legislative Drafting in Transitional States: The Case of Palestine." *International Journal of Legislative Drafting and Law Reform* 2, no. 1 (2013): 7–34.

———. "Notification in Case of Polygamy Is Not Enough." September 16, 2014. www.qanon.ps/news.php?action=view&id=18220.

———. "The Interplay between International Human Rights and Labour Rights in Palestine." *Journal of Islamic State Practices in International Law* 9 (2013): 121–146.

———. "Who Has the Right to Become a Palestinian Citizen? An International Law Analysis." *Yearbook of Islamic and Middle Eastern Law 2014* 18 (2017): 112–152.

Ramadan, Aref, ed. *Completion of Laws: Ottoman Laws Valid in Arab States Detached from the Ottoman Government.* Beirut: Science Press, 1928.

Samara, Abedlkarim. "Palestinian Academic is Accused to be Infidel Due to His Courageous Opinions." Accessed May 6, 2014. https://tinyurl.com/yd6xetjz.

Touqan, Talal. *The Necessity Decree-Laws Enacted by the President.* Ramallah: Miftah, 2008.

Tripathi, Anushree, and Supriya Yadav. "For the Sake of Honour: But Whose Honour? Honour Crimes against Women." *Asia-Pacific Journal on Human Rights and the Law* 5, no. 2 (2004): 63–78.

Women NGO Coalition on the Implementation of CEDAW in the Occupied State of Palestine. "Report on the Status of Women and Girls in the State of Palestine [submitted to the UN CEDAW Committee in Geneva]." *Seyasat* no. 41 (September 2017).

Zayat, Iman. "Tunisian President Triggers Debate after Call for Gender Equality in Inheritance, Marriage." *Arab Weekly*, August 16, 2017. https://thearabweekly.com/tunisian-president-triggers-debate-after-call-gender-equality-inheritance-marriage.

Part II

At home

Arab Spring, gender, and human rights

3 The sources of public patriarchal authority in Morocco

Fatima Sadiqi

Introduction

This chapter focuses on the major sources of public patriarchy and their impact on the main social changes in Morocco from precolonial times, to the 2004 law reform, to the present.[1] This chapter builds on the author's previous work, "The Central Role of the Family Law in the Moroccan Feminist Movement," which conceptualized patriarchy in North Africa as both private and public, with the latter regulating social change and law. This chapter narrows the focus to the operation of patriarchy in Morocco.

To address these issues, this chapter proceeds in three sections. First, given the complexity of the Moroccan multilingual and multicultural realities, and the overarching sociocultural and historical conditionings, Section "On the concept of authority" examines and defines the primary and secondary sources of authority in this country that affect how patriarchal structures operate in Morocco. Section "History of patriarchy in Morocco" provides a brief historical overview from pre- to postcolonialism on the operation of patriarchy in Morocco. This section is important because it establishes the foundation for Section "Impact of primary and secondary sources of patriarchal authority in Morocco and primary sources of patriarchal authority in Morocco," which interrogates the primary sources (religion and the monarchy) and secondary sources of patriarchal authority in Morocco (the family, the mosque, the school, the street, the workplace, and the systems of justice). In conclusion, I state that, without understanding the sources of authority in Morocco, it is impossible to envisage any ways of addressing patriarchy in the Moroccan context.

On the concept of authority

The term *authority* refers to a complex abstract concept with sociological and psychological components. I conceptualize authority into primary and secondary sources. Primary sources have stronger abstract cultural weight and include religion, language, the urban/modernity nexus, and monarchy. Secondary sources include the family; the mosque; the school; the urban street and workplace; and modern institutions, particularly the invisible rulers' immediate circles, the parliament, and the court of justice. Each primary source is "relayed" or "executed" by a secondary source: for instance, patriarchy is relayed by the family, religion by the mosque, language by the school, the urban/modernity nexus by the street and workplace, and the invisible entourage by the parliament and the court of justice. Accordingly, the two sources of authority feed into, intersect with, and strengthen each other.

Gender is central to the maintenance of this cross-feeding and the power dynamics it generates. The most important source of authority in Morocco is patriarchy, and, in an endeavor to circumvent its tantalizing impact, a periodization framework is adopted with regard to this particular source. This framework has the advantage of contextualizing the nature and status of patriarchy within larger sociocultural and political boundaries, and gives meaning to the various types of impact it has on the other sources of authority. Patriarchy and its periodization are indeed central in understanding Moroccan women's changing status and their corresponding agency potential, or lack thereof.

The complexity of the concept is rooted in its entanglement with two other concepts: *power* and *legitimacy*. Power is often defined as either a personal or social ability to achieve certain ends.[2] Thus, the ability to impose one's will (or that of a group) over others is an example of individual or social power, respectively. As for legitimacy, it is often characterized as the right to exercise power as constructed by society and psychologically internalized by the members of that society.

As a result, a monarch's rule or a *fqih*'s (religious man) *fatwa* (religious decision) is generally accepted as legitimate in Morocco. In theory, an individual may possess legitimacy without having actual power or possess power without having actual legitimacy. A classic example of the former is the legitimate heir of monarchical power, who is forced to live in exile and, of the latter, the usurper who exiled the heir to the throne and appropriated his monarchical functions. Power and legitimacy relate to authority in the sense that an individual or a group possesses authority only when they have both power (social sanctioning) and legitimacy (unconditional acknowledgment and acceptance). In other words, the social and psychological aspects of authority are essential for its viability and its inclusiveness of power and legitimacy—hence, its cultural strength.

With the advent of social sciences, the concept of authority began to occupy center stage in explaining various power dynamics in a given society and culture. The most influential theory of authority in modern times is that of sociologist Max Weber, who proposed three types of authority: *traditional*, *charismatic*, and *legal-rational*.[3] The first type is typically embodied in the traditional norms of feudalism or patrimonialism, which strived to maintain a grip on individuals and communities by blocking any law that opposed feudal interests. *Traditional authority* depends on long-established customs, habits, and social structures, and its legitimation resides in the sanctity of tradition itself. This type of authority often creates systems of structure that do not change or evolve;[4] additionally, it perpetuates the status quo and does not facilitate social progress. The second type of authority, *charismatic authority*, is typically embodied in a leader whose vision and mission constitute a source of inspiration for others. Weber associates such a leader—for example, a prophet—with perceived extraordinary characteristics and divine or supernatural powers. In the realm of religion, charismatic authority plays an integral role in traditional authority in the sense that charismatic authority is "routinized" or "ritualized" by becoming "traditionalized."[5] In other words, a specific charisma in a specific culture tends to melt into tradition, and followers change into legal or "estate-like" (traditional) buttressing "staff."[6] The third type of authority, ***legal-rational authority***, is typically embodied in the formalistic belief in the content of the legal law as natural rational law.[7] According to Weber, political and economic bureaucracy is the typical example of legal-rational authority.[8] Such a form of authority is best embodied by the modern state, the city government, the private and public corporations, and various voluntary associations. In Morocco, the rational-legal authority is embodied in the *Maliki* School legalized interpretations of the Qur'an, which the Moroccan state adopted after independence and turned into state laws. These are generally perceived as "natural" laws.[9]

In sum, the importance of Weber's types of authority resides in the fact that they create solid belief systems that are difficult to resist or change. Weber's thoughts opened the door to further research on authority. For example, Coser highlights the interconnectedness and overlapping nature of Weber's types, which, in theory, may give rise to other types of authority.[10] This distinction demonstrates how the nuances of Weber's categorizations were singled out by scholars such as Blau, who qualifies traditional authority as "impersonal" in opposition to charismatic authority, which he describes as "personal," and associates the legal-rational authority with "irrational" traditional authority.[11] Blau also notes that whereas charismatic authority is dynamic, the traditional one is not. For Blau, the viability and power of a specific type of authority depend on its ability to retain the traits that make the authority type unique.

Therefore, traditional authority may be weakened by a charismatic authority's revolutionary ideals or by a rational authority's pursuit of ends via abstract formal principles. Conversely, a charismatic, revolutionary movement can be translated into a traditional order or incorporated into a rational, formal organization. Similarly, the irrational power of tradition or charisma can weaken legal-rational authority. In addition, humanity has witnessed several social movements started by charismatic authorities who rose in the face of traditional or legal-rational authority. In sum, there are ways of circumventing what would appear as solid authority.

Authority is linked to hierarchy, as the latter ensures the necessary superior–subordinate relationship that defines the former. Being a concept where items (objects, names, values, categories, etc.) are represented as being "above," "below," or "at the same level as" one another, hierarchy can link entities directly, indirectly, vertically, or horizontally. Indeed, a combination of authority and hierarchy is crucial for an efficient organization of power structure in the sense that, for the latter to work, it needs an intersection of hierarchy and authority at some point. This intersection is deemed necessary for a well-ordered society, as it is supposed to ensure and maintain a certain status quo or serve a specific party. In turn, this specific party will endeavor to maintain the status quo. It is these various intersections that make challenges to authority difficult and explain the fact that authority can and usually is delegated or transferred. Yet another significant development of Weber's characterization of authority is the work of Collins, which links Weber's categories of authority to a larger network of concepts that include class, status groups, and parties. Collins argues that while traditional authority underlies status groups, charismatic authority underlies market schemes, such as the potential for life chances.[12] This view runs counter to Weber's, which sees charismatic authority as an outcome of class and parties as the codification of legal-rational authority, especially in the case of bureaucracies.

Today, authority is generally understood as a function of power—that is, as the supposed legitimacy and symbolic power that institutionalize it. In modern social sciences, authority is becoming increasingly important in researching a variety of empirical settings, social patterns, and human behavior, such as the family (patriarchal or "father" authority), the mosque (religious authority), the school (knowledge authority), and politics (institutional authority).[13] These sources are created locally and tend to be culture specific. In Morocco, for example, authority is primarily perceived and lived through the prism of culture. A consideration of the sources of authority in Morocco suggests that they are of two main types: primary and secondary. The primary sources have strong cultural weight and include patriarchy. This chapter addresses the roots of current patriarchy in Morocco because without knowing the nature, history, and workings of these roots, we cannot understand the overall status of women in today's Morocco. Knowledge and appreciation of the roots also allow better ways of reforming the state's legal system, which still restricts women in private and public spaces. Education has been instrumental in giving Moroccan women a female consciousness of their roles and potentials in society; however, these roles and potentials can be further enhanced by their knowledge of the sources of patriarchy that still reinforce a restrictive legal system: (and its immediate circles),[14] the parliament, and the court of justice. The Moroccan historian Abdallah Laroui defines the term *makhzen,* which literally means "warehouse," in the following terms: "*Makhzen* refers both to an administrative apparatus and to particular social and cultural symbols, as well as to practices and rituals that have always buttressed functions of the state."[15]

Administratively, the *Makhzen* relies on a system of advisors with a full-fledged and highly influential administrative structure that focuses on specific issues, such as education, business, civil society, and so on. The sociocultural and symbolic aspects of the *Makhzen* are mainly embodied in the practices and rituals that reinforce the state, such as the annual formal allegiance, whereby representatives of the various regions in Morocco express their formal allegiance and that of the people they represent to the king. The *Makhzen* concretizes the primary authority of monarchy (and the state) and constitutes a notorious source of political power in Morocco. Its longevity stems from its capacity to adapt to changing times.

History of patriarchy in Morocco

Patriarchy (derived from *patri*—father) is the strongest and most pervasive source of primary authority in Morocco. As a concept, patriarchy has been defined in various ways. Two such definitions are relevant for the purposes of this chapter. The first one is from the anthropologist Michael Hughes, who defines patriarchy as

> a system of social organizations in which men have a disproportionate share of power. [Patriarchy] is rooted in cultural and legal systems that historically gave fathers authority in family and clan matters, made wives and children dependent on husbands and fathers, and organized descent and inheritance through the male line.[16]

The second definition is from anthropologist Allan Johnson, who considers patriarchy as a social structure with four dimensions: (1) male domination (men hold the most powerful roles and women the least powerful ones), (2) male control (women are subject to physical and psychological control and violence in exchange for supervision and protection), (3) male identification (valued aspects are associated with men and devalued ones with women), and (4) male centricity (more attention is granted to men than women in (media) representations).[17]

In highlighting the sociocultural, legal, and political roots of the patriarchal order, both definitions are central to the themes of this chapter.[18] For example, in addition to a patriarchal family structure, the patriarchal interpretations of the sacred texts resulted in a male-biased legal Islam. In addition, in Morocco, manifestations of state patriarchy take the form of state feminization of anything connected with the indigenous ethnic Moroccan Berber population or anything characterized as "rural."

Historically, patriarchy rose as a social institution with the rise of urban centers and the emergence of property owning.[19] According to Gerda Lerner, the appropriation of women's sexual and reproductive capacity by men took place before the formation of private property and class society.[20] With the advent of the latter, men linked class to the means of production in the sense that whoever owns production (men) dominates those who do not (women). Women had a mediated relationship to class because they had access to the means of production and material resources through ties with men. This view was corroborated by the author's own observation that the economic importance of what men and women do is not often related to their social preeminence; thus, the norm is that dominant classes tend to make subordinate classes do the work for them. Subsequently, what women produced was always important for their communities and societies, but women themselves were systematically excluded from the exchange market as genuine economic agents and from accessing the benefits of their work. This resulted in the division of women into "respectable" (tied to a man) and "nonrespectable" (free, that is attached to all men) categories, regardless of what they did.[21] To consolidate its grip, patriarchy manifests itself in both concrete ways (such as disqualifying women as voters, preventing them from royal succession, or leading public prayers) and representational ways (such as representing the male-dominated order as normal or true and women as respectable and nonrespectable).

As a source of authority, patriarchy is not static; it is an ongoing process that is continuously shaped and reshaped by both men and women. Throughout the long history of Morocco, various patriarchies have held sway over five major periods that may be singled out: pre-Islamic, early Islamic, precolonial, colonial, and postcolonial. Continuity and change characterize this periodization.

Patriarchy in early Islamic Morroco

Islam was introduced to North Africa by Musa Ibn Nusayr and his warriors in the seventh century.[22] The newcomers brought with them an already well-entrenched Arab–Islamic patriarchy. The major forces that shaped this patriarchy were Berber tribalism, Arab Beduin tribalism, and legal Islam.[23] The notion of "tribe" is important in any discussion of patriarchy in North Africa because it is based on male lineage and supremacy. The most widely recognized authority on North African tribalism is Ibn Khaldun.[24] For this author, fourteenth-century North Africa was made up of two social groups: the urban (*al ʿumarn al-madani*) and the rural (*al-ʾumran al-badawi*). As urbans were then fewer in number, they lived in fortified cities, had urban jobs, organized dynasties, and depended on rurals for their protection. The latter were greater in number; indeed, they constituted the majority of the North African populations at the time. It is for this reason that Ibn Khaldun gave them special attention: "J'ai mis en tête la civilization bédouine parce qu'elle est la première à se manifester sur la terre [I start with the Beduin civilization because it was the first one to manifest itself on earth.]"[25]

People residing in rural Morocco were seminomads, lived in tents, raised animals, and organized themselves in tribes. Although their tribal structure differed from tribe to tribe and had to accommodate local specificities, the tribes themselves shared a common feature: they had a common male ancestor, whose name they carried. Tribes branched into subtribes and bigger tribes branched into smaller ones with their own oldest male ancestors. Whatever the size of the tribe, it commanded loyalty and solidarity among its members; the notion of an individual who was isolated from the tribe was an alien concept. When a member of a tribe was attacked, all the other members mobilized like one single body to defend the individual. This was expressed in Ibn Khaldun's term "ʿa*sabiyyah*" (the singular form, *asab*, meaning "nerve," and the collective noun, *ʿasabiyya*, meaning "the spirit-nerve of the clan").[26] In tribal social organization, ancestral lineage was the foundation of human identity, and the identity of a human subject came before anything else, including his or her tribal or dynastic history.[27] *ʿAsabiyya* was, thus, the basis of tribal organization and the nerve of North African patriarchy. It created a belief system with strong cultural and/or ethnic identity aspects that separated members of one tribal group from those of another one. The next section describes the two major types of tribalism that existed in Morocco, Berber and Arab, and elucidates commonalities and distinctions.

Berber tribalism

Modern scholars have identified four major traits that differentiate the most salient characteristics of traditional Berber society from Arab society: segmentarianism, cephalousness, kinship, and egalitarianism.[28] Segmentarianism is a tribal system that stresses the existence of a common ancestor or a common territory that would keep balance and opposition in the tribe. This trait is more prevalent in mountainous regions than in pastoral ones, a characteristic that differentiates Berber tribes (often mountainous) from the Arab Beduin ones (often pastoral). This particular characteristic is still prevalent in contemporary Moroccan Berber tribes. The second trait, cephalousness, denotes a structure with minimally established political power and hierarchy. Contemporary Moroccan Berber tribes still adhere to this structure. The third trait, kinship, refers to family relationships that are distinctive to a single tribe. Kinship ensures loyalty and solidarity. The last trait, egalitarianism, describes the need for power to be fair when administrating intratribal affairs. It is important to note that tribal egalitarianism was only applied to men.

In sum, the Berber tribe was based on a relatively simple internal social structure with few (if any) significant social distinctions between individuals. Being kinship based and intrinsically agnatic, this type of tribal system was inherently patriarchal and self-sufficient; hence, Berber tribesmen rejected any imposition of centralized authority.[29]

The transmission of Islam to the North African region resulted in an increasing number of Berber mountainous tribes' migration to urbanized areas. Their migration resulted in the expansion of tribes with more pronounced notions of "clans." Clans became defined as federations of several extended families whose male members claimed to be sons of the paternal uncle without specifying the degree of that relationship. During this time, the concept of clans began to spread in North Africa. The Islamic Berber tribal patriarchy was characterized by a typically rigid sexual segregation and stratification, referred to by Bourdieu as a "mythico-ritual system" founded on "male self-esteem and male self-image in the company of peers."[30] This segregation was typically based on space and is best expressed in Bourdieu's terms as

> the opposition between the inside and the outside. [It] is expressed concretely in the sharp division between the women's space—the house and its garden, a closed, secret, away from intrusions and the public gaze—and the men's space—the place of assembly, the mosque […], the fields and the market.[31]

This space-based patriarchy was motivated by a cardinal pillar of the Islamic Berber patrilineal system: safeguarding and preserving loyalty to family honor, which meant male honor.[32]

In traditional Berber culture, spatial sexual division of labor assigned a man the duty of defending his honor, which included his extended female kin (especially the wife/wives and children), and assigned a woman the duty to seek a man's protection. In such a context, the conception of honor among Berbers was based on the socialization of the male members of the tribe in a manner that would make them shelter the private sphere of intimacy and women with a duty to protect that power while expecting the protection to do so from men. In this overall socialization framework, the masculine and feminine spaces had to be clearly separated.[33] As some Berber communities became gradually urbanized, men's spaces started to overlap with women's, leading to new patriarchal strategies, such as confinement and/or the wearing of the veil, as a way of safeguarding intimacy.

Space-based patriarchy also meant sustained and continuous protection of male self-esteem and honor, especially in the presence of other males. Accordingly, men's weaknesses (especially psychological ones), as well as any shortcomings, failures, or internal dissensions, were not to be exposed in the presence of other men—especially strangers to one's own tribe or clan—and, more importantly, in the presence of women. Wives were expected to keep their husbands' secrets and never divulge them, not even to their own families, hence the general reluctance of husbands and mothers-in-law to let wives pay frequent visits to their blood relatives. Women's failure to abide by these unwritten rules could lead to tarnished male reputation, which, in some instances, could lead the husband to unilaterally divorce his wife. Thus, within this system, women's subordinate statuses were necessary. According to Bourdieu,

> The ethos of male honor is opposed in its very principle to a universal, formal code affirming the equal dignity of all men and therefore the identity of their rights and duties. Not only do the rules imposed upon men differ from those imposed upon women [...] but also the commands of honor, directly applied to particular cases and varying according to the situation, are in no way capable of being universalized.[34]

Ironically, in subordinating women, the patriarchal order facilitated the establishment of the tribal "egalitarian" system (alluded to above) in the sense that male subordination of women did not exclude equality among men. This equality meant the creation and maintenance of homogeneity in the tribe. Indeed, the typical Berber Islamic tribe continued to be a homogeneous group of clans whose members held claims of descent from a common male ancestor. These characteristics made the Berber Islamic tribe a patrilineal, patrilocal, and patriarchal system built on the absolute subordination of women's rights to those of their male kin. To reinforce and maintain its authority, the tribe sacralized the institution of the "father-patriarch," whereby the father was granted absolute authority over his wife (wives) and children and absolute power to disinherit potential male heirs if they violated tribal norms. According to Bourdieu, the father had an even more potent authority: the power to "call down curses" and bring down divine punishment on the rebel, the ungrateful, or the prodigal.[35]

However, the authority of the father-patriarch was not total. It was subjected to the indirect control of another tribal institution: the djemaa, a group of men who functioned as heads of the clan lineage.[36] The djemaa had direct control over the tribe and indirect control over the family. The main authority of the djemaa resided in its control of what was known as arch lands, which it distributed to members of the tribe each year in accordance with their needs. The land allotment took place annually in the fall after the first rains. Other prerogatives of the djemaa were the capacity to adjudicate conflicts between clans and expel individuals for offenses against the tribe. Among these offenses, adultery held a prominent place. In this way, the dialectic relationship between the tribe and the family underscored the family and social aspect of the patriarchal system: the social role of fatherhood (power over women and children) was supported by a political economy (control of arch lands) in which the family unit retained a significant productive role (cultivation of land).[37]

Another foundational aspect of Islamic Berber tribal organization was the veneration of overarching saints. Saints were considered figures that transcended the social organization of the tribe and ensured a continuity that the tribal organization might not maintain. Each local area had its saint, and the whole nation had a monarch or a political leader. The saints were produced and constrained by the functional needs of the tribes.[38] Each tribe had its preferred saint, who was seen as a spiritual protector of the tribe and its gifts, and annual festivals (moussems) were organized by the tribes in their honor. Visiting saints in search of "baraka" (divine blessings) is still practiced in today's Berber communities in Morocco and Algeria, and is considered a typical way for women to gather and socialize.

Patriarchy in Islamic Morocco—the precolonial era[39]

The precolonial era spans the centuries that followed the coming of Islam to Morocco, from the eighth to the beginning of the twentieth centuries.[40] During this period, the early Islamic cohabitation of Berber and Arab tribalisms intensified, which constituted the heart of Arab tribalism, and appealed to Berber tribesmen who were converting to Islam en masse, mainly through military enlisting. This greatly facilitated the cohabitation of the two tribalisms and resonated well with the Berber and Arab patriarchal social systems.[41]

Patriarchy in precolonial Morocco was reinforced by the factors that marked the period: economic hardship, famine, and protests.[42] This hardship culminated into the nineteenth century and paved the way to colonization. Precolonial patriarchy manifested itself through three things: a more sophisticated tribalism, a harsher Islamic doctrine, and "men-friendly" architecture.[43] As a tool of segregation between men and women, space was again incorporated into the three. With respect to the first manifestation, Islamic Berber tribalism became more complex and more hierarchical with the coming of Islam because it needed to integrate core aspects of Arab tribalism as well as use religion to consolidate the varied tribalisms. As for the harsher Islamic doctrine, Berber tribesmen during this period adopted a rigid version of legal Islam and a strong sense of the "community of the faithful" (*Umma*), which was unified by religion and rendered Berber Islamic tribalism more sophisticated. As non-Arab tribes, Berber elites adopted a harsher Islamic doctrine that took them to the highest levels of political authority. Indeed, various Berber dynasties[44] ruled Morocco from the eleventh to the fifteenth century and could extend their political domination to Senegal in Africa and to Spain and Portugal in Europe. It is important to note that none of these dynasties claimed descent from the Prophet Muhammad; they came from local regions and spoke Berber as their mother tongue. Within this overall system, women continued to occupy subordinate societal roles. They had to live in households where, together with their children, they occupied the lowest positions and had the least power. This is in accordance with Kandiyoti's characterization of the "precolonial" households as "paterfamilias," where women had an intrinsically unequal position.[45] In this type of family, young women married older men and gained more status when they bore sons and eventually became mothers-in-law. In fact, the logic behind girls' marrying at a very young age was to extend the length of the time they could bear children, and thus garner power and status for their families.[46] Such households also survived because in the face of women's illiteracy, poverty, and the burden of cultural norms, young girls socialized more easily to unequal roles and inequitable entitlement to their family resources.[47] At the same time, however, they were the bearers of family and community honor and reputation. Nevertheless, in exchange for abiding by these patriarchal rules that lowered their status, they gained protection and maintenance.[48]

As for architecture, the spatial organization of houses was based on gender segregation, with the visible parts of the house being allocated to men, and the less visible parts allocated to women. In this architectural logic, endogamous sexuality, a cardinal cornerstone of patriarchy, necessitated an introvert spatial organization of homes. This was concretized with the rise of cities in the premodern Morocco. For example, the architecture of the precolonial city (*medina*)[49] of Fez, founded by Moulay Idriss II in A.D. 789, was meant to express a combination of tribal and Islamic patriarchal ideologies. This explains the building of distinct quarters specializing in distinct crafts and skills throughout the *medina*, with each quarter denoting a specific tribe of origin. In other words, it was tribal logic that dictated the division of the city into quarters offering services in different skills. These skills, in turn, gave names to these quarters. Hence, there were quarters for *nnajarin* (carpenters), *dabbaghin* (leather workers), and *attarin* (spice vendors), which expressed not only tribal divisions but also a desire to segregate tribal families and ensure endogamy.

As for the expression of Islamic patriarchy, it was based on hegemony in the name of Islam. Fez was called *dar al-Islam* (the house of Islam), and its architecture reflected this: an overall round shape that engulfed all identities in its controlled space.[50] The introvert and labyrinthine architecture of the *medina* of Fez as well as that of its houses was meant to express the integration of various identities in one space in the name of an Islamic universalist faith. The founder's sacralized tomb was positioned at the center of the *medina* as the most important piece of architecture, with places such as the tombs of other religious saints, a religious university, *zaouias* (Islamic *fiqhic* schools), *medersas* (religious schools), *souqs* (public markets), *hammams* (public baths), and "noble" trades surrounding it in a protectively circular introvert and labyrinthine arrangement. Furthermore, both the tribal and Islamic patriarchal logics thrived on displaying public pride in a glorious past, which was reflected in the glamorous design and decorated entrances of religious and public places that contrasted sharply with the shabbiness of the doors of ordinary houses.[51]

The meeting of the tribal and Islamic patriarchal systems produced an architectural logic where the veiling of women was necessary to both keep tribal segregation and enforce Islamic law. With respect to tribal segregation, ensuring paternal genealogical descent was crucial and, with respect to Islamic law enforcement, producing legal human beings who could own and transmit money and property was important. However, as women's virginity was a way of ensuring lineage in spite of the fact that women did not inherit in the same way as men in Islamic law, they needed to be controlled with veiling.[52] Thus, in both the tribal mentality and the Islamic law logic, women had to be banned from free circulation in mixed public spaces, which could lead to unwanted promiscuity or "mixed" marriages that would threaten family cohesion and wealth. Women's veiling in public spaces was also a manifestation of a space-based patriarchy that imposed clear gender distinctions on men and women. As an extension of this, the streets of the *medina* were designed as places for men only; narrow and tortuous, they could accommodate only animals (especially donkeys and mules) to transport people (usually men) and goods. In addition, the fact that the houses of the *medina* had no windows or balconies looking on the outside made the overall architecture of the houses introversive.

Despite the convergence of the tribal and Islamic patriarchies in architecture, there existed some differences between the Berber and the Arab in the ways in which women related to the territorial spaces they occupied. The Arab house typically consisted of a large courtyard, which dominated a series of long, narrow rooms or "dependencies" that opened on it. In comparison, the Berber house consisted of large independent rooms opening on the courtyard.[53] In a sense, the structure of the Arab house imposed asexuality designed to serve and protect the patriarchal prerogative of "hiding women,"[54] while the structure of the Berber house relatively gave women more freedom and visibility. In Berber communities, the mother or wife of the eldest male was considered "the pillar of the house."[55] She was responsible for the household economy and the behavior of younger women living with her—daughters and daughters-in-law. In the Berber *Tuareg* societies, women had an important role in their communities, as they influenced decision-making at all levels.[56] Monogamy, which is general in Berber areas in spite of legal and religious customs permitting up to four wives, also reinforced the unity of the household.

Patriarchy in colonial Morocco

The French colonization (Protectorate) of Morocco was officially established by the so-called Traité de Fès (the Fez Treaty), signed on March 30, 1912, and lasting until November 18, 1956.[57] Under the cover of a *mission civilisatrice* (civilizing mission), the French colonizers reinforced patriarchy and never considered empowering Moroccan women. The interaction between patriarchy and colonialism in Morocco was facilitated by a set of commonalities the two shared. Both patriarchy and colonialism entrapped and unfairly defined minority groups (women in the case of patriarchy and the natives in the case of colonialism), and both used their intrusive "male gaze" to reduce these groups to stereotypes: "virgins," "whores," "savages," and "heathens," thus denying their identities.[58]

Similarly, patriarchy and colonialism manifested themselves in both material and symbolic ways. On the material level, they disqualified women from education, jobs, and politics, and on the symbolic or imaginative level, they used strong representational systems to make their projects seem "normal" and "true."[59] Patriarchy and colonialism also fed into each other; by being unequivocally male centered and Eurocentric, colonialism (and imperialism) often engendered patriarchal beliefs and misogyny, thus immediately categorizing native women as "alien" and "subaltern."[60] Finally, both patriarchy and colonialism, as sources of authority, engendered resistance in the forms of nationalist and feminist movements.

The meeting of the colonial and local patriarchies was detrimental to Moroccan women. French colonial oppression affected the lives of women, both socially and economically, resulting in a type of "double colonization," as women were discriminated against for their positions as colonized people and as women.[61] It is a proven fact that patriarchy becomes stronger in times of crises.[62] Augmented by colonization, a combination of the precolonial, space-based patriarchy and an increasing colonization tightened its grip during the colonial period under two apparently similar but deeply different pretexts: the preservation of local religion, family structure, and traditions, on the one hand, and the respect (and distance from) those very traditions, on the other. Hence, in the face of the homogenizing colonization, local patriarchy was further reinforced as the "shelter" of Morocco's collective self that fueled nationalism and the struggle for liberation.

The nationalists facilitated the role of women as the "producers" of heroes that would stand in the face of the French invaders. Indeed, Moroccans in general designated women as guardians of the patriarchal order during colonization. In parallel, the colonialists targeted their "civilizing mission" to future male state-builders and potential male interlocutors by exploiting women only for prostitution. For this purpose, the colonialists built all-male schools, cafés, and brothels.[63] The nationalists' and the colonizers' perspectives on women produced a complex patriarchal system where authority was male and where women were relegated to the background. This period of Morocco's history was documented in novels, poems, and social history.[64]

During this time, literary art documented a difficult period of disillusionment, paradoxes, contrasts, and ambiguities.[65] Nevertheless, women were conscious of these complex challenges and participated in the struggles for independence.

Moroccan women's participation in the fight for decolonization was generally characterized as "liminal," "transitory," and "mobile": gender segregation boundaries temporarily disappeared, allowing Moroccan women "temporary" access and authority in the public sphere of power.[66] The boundaries of the male–female spaces were briefly blurred during this period, as women were encouraged to circulate freely in public spaces when assisting in the armed struggle and engaging in tasks such as transferring ammunition and bringing food and medical help to the freedom fighters.[67]

It is important to note here that the nationalist and colonialist patriarchal discourses did not highlight the roles of Berbers, especially Berber women, in the struggle for independence. This attitude is clearly documented in the narratives of nationalism and struggles for independence. According to Chafik, Moroccan historians did not show interest in the long colonial war waged by colonial armies on the populations of the Atlas Mountains of Morocco during a period of time that stretched from 1912 to 1934, which constitutes almost half the length of the French Protectorate.[68] Ironically, it was the French colonizers who were unintentionally forced to recognize the courage, pride, and resilience of the Berber mountainous people, who performed heroically for independence and paid a high price on human, economic, and political levels. With the gradual extinction of the Moroccan generations who lived through the period of armed resistance, all that has survived of this period is oral or written testimonies. For example, Berber oral poetry and literature, most of it authored and preserved by women, was used to echo men's and women's resistance to the French colonization in remote areas.[69] The significance and function of illiterate women's oral poetry of resistance is an example of women's authority in a patriarchal system going through mass mobilization for a noble national cause. However, as Leila Abouzeid brilliantly depicts in her novel *The Year of the Elephant*, Moroccan women's authority (she calls it "public utility") disappeared after independence.[70] Indeed, the first law that the newly independent elite in Morocco promulgated was a family law where women figured as "second-class" citizens.[71] Such examples express the tenacity of patriarchy in Moroccan society. Indeed, despite lip service to women's heroism in both the private and public spheres, little was done to concretely reward these women.

In sum, patriarchy was substantially reinforced during the colonial period, and women's issues were not on politicians' agendas at the time. Even so, this did not prevent Berber rural women from expressing anger and urban women from demanding rights. Indeed, Moroccan modern social history has largely fed on the female oral literature of the period, and the Moroccan urban feminist movement was born in 1946—that is, during the Protectorate.

Patriarchy in postcolonial Morocco (neopatriarchy)

This section analyzes patriarchy in postcolonial Moroccan society through the present day. Assuming that present-day human societies are all patriarchal, patriarchy does not manifest itself in the same way everywhere. For example,

Arab–Muslim patriarchy is based on space, while mainstream Western patriarchy is based on imagery: large, economy-controlling multinationals create images of women they impose on consumers (men and women). The power of economy and wealth in mainstream Western societies also creates a dynamic in which the economy controllers attempt to guess women's needs, sometimes before the women themselves can articulate them. Consequently, the basic difference between Arab–Islamic patriarchy and mainstream Western patriarchy is the prominent status of the father in the former, not only at the family level (women keep their fathers' names after marriage) but also at the state level (the supreme leader is also the "father" of the nation). In mainstream Western societies, it is more appropriate to speak of "male dominance," where tension is located between the "husband" and "wife" rather than between the father and the women in the family.

Patriarchy in independent Morocco has been deeply affected by postcolonialism and state policies. Postcolonialism can be characterized as the overall reaction to colonialism with a focus on power relations between the dominating and the dominated groups. In postcolonial Morocco, it is evident that patriarchy weakened but was not substantially dismantled. The weakening manifested itself in the war on social representations, the powers they served, the cultural hierarchies they constructed, and the inequalities they consolidated, which opened some intellectual space within which patriarchy was addressed, sometimes in severe terms. However, these attacks were levered by what may be called "state patriarchy" or "neo-patriarchy." Neopatriarchy is the product of the encounter of modernity and patriarchy (in its traditional sense) in an overarching context where global capitalism dictates the laws of economy to dependent nations.[72] This encounter created two conflicting demands in postcolonial Morocco: a need for material prosperity, which necessitated modernization, and a need for a national identity, which necessitated the maintaining of tradition. By Islamizing the state (Islam is the official religion of the state), pushing for rather conservative family law, favoring urban over rural areas, and favoring Arabic over Berber, the postindependence state enhanced patriarchy.[73] While postcolonial patriarchy was the target of the pioneer feminists in Morocco, it has also opened the door to the second source of authority: religion and, more specifically, legal Islam.

Impact of primary and secondary sources of patriarchal authority in Morocco

Patriarchy, religion, language, the urban/modernity nexus, and monarchy are the primary sources of authority in the Moroccan culture. The strength of these sources resides in their capacity to create, maintain, and monitor a system of sociocultural values that span family (social organization), the mosque, the street and workplace, as well as political institutions. These sources interact and often feed into each other, and subsequently have a tantalizing power.

Religion

As a concept, religion is so encompassing that it may be approached from various angles. In this section, religion is perceived in its sociological dimension, namely, as an institutionalized system of beliefs, symbols, and values that are significant on the personal, social, economic, legal, and political levels.[74] On the personal level, religion provides members of a social community with solutions to otherwise complex and apparently unsolvable questions, such as the deep suffering following the death of a beloved or unexpected failure, and endows them with ultimate and convincing answers to such questions and dilemmas. As such, religion is a powerful source of individual fulfillment and integrity, and a panacea to fear and frustration. By spanning both life and the afterlife, religion opens metaphysical horizons for humans and positions them at the center of both worlds, endowing them with possibilities of infinite, uplifting self-expansion, self-growth, and self-empowerment. Within this framework of thought, humans do not live by knowledge alone and need religion to cope with the unknown.

On the social level, religion is a powerful means of social cohesion, social welfare, and social control. As far as social cohesion is concerned, the social values by which individuals control the actions of the self and others are founded on religion. For example, "children should obey their parents," "women should be faithful to men," or "people should be honest and virtuous," are examples of social values which maintain social cohesion and perpetuation. This social role of religion can never be completely replaced by advanced human thought, science, or technology. Indeed, society thrives on confident citizens who are willing to fulfill their social roles. With respect to social welfare, religion provides humanity with important services, such as employment, encouragement of culture, and so forth. For example, religion is widely recognized to have laid the foundations for philosophy, medicine, and other sciences. It also helped to spread education, encourage philanthropy, and draw attention to the suffering of the poor. As for social control, through its system of values, religion designs moral, disciplined, and socialized citizens.

By endowing humans, especially the youth, with a model of living, religion also spreads and sustains specific values and ideals that believers/citizens adopt easily. On an economic level, religion influences the adopted trends in the management of economic life. According to Weber, the reason why Hindus highlight the spiritual aspect of their lives is that materialism did not firmly take root in the Indian economic fabric.[75] In contrast, capitalism grew more in Protestant countries such as the United States and Great Britain, and less in Catholic Italy or Spain. On the legal level, religion often regulates human behavior in vital ways. This is often reflected in family laws, which assume a significant role in the entire legal apparatus of countries where religion functions at the state level. On the political level, religious authority may be channeled, with various degrees of intensity, through powerful public institutions, such as ministries and schools. All these aspects make religion a strong source of authority, especially when facilitated by ruling patriarchs.

Throughout the ages in Morocco, religion has been manifested in Paganism, Judaism, Christianity, and Islam.[76] While documentation on transitions from Paganism to Judaism and from the latter to Christianity is scarce, the transition from the pre-Islamic to the Islamic period is well documented. This transition was a monumental one in the history of Morocco, and, in order to appreciate it, we must briefly consider some women-related changes that took place before Islam reached Morocco.

Islam appeared first in Arabia (the Middle East), an already heavily patriarchal and tribal society. Arab patriarchy witnessed an ebb and flow in its status during the transition from the pre-Islamic to the Islamic eras. The very first decades of Islam in Arabia were rather beneficial to women.[77] Indeed, before the advent of Islam, Arabian women had few if any rights, and even the right of life could be jeopardized, as small girls were often buried alive in times of scarcity because the little food that was available went to boys, as girls were considered a perpetual potential source of *fitna* (chaos) that would bring dishonor to the family. This situation changed with the coming of Islam, as the Qur'an states that on the Day of Judgment, "buried girls" will rise from their graves and ask for what crime they were killed.[78] Polyandrous relationships, which some authors[79] believe existed in pre-Islamic societies, were replaced by polygamous ones under Islam. In addition, Islam taught that men and women were equal before God.

The advent of Islam was also accompanied with a number of real and alleged changes in the overall status of women. For example, Islam allowed women to retain their fathers' names after marriage (thus acquiring a legal personality) and legally own property (up to one-half of the property in a marriage). It also granted them divinely sanctioned inheritance and the right to reject the terms of a proposal and initiate divorce. Women also acquired a Qur'an-codified right to own a *mahr* (dowry).[80] Furthermore, in early Islam, women were professionals and property owners.

However, things gradually changed over the century and a half after the death of Prophet Muhammad, and strict patriarchy resumed with force in the institutionalization of legal Islam, as is reflected in the development of Muslim schools of law or *fiqh* (religious jurisprudence) some three centuries after the Prophet's death.

Legal, doctrinal, or man-made Islam must be differentiated from popular and spiritual Islam. While the former is linked to the public spaces of authority and male control, the latter is more related to the private sphere and women. By securing both spiritual (universal) Islam and legal Islam, patriarchy made it possible to maintain the presumption of equality between males by allowing reference to the moral force of Islam while simultaneously sustaining a system of subordinating females.

The type of Islam that reached North Africa in the seventh century A.D. was mainly legal Islam. Legal Islam gradually but drastically changed various aspects in the lives of people in Morocco.[81] The indigenous tribes, themselves heavily patriarchal, gradually adopted the *Maliki* School of jurisprudence. According to the Moroccan historian Mohamed el-Mansour, when Islam reached Morocco, the *Maliki Madhab* doctrine was chosen because it was the simplest and most straightforward of the four Islamic *Madhabs*, and was thus best suited for the needs of Berber tribes, who were supposedly not well versed in Arabic.[82] According to el-Mansour, *Maliki* rites and jurisprudence were formulated in ways that resembled the Berber customary law tables (*alwah*), which still exist in some Berber villages. As Maddy-Weitzman states,

> Given the fact that Maliki rites and jurisprudence are considered to be the most straightforward and least philosophical of the four Islamic schools of law, they could easily be transmitted in a simplified fashion, making them appropriate for illiterate Berber tribesmen who had difficulty mastering Arabic.[83]

The simplicity of the Maliki School did not make it less patriarchal than the other schools of Islamic jurisprudence. As Berbers outnumbered Arabs at the onset of the Islamization of what is now Morocco, their type of tribalism was more pervasive and dominant. Because they were not Arab, they strived—perhaps more than the latter—to impose legal Islam. The meeting of legal Islam and tribalism (Arab and Berber) created tension; each one of these sought to assert itself through some kind of gender segregation. This tension intensified the grip over family and social organization in the name of establishing and keeping order. This legal aspect of Islam was greatly exploited by conservatives throughout the following centuries to resist social transformations in Morocco. This, in turn, resulted in continuous controversy as to what the Qur'an concedes to women. Accordingly, early Islamic patriarchy in North Africa was disseminated through a combination of Berber and Arab tribalisms, on the one hand, and Islamic doctrine, on the other. Both of these implemented spatial segregation to separate men from women and designated women to inculcate and implement this segregation. Bourdieu rightly claims that legal Islam reinforced patriarchy by positioning the agnatic family at the center stage of the greater *Umma* (Muslim nation or "bigger family"), hence making it central in Islamic law-making.[84] Therefore, the regulations of marriage, repudiation, and inheritance could only be expected to give priority to the group and the patriarch, relegating women to an inferior rank.

Along the same line of thought, but from a different perspective, Nikki Keddie posits that by favoring male children over female ones in Islamic inheritance rules, patrilineage was supported by legal Islam.[85] It is important to note that it was the rise of private property (itself brought about by the increasing emergence of new cities) that positioned inheritance rules at the center of the laws that regulated men–women unions. Male property owners needed to control the flow of wealth by ensuring regulated succession. In other words, by dictating family laws, legal Islam provided a religious rationale to institutionalize patriarchy and position it at the center of Muslim family organization.[86] This powerful relationship between legal Islam and patriarchy continued to be reinforced in the centuries that followed the coming of Islam to North Africa.

The overall subordination of women to men in legal Islam resulted in the "automatic" interpretation of female attributes as inferior to men's. As such, the assumption that women cannot call for prayers or lead mixed-gender prayers[87] because their voices are *ʿawra* (taboo) and their bodies *fitna* (chaos) fostered cultural and social resistance to their political leadership (such as leading a political party or a state) and their religious authority (such as issuing *fatwas*, which are scholarly commentaries). The obvious logic was that if women's voices were not important in religion, why should they be important in the media, the parliament, or the government? While it is true that patriarchal legislation was challenged by Islamic reform in the nineteenth century, that was interrupted by colonization, and was resumed decades after the independence of North African countries, including Morocco. Indeed, a number of women and men are now challenging Islamic patriarchal legal laws.

Today, religion is still a genuine source of authority in Morocco. The term "religion" is largely equated with "Islam," which is the central element in the lives of Moroccans;[88] it is the propagator of the values and ethical codes that provide the integration of personality, cohesion to society, and stability in the economy. This "packaged" understanding of Islam blurs an important dichotomy that characterizes this religion: both a faith/spiritual aspect and a legal/doctrinal one. While the former aspect is personal and egalitarian, the latter is more related to social control and culture. The latter aspect also constitutes a genuine source of authority and interacts with patriarchy in a very significant way: Both patriarchy and legal Islam were created by men, and both have defined the dominant family order in Moroccan culture.[89]

The Moroccan Monarchy

The institution of monarchy is another source of authority in Morocco. The Moroccan monarchy is the oldest ruling one in the world.[90] A number of American, European, and North African anthropologists have spent considerable time and energy trying to understand this monarchy—its nature; structure; strategies; and, above all, its longevity.[91] One of the most convincing arguments that most of these anthropologists stress is the fact that monarchal rule came to Morocco hand in hand with Islam in the eighth century, and thus has strong cultural roots, which gave it uncontested legitimacy. Moroccan monarchs have always embodied the highest executive and religious authority, thus combining both temporal and spiritual powers. After independence, the monarch is also the supreme "arbiter" in national controversial debates that often oppose conservatives and modernists on issues such as women's and language rights. Royal authority was sought to balance conservatism and modernity during the long debates that lasted decades and led to the promulgation of the 1993 and 2004 Family Laws, as well as those that led to the promotion of the preservation of Berber identity. This "arbiter" function of monarchy is indeed a characterizing feature of Moroccan politics that tends to privilege moderation and modernity.[92] This is best reflected in the promotion of the modern state, the city governments (regionalization), the private and public corporations, and the various nongovernmental associations. Moroccan monarchy is also characterized by flexibility, pragmatism, and adaptability to the changing global and local circumstances and, thus, has managed to keep its authority in the face of colonialism, modernity, socialism, and now the so-called Arab Spring.[93]

As far as women's issues are concerned, and as legal Islam (*Shari'a* law) is gaining momentum in Morocco, monarchy has served as a deterrent and a pro-modernity (pro-women's rights) institution. By upholding state modernity, monarchy has, throughout the decades that followed independence, been more pro-women's rights than conservative. This was often referred to as "state feminism" or "a top-down empowerment."[94] Taken together, patriarchy, religion, language, and monarchy constitute the core sources of primary authority in Morocco. These sources have secondary "relaying" mechanisms, which are no less important in understanding the nature of authority in Moroccan society and culture.

Secondary sources of patriarchal authority in Morocco

The secondary sources of patriarchal authority in the Moroccan sociocultural context may be qualified as "relay institutions," which "concretize" the authority of the primary sources on the ground.[95] Patriarchy is relayed by the family institution, religion by the mosque, language by the school, the modernity/urbanity nexus by the street and workplace, and monarchy by political institutions such as the *Makhzen* (the monarch's immediate circle, such as his advisors), the parliament, and the court of justice. These secondary sources of authority interact in a dialectic manner with the primary sources in the sense that the latter sanction the former and vice versa.

The family

Family is the site where the core patriarchal order is implemented. Although designed by the space-based patriarchy as the realm of women, it is in the family that the patriarchal order is honed as the most essential part of the socialization process. Because of this fundamental role, the family has been constructed as the most important unit of Moroccan society and culture. Within this unit, the husband/father (and, in the absence of these, the next male kin) is the supreme detainer of *lahkam* (physical and symbolic authority) over his wife (or wives) and children. The supremacy of the father's authority in the family and the central role of patrilineal affiliation in inheritance laws entail the legal dependence of wives and children on their closest male relatives.

In the Moroccan conception of the family, the group or the community predominates over the individual, and virtue is inexorably at the service of the honor of the group. This is why a woman only acquires identity through masculine intermediation (belonging to a family in which she is "the daughter," "wife," or mother"). In this system, women are primarily defined in the family as "homemakers" and "mothers."

The cultural importance of the family in Morocco resides in the fact that it is the basic structure of socialization, where relations between men and women are engineered at a very early age. Various sociocultural, economic, and political factors influence and determine lasting patriarchal family relations. Socioculturally, the identity of a family is associated with its male head. Economically, the male head of the family is expected to be the breadwinner, and politically, power is expected to lie in the hands of men. These male prerogatives are sustained by the prevalent cultural assumption that men have more reason than women and should lead at all levels. These unwritten rules change very slowly, in spite of the rapid evolution in familial structures in the last few decades. Thus, despite the spectacular changes in gender roles and the job market, very little change has operated at the deep cultural level of the family.

The family structure in Morocco is of three main types: extended, nuclear, and single parent. These types of family structures are all hierarchical. At the top of the hierarchy figures the father (patriarch) or a male member in his absence (a brother, for example). The father has the absolute real and symbolic dominance over the other members of the family. His authority is socially sanctioned and psychologically legitimized by society at large. His will is forced through consensus, ritual, or coercion. In such a structure, the wife and children blend into the family structure as individuals, and, in return, they are provided with a strong sense of belonging and a collective safety net when in trouble. Girls gain more status through marriage, with younger wives gaining further status after the birth of the first son. Marriage does not only have religious importance but also has economic, political, social, emotional, and symbolic importance. It keeps the structure of the social order through binary hierarchal authority and a fixated distribution of gender roles. In the family, women are more responsible than men for the honor of the family. Honor exists both individually and collectively. A mechanism of strict discipline is imposed in the family because "honorable" or "dishonorable" behavior by a family member affects its other members. Honor is also linked to reputation and to people's perceptions thereof. A loss of honor by one family member can affect all the others, to the extent that brothers and sisters may become ineligible for trust or marriage.

Family hierarchy also regulates gender role assignment in significant ways. By privileging male sexuality and charging women with upholding family honor, girls and young women become eternal sources of the potential threat to the cohesion of the family (and social order). Virginity is closely "watched over" by mothers and other women in the family. Indeed, the way in which female sexuality is stigmatized within the family unit strips women of authority. Moroccan family culture also perpetuates gender roles by enforcing a hierarchy of women within the family unit. While the mother has no authority over her husband, she wields power over the younger women of the household, and particularly over her daughter(s)-in-law or, in the nuclear family structure, the housemaid (domestic).

In sum, both the paradoxical pressure and stigma placed on young women's sexuality as a foundation of familial honor, and the cyclical hierarchy perpetuated by the denial of matriarchal authority exemplify how the family unit strongly reinforces patriarchal gender roles within Moroccan society. As such, the institution of the family is a genuine "engine" that the patriarchy uses to "manufacture" the right type of citizens who will later serve the state.

The mosque

The mosque is the site of physical and symbolic religious authority. The concept that the term "mosque" refers to has evolved through centuries. In the early days of Islam, the mosque served as a place for prayer as well as a space where various other activities took place. For example, the mosque functioned as a place for teaching and learning, a place where political issues were debated in dialogical ways, a courthouse where people's legal issues were resolved and judgments adjudicated, and a community center where families gathered to meet friends and neighbors or celebrate family events.[96] The mosque was the locus of public life for the emerging Muslim community, and, as such, it was open to women. According to Mernissi, in those ages, the mosque was a friendly place for women because they could access any aspect of public life by going to the mosque.[97] With the gradual emergence of gender segregation in the centuries that followed the death of the Prophet, and under the impact of patriarchy, women's access to the mosque began to shrink. This restriction hampered women's participation in mosque activities and gradually distanced them from public life. The first sign of segregation was the provision of a screen (*hijab*) that literally separated men from women and placed the latter behind men during congregational prayers. Ever since, the mosque has become a typical male space and a secondary source of authority, which relays the patriarchal doctrine of legal Islam and distances women from exposure and participation in scholarly commentaries. Today, one of the functions of the mosque is to reinforce the importance of the family and its patriarchal order through selected interpretations of the sacred texts. Even with the advent of female religious guides that give advice to men and women in the mosque, a man's decision cannot be supplanted by a woman's.[98] Women have their own space at the back of the mosque and listen to sermons by religious women, but those are usually concerning matters relating to women only.

As a secondary source of authority in today's Moroccan culture, the mosque is a "sacred" and male-dominated site. In addition to serving as a prayer place, the mosque is also a site where political and social affairs are presented by the *Imam* (male leader of mixed prayers). The contents of *Imam*'s sermons are often carried over to homes and the street, which strengthen the *Imams'* notorious authority.

The school

The school is a powerful site where language authority is performed. Bourdieu qualifies education as

> one of the most effective means of perpetuating the existing social pattern, as it both provides an apparent justification for social inequalities and gives recognition to the cultural heritage, that is, to a social gift treated as a natural one.[99]

Given this prominent role of education, the vehicle of instruction in schools is bound to be authority laden. Pupils associate the language of school with the values it carries. In the multilingual Moroccan context, where the school is bilingual (Standard Arabic and French), each language carries specific values: Standard Arabic carries religious values, while French carries modern values. The school is also a site that further consolidates the authority of the family, the mosque, and the street. Gender role assignment and perception are engineered in the family but solidified at school. The transition from home to school is an enhancement of these gender roles, as deeply rooted social beliefs are perpetuated in the unequal treatment of girls and boys. This creates a subtle "hidden curriculum" that continues to send harmful messages at a crucial time when children develop their belief systems.[100] The school implements its authority through three powerful channels: the behavior of the teacher, the classroom setting and methods of teaching, and the textbooks. These channels are interrelated, as individual and contextual factors are intertwined in a classroom experience.[101]

The teacher is the central element in the entire teaching enterprise. The increasingly spectacular use of technology in the classroom has not altered this fact; instead, it has enhanced it.[102] As a product of Moroccan society and culture, the teacher (male or female) comes to class with his or her gender stereotypes (the portrayal of males as dominant and females as subordinate). Some scholars such as Clarricoates as well as Yogev and Ayalon associate these stereotypes with the choice of disciplines by students: while males tend to opt for science and technology, females tend to opt for humanistic disciplines.[103] Whatever the case, these stereotypes make teachers (of both genders) give more attention to male rather than female students in teacher–student interactions.[104] This is also true in Moroccan society.[105] Beyond educational and economic implications, textbooks promote strong ideological implications. They are a basic vehicle of socialization, as they convey both knowledge and a system of values. In depicting women doing housework and men reading a book or a newspaper, most Moroccan textbooks perpetuate already-entrenched stereotypes about women. In Morocco, stereotypes are significant because Moroccan culture regulates men's and women's lives in rather strict ways and creates a strong common cultural mind-set that is translated into sociolinguistic patterns of thought and behavior. In the largest part of the Moroccan educational system, textbooks do not reflect the real progress made by women and rarely use gender-sensitive language. Furthermore, rural and semiurban women are marginalized in these textbooks and are generally depicted in relation to poverty and illiteracy.

The street

The Moroccan street is not a homogeneous space; it may have either a traditional or a modern aspect, hence its function as a secondary source of authority, which reflects the urban/modernity nexus. Some examples of the traditional street are the rural (*village*) street and the semiurban street (*medina*). Both types serve as extensions of the home.[106] This is attested at both the physical and the sociological levels. At the physical level, these streets are narrower and tortuous (people are physically closer and may literally rub shoulders). On the sociological level, neighbors in these streets generally know each other and can easily spot strangers. Promiscuity and intimacy create homelike solidarity between the inhabitants but also enforce more social control over girls and young women, as the street is the site where male power is socially sanctioned.

These two characteristics of the Moroccan traditional street are frequently invoked in the writings of Moroccans who lived in old *medinas*, such as Fez, often likening it to a "labyrinth" or a "womb."[107] For example, in his semiautobiographical novel *Fi at-Tufula* [*In Childhood*], the Moroccan writer Abdelmajid Benjelloune (also the narrator in the book) describes his experience of the "labyrinth" of Fez as a landmark in his late childhood.[108] He contrasts this space with that of Manchester, where he grew up. The open and spread-out English urban organization is presented in Benjelloune's novel as different from the closed and circular old city of Fez, which he equates with "home":

> We quickly entered the city to pass through its narrow streets ... Is this the city that my uncle had been saying from the first day that it exemplified the truth of the country? The people must not be able to walk in the street without bumping shoulders. We entered at night, and saw the pale, sad streetlamps as if they were lamps left in place after a funeral.[109]

Indeed, a characteristic of the traditional type of Moroccan street is that human interactions and natural features are very real, which makes them closed to the outsider gaze. Interestingly, however, this space seems to be owned by men: while men in this space appear relaxed, spontaneous, and natural, taking their time in doing things, women often appear to move hurriedly, hardly relaxed, and somewhat apologetic.

In contrast to the traditional street, the modern street in Morocco may be characterized as "open" and less complex. Historically, the transition from traditional to modern cities was accompanied by a transition from traditional agricultural ways of production to the capitalist modes of production. While various trades are organized in a circular manner in old Moroccan cities, they are displayed in an aligned manner to attract consumers in modern cities. This difference entails different interactions between people on the modern street.[110] Hence, gender relations have become relatively more flexible on the modern street, though a closer look shows that patriarchy is well at work on the urban street as well.

Indeed, as Graiouid explains, despite their differences, traditional, semiurban, and urban Moroccan streets are generally used to monitor the social and political behavior of men and women.[111] Thus, the patriarchy-monitored behavior in the family is often extended to the street, where men feel responsible for the protection of their wives', sisters', and daughters' behavior. This responsibility drops in the presence of nonkin girls and women on the street; these women are often regarded as approachable.

The Moroccan urban street is a genuine site of patriarchal performance via two seemingly paradoxical forms: female veiling and sexual harassment. While the veil is subject to sanctions and facilitates women's access to the public space, sexual harassment is the penalty for their transgressing the frontiers of private space (even if veiled) and serves as a weapon in the hands of men who see the public space as solely theirs. From unwelcomed verbal comments to nonconsensual grabbing and assault, street harassment is a daily characteristic of today's Moroccan urban street, regardless of how women are dressed or what they are doing. Both a product and a perpetrator of Morocco's space-based patriarchy, street harassment forces women into subordinate roles and encourages them to return to the private realm, while allowing men to fill their traditional gender roles as the authoritative figures in this space. Sexual harassment may also be understood as the manifestation of the tensions and conflicts surrounding modern Morocco's space-based patriarchal system. While street harassment is clearly a power-based relationship between the male assaulter and the female victim, both individuals ultimately fall into a socially dictated gender role assignment order.

Within Moroccan society, male sexual harassment is part of the general tendency of men to constantly remind nonkin women on the street that they are primarily "sexual objects." It is a verbal, physical, psychological, and symbolic act that "comforts" men who generally perceive women's education and work as a threat to their "territory": the public space.[112] On the other hand, sexual harassment in Moroccan streets expresses a deep crisis of masculinity in this country. With male unemployment on the rise and female visibility in the workplace increasing, constructed masculinity is challenged on a daily basis.

The workplace

Together with the street, the workplace relays the urban/modernity nexus of authority. It is a site where the tension of gender roles is mitigated by concrete or symbolic segregation. Because the workplace is a space where people are supposed to be free of family patriarchal shackles, it is closely monitored by male family members—particularly husbands—and constitutes a site where women are supposed to exercise maximum self-control. It is often the case that women trade their economic independence by putting their salaries to the service of the family, even though Islamic law allows women to manage their property and use it for their own needs. As such, the workplace is a site of social and economic authority trading. The Moroccan workplace is generally understood as an urban and mixed space; yet, women are neither encouraged nor invited to invest themselves in the paid labor force because men, rather than women, are culturally viewed as the breadwinners. Cultural norms also tend to restrict interaction between women with men outside their kin and inhibit women's entry into the paid labor force unless it is necessary. This reality is enhanced by a typically patrilineal family and kinship system. Moroccan space-based patriarchy encourages the patriarchal family, the separation of the sexes, and the division of labor, even in spaces outside the home. Despite the fact that Moroccan women are present in the workforce, the majority of them are employed in lower-paying jobs, while men monopolize the more prestigious and better-paid jobs.[113]

Like the street, the workplace is a site of sexual harassment (often performed by male employers on female employees), with the difference that, in the latter case, there is a law that precludes it.[114] Sexual harassment is a product of the urban/modernity nexus, which creates anonymity and encourages male harassment of women. This type of harassment is less common in rural areas, where people better know each other and tend to shun this behavior.

The invisible ruling elite: "the Makhzen" and systems of justice

For the layman, the *Makhzen* is generally perceived as an overwhelming, anonymous authority and a source of fear in the face of which people are helpless. This deeply engrained psychological fear of the *Makhzen* was intensified in the period between the 1960s and the 1980s, which witnessed a high degree of state violence, also known as the "Years of Lead." This perception stems from the fact the *Makhzen* is both a government institution and a social organization, which basically garners the historical and symbolic legitimacy of the regime and guarantees political stability, even if this necessitates the use of violence.

The parliament

As a modern institution, the Moroccan Parliament is a powerful source of legal authority that, among other things, regulates rights and buttresses monarchy as a primary source of authority. Although there are several sources of law, the parliament remains the dominant source as it gathers politicians who represent political parties, who are elected by the people, who are supposed to initiate debates on issues related to these people, and who may lead to law promulgation. Issues that are debated in the parliament are usually national issues that directly affect citizens. The prerogatives of the Moroccan Parliament witnessed significant reforms in the last decades, and the parliament now has more authority on the eve of independence. More and more laws that were once sanctioned by royal decrees are now required to secure parliamentary sanction. For example, the 1957–1958 and 1993 Family Laws were promulgated without parliamentary sanction, but the 2004 Family Law was sanctioned by the parliament.

On the other hand, the number of women in the Moroccan Parliament has always been a litmus test for Moroccan democracy. The 2002 quota system allowed thirty-five women (out of 325) to be elected to the lower house of legislature; in 2007, the number decreased to thirty-four. Later, however, the quota system was adopted, and in 2011, the number of women jumped to sixty-seven (out of 395 this time), thanks to the quota system.[115] Together with the 2004 Family Law, these increasing numbers of women in the highest spheres of decision-making have been used as a token of Morocco's openness about democratic practices. On the social and cultural levels, the parliament is generally associated with election and representation.

The court of justice

Together with the *Makhzen* and the parliament, the court of justice is an authority relay of the monarch's authority. As a modern institution, the court of justice is a source of social, legal, and political authority. On the social level, it is generally perceived as a relay of the family patriarch's *lahkam* (control) outside the family. In this sense, reaching the court of justice is generally understood as "not abiding" by this *lahkam*. Hence, the act of appearing in court for women seriously jeopardizes their reputation and constitutes serious harm into their family's honor. It is common for women to relinquish their rights to avoid appearing in court, which benefits men. The court of justice may also be a source of legal authority. Judges may make laws through court decisions; this is often referred to as *Ijtihad*.[116] The type of *Ijtihad* applied by judges in court is determined by factors such as the overall personality of the judge, the setting, and the particular cases. In addition to social and legal authority, the court of justice is also a source of political authority. Like those of the parliament, the nature and structure of the judiciary have been subject to reform and are a test for Moroccan openness and democratization. For example, one of the core demands of the Berber movement is to have translators (from Berber to Arabic and vice versa) in courts of justice.

In sum, the family, the mosque, the school, the street, the workplace, and the *Makhzen* are systems of justice that are powerful secondary sources of authority in Moroccan culture. These sources feed into each other and reinforce patriarchy, religion, language, the urban/modernity nexus, and monarchy, which constitute the primary sources of authority. Because patriarchy is the strongest primary source of authority, its tantalizing impact is promulgated in all the other types of authority (both primary and secondary).

Conclusion

This chapter has addressed the roots of current patriarchy in Morocco. Without knowing the nature, history, and workings of these roots, we cannot understand the overall status of women in today's Morocco. Knowledge and appreciation of the roots also allow better ways of reforming the state's legal system, which still restricts women in private and public spaces. Education has been instrumental in giving Moroccan women a female consciousness of their roles and potential in society; however, both could be further enhanced by their knowledge of the sources of patriarchy that still reinforce a restrictive legal system.

Notes

1 This chapter is based on research from my book Fatima Sadiqi, *Moroccan Feminist Discourses* (New York: Palgrave Macmillan, 2014).
2 Michel Foucault, "Subjectivity and Truth," in *Ethics: Subjectivity and Truth*, edited by Paul Rabinow (New York: The New Press, 1997), 87–92.
3 Max Weber, "The Three Types of Legitimate Rule," translated by Hans Gerth, *Berkeley Publications in Society and Institutions* 4, no. 1 (1958): 1–11.

4 For example, through heredity, the ability and right to rule do not change as they are passed down from father to eldest son.
5 Martin Riesebrodt, "Charisma in Max Weber's *Sociology of Religion*," *Religion* 29 (1999): 1–14.
6 Max Weber, "Chapter 7: Three Types of Legitimate Rule," in *The Essential Weber: A Reader*, edited by Sam Whimster (London and New York: Routledge Press, 2003), 133–138.
7 Riesebrodt, "Charisma in Max Weber's *Sociology of Religion*," 1–14.
8 Weber, *Three Types of Legitimate Rule*, 133–138.
9 More details on legal Islam are given in this chapter.
10 Lewis A. Coser, *Masters of Sociological Thought* (New York: Harcourt Brace Jovanovich, 1971).
11 Peter M. Blau, "Critical Remarks on Weber's Theory of Authority," *The American Political Science Review* 57, no. 2 (1963): 305–316.
12 Randall Collins, *Weberian Sociological Theory* (Cambridge: Cambridge University Press, 1986).
13 See Fatima Sadiqi, *Moroccan Feminist Discourses* (New York: Palgrave Macmillan, 2014).
14 In Morocco, the Makhzen connotes the king, top-ranking military personnel, landowners, civil servants, and other well-connected members of the establishment; see generally, Abdallah Laroui, *The History of the Maghrib: An Interpretive Essay* (Princeton, NJ: Princeton University Press, 1977): 209–201.
15 *Ibid.*
16 Michael Hughes, Carolyn J. Kroehler, and James W. Vander Zanden, *Sociology, the Core*, 11th ed. (Boston, MA: McGraw Hill, 1999), 250.
17 Allan Johnson, *The Gender Knot: Unraveling Our Patriarchal Legacy* (Philadelphia, PA: Temple University Press, 1997), 7–14.
18 In this section, focus is put on patriarchy as a system. Family is dealt with below as a secondary source of authority that relays the primary authority of patriarchy.
19 Gerda Lerner, *The Creation of Patriarchy* (New York: Oxford University Press, 1986).
20 *Ibid.*
21 *Ibid.*, Lerner takes these facts to lie at the origin of the institutionalization of laws veiling women.
22 Sadiqi, *Moroccan Feminist Discourses.*
23 Berber and Arab tribalisms are dealt with in this section, and legal Islam is dealt with in the religion section below.
24 Ibn Khaldun, *The Muqaddimah: An Introduction to History*, abridged edition, translated and introduced by Franz Rosenthal, edited and abridged by N.J. Dawood, with a new introduction by Bruce B. Lawrence (Princeton, NJ: Princeton University Press, 1969).
25 *Ibid.*, 83.
26 *Ibid.*, 256, 777, and 741; Ibn Khaldun detailed the genealogy of the smaller and larger Beduin tribes in North Africa, as well as that of small and bigger urban dynasties. Thousands of genealogical trees, including minute details in remarkable precision, and covering the countries of Morocco, Algeria, and Tunisia were worked out by the author.
27 *Ibid.*; today, Ibn Khaldun is recognized as the first scholar to construct a scientific theory of history, and his notion of *'asabiya* is still a valid category of analysis in the sociology of tribes.
28 Pierre Bourdieu, *Outline of a Theory of Practice* (Cambridge: Cambridge University Press, 1977); Michael Brettand and Elizabeth Fentress, *The Berbers* (Oxford: Blackwell Publishers, 1996); and Bruce Maddy-Weitzman, *The Berber Identity Movement and the Challenge to North African States* (Austin: Texas University Press, 2011).

29 Ibn Khaldun, *The Muqaddimah: An Introduction to History*, highlights the centrality of social principles, such as accountability to the tribe in tribal organization.
30 Bourdieu, *Outline of a Theory of Practice*, 56.
31 *Ibid.*, 56.
32 Sadiqi, *Moroccan Feminist Discourses.*
33 Bourdieu, *Outline of a Theory of Practice*; according to Bourdieu, masculine and feminine physical spaces were physically separated by paths or fountains. If a fountain was shared by two tribes, women would fetch water at nightfall. Ironically, women often used this opportunity to exchange gossip about daily concerns, including men, something they could not indulge in private without incurring the wrath and retaliation of their male kin, especially their husbands and in-laws.
34 *Ibid.*, 21.
35 *Ibid.*, 21.
36 There is no record of women participating as members of a tribal or clan assembly. See generally, Sadiqi, *Moroccan Feminist Discourses.*
37 *Ibid.*, 81.
38 Berber tribes were instrumental in the maintenance of the Moroccan monarchy. According to Burke, Gellner, and Hart, Morocco's monarchy was very weak in the 1800s, and only the organizational strength of outlying tribes rescued it. For these authors, the center-periphery dynamics constituted the practical foundations of central rule in Morocco at that time; see generally, Edmund Burke, *Prelude to the Protectorate in Morocco* (Chicago, IL: University of Chicago Press, 1976); Ernest Gellner, *Saints of the Atlas* (Chicago, IL: University of Chicago Press, 1969); David. M. Hart, "The Tribe in Modern Morocco," in *Arabs and Berbers: From Tribe to Nation*, edited by Ernest Gellner and Charles Antoine Micaud (Lexington, KY: Heath, 1972), 25–58.
39 This period witnessed the emergence of Morocco as a state in 708 A.D., giving the country an independent geographical entity.
40 The French Protectorate was established in Morocco in 1912 and lasted until 1956.
41 Islam and Arabic have always served as the idiom of unity in North Africa. Pre- and post-Islamic Berber kings adopted the two as official means of ruling in the region. They adopted Islam because it allowed the unification of tribes, hence facilitating the process of ruling the region, and Arabic because the Qur'an was introduced to the region in this language.
42 See Fatima Sadiqi, Amira Nowaira, Azza El Khouly, and Moha Ennaji, eds., *Women Writing Africa: The Northern Region* (New York: The Feminist Press, 2009).
43 Sadiqi, *Moroccan Feminist Discourses*: 82.
44 Sadiqi, *Moroccan Feminist Discourses*; the Berber dynasties were the Almoravids (who formed an empire in the twelfth century and spread their rule over the western Maghrib and Andalusia), the Almohads (who overthrew the Almoravids and formed an empire in the twelfth century and whose reign breached Libya in North Africa as well as Spain and Portugal), and the Merinid (who overthrew the Almohads and ruled over a longer period, from 1269 to 1465 A.D.).
45 Deniz Kandiyoti, "Identity and Its Discontents: Women and the Nation," *Millennium* 20, no. 3 (1992): 429–443.
46 *Ibid.*; see also Valentine M. Moghadam, *Modernizing Women: Gender and Social Change in the Middle East* (Boulder, CO: Lynne Rienner Publishers, 1993).
47 Patriarchal societies emphasize women's modesty and the practice of veiling (*hijab*).
48 Deniz Kandiyoti, "Bargaining with Patriarchy," *Gender and Society* 2, no. 3, (1988): 274–275.
49 The term *medina* is derived from the term *madaniyyah* (urbanization, civilization). See Rachel Newcomb, *Women of Fez: Ambiguities of Urban Life in Morocco*

(Philadelphia: University of Pennsylvania Press, 2009): 15, for details of the "ville nouvelle" (new town) which contrasts sharply with the *medina*.

50 Sadiqi, *Moroccan Feminist Discourses*, 83.
51 *Ibid.*
52 *Ibid.*; in Morocco, the emergence of the veil was historically associated with the rise of cities and moments of transitional crises.
53 Sadiqi, *Moroccan Feminist Discourses*, 84.
54 *Ibid.*, 84.
55 *Ibid.*, 84.
56 Bourdieu, *Outline of a Theory of Practice.*
57 Sadiqi, *Moroccan Feminist Discourses*, 85.
58 *Ibid.*, 84.
59 *Ibid.*, 85.
60 *Ibid.*, 85.
61 *Ibid.*
62 *Ibid.*
63 Indeed, cafés still carry a notorious connotation in the Moroccan consciousness because they used to serve as meeting points for the colonizers, local collaborators, and prostitutes. See generally, Sadiqi, *Moroccan Feminist Discourses* (citing Said Graiouid, "A Place on the Terrace: Café Culture and the Public Sphere in Morocco," *The Journal of North African Studies* 12, no. 4 (2007): 531–550).
64 Ahmed Sefrioui, *La Boîte à Merveille* (Paris: Le Seuil, 1954); Leila Abouzeid, *Year of the Elephant: A Moroccan Woman's Journey Toward Independence* (Austin: University of Texas at Austin Press, 1989); Fatima Mernissi, *Dreams of Trespass* (Cambridge, MA: Perseus Books, 1994).
65 Sefrioui, *La Boîte à Merveille.*
66 Sadiqi, *Moroccan Feminist Discourses*, 186.
67 Liat Kozma, "Moroccan Women's Narratives of Liberation: A Passive Revolution?" *The Journal of North African Studies* 8, no. 1 (2003): 112–130; and Marnia Lazreg, *The Eloquence of Silence: Algerian Women in Question* (London: Routledge, 1994).
68 Mohamed Chafik, "La Poésie Amazighe et la Résistance Armée au Moyen et au Haut Atlas Entre 1912–1934," *Al-Akadimiyyah* 4 (November 1987): 11.
69 See Fatima Sadiqi, Amira Nowaira, Azza El Khouly, and Moha Ennaji, eds., *Women Writing Africa: The Northern Region (French Version)* (New York: The Feminist Press, 2013); this book provides examples of this female oral genre, together with a historicizing of its role in the making of Moroccan modern history.
70 Abouzeid, *Year of the Elephant.*
71 Sadiqi, *Moroccan Feminist Discourses*, 87.
72 *Ibid.*, 88.
73 As'ad Abu Khalil, "Gender Boundaries and Sexual Categories in the Arab World," *Feminist Issues* 15, no. 1–2 (1997): 91–104.
74 I adopt Weber's views in this section. See generally, Weber, "The Three Types of Legitimate Rule," 1–11.
75 *Ibid.*
76 Today, the overwhelming majority of Maghribians are Muslim.
77 According to Mernissi, women had more rights during the Prophet Muhammad's life than in later periods. See generally, Fatima Mernissi, *Beyond the Veil, Male-Female Dynamics in Muslim Society* (Cambridge, MA: Schenkman Publishing Company, 1975); other scholars such as Al-Hibri confirm this view in Azizah Al-Hibri, *A Study of Islamic Herstory: Or How Did We Ever Get into This Mess?* (Oxford: Pergamon Pres, 1982).
78 Sadiqi, *Moroccan Feminist Discourses*, 92.

79 See Marjorie Lightman and Benjamin Lightman, *A to Z of Ancient Greek and Roman Women* (New York: Facts on File, 2008).

80 According to Tillion, the *mahr* (dowry given by the would-be husband) was divided into two with a part deferred to death or divorce, and the man was entitled to take as many concubines as he could afford. See Germaine Tillion, *Le Harem et les Cousins* (Paris: Editions du Seuil, 1982).

81 John L. Esposito and Natana J. DeLong-Bas, *Women in Muslim Family Law* (New York: Syracuse University Press, 2001); L. Léon Buskens, "Recent Debates on Family Law Reform in Morocco: Islamic Law as Politics in an Emerging Public Sphere," *Islamic Law and Society* 10, no. 1 (2003): 70–131.

82 Sadiqi, *Moroccan Feminist Discourses*, 92–93.

83 Maddy-Weitzman, *The Berber Identity Movement and the Challenge to North African States*, 35.

84 Bourdieu, *Outline of a Theory of Practice*, 70.

85 Nikki Keddie, *Modern Iran: Roots and Results of Revolution* (New Haven, CT: Yale University Press, 2003): 30–31.

86 It is from this perspective that Islam outlawed *sadica* marriages on the premise that such unions were adulterous, while retaining certain forms of *ba'al* dominion marriages. See generally, Sadiqi, *Moroccan Feminist Discourses.*

87 See generally, *Ibid.*; whereas men can lead prayers in all-male or mixed groups, women can lead prayers only in all-women groups.

88 See generally, *Ibid.*; it is a *din* (religion) and *dunia* (life.)

89 Many scholars went into detail, both explaining how legal Islam is biased toward men and how this can be remedied; see Lena Larsen, Ziba Mir-Hosseini, Christian Moe, and Kari Vogt, eds., *Gender and Equality in Muslim Family Law: Justice and Ethics in the Islamic Legal Tradition* (London: I. B. Tauris, 2013); Amina Wadud, *Inside the Gender Jihad: Reform in Islam* (Oxford: One World Publishers, 2006); Asma Barlas, *Believing Women" in Islam: Unreading Patriarchal Interpretations of the Qur'ān* (Austin: University of Texas Press, 2006); and Mernissi, *Beyond the Veil.*

90 The Japanese monarchy is the oldest one in the world, but it is not ruling; linguistically, the term *Sultan* was used at the onset of monarchy, and the term *malik* (king) was used after the independence of Morocco in 1956.

91 Clifford Geertz, *Islam Observed: Religious Development in Morocco and Indonesia* (Chicago, IL: University of Chicago Press, 1968); Gellner, *Saints of the Atlas*; Dale F. Eickelman, *Moroccan Islam, Tradition and Society in a Pilgrimage Center* (Austin and London: University of Texas Press, 1976); Laroui, *The History of the Maghrib: An Interpretive Essay*; Margaret Elaine Combs-Schilling, Sacred Performances: Islam, Sexuality, and Sacrifice (New York: Columbia University Press, 1989); Abdellah Hammoudi, *Master and Disciple*, (Chicago, IL: University of Chicago Press, 1997).

92 Sadiqi, *Moroccan Feminist Discourses*, 99.

93 Moroccan monarchy is the only ruling system that has not been removed by French colonialism in North Africa. Furthermore, no monarch's rule duplicates his father's, a fact which helped absorb the tensions that accompany the death of a monarch. In the aftermath of the recent uprisings in the region, King Mohamed VI gave a speech on March 9, 2011, where he reduced some of the prerogatives of the king and announced the creation of the independent office of "Head of the Government," who would belong to a party elected democratically by the people. It is also worth mentioning that the 2011 uprisings in Morocco resulted in the creation of the youth's February 20 Movement, which demanded more limits on the authority of the king without demanding a regime change, as was the case in Tunisia, Libya, and Egypt.

94 Sadiqi, *Moroccan Feminist Discourses*, 99.

95 *Ibid.*, 99–100.

96 Mernissi, *Beyond the Veil.*

97 *Ibid.*

98 Sadiqi, *Moroccan Feminist Discourses.*

99 Pierre Bourdieu, "The School as a Conservative Force: Scholastic and Cultural Inequalities," in *Contemporary Research in the Sociology of Education*, ed. John Eggleton (London: Methuen, 1974): 32.

100 Jo Sanders, "Teaching Gender Equity in Teacher Education," *Education Digest* 68, no. 5 (2003): 25–29, and Timothy Frawley, "Gender Bias in the Classroom: Current Controversies and Implications for Teachers," *Childhood Education* 8, no. 4 (2005): 221.

101 There is growing research documenting gender inequity in the Moroccan educational system.

102 Janice L. Streitmatter, "Ethnic/Racial and Gender Equity in School Suspensions," *The High School Journal* 68 (1985–1986): 139–143; Dyanne M. Tracy, "Toys, Spatial Ability, and Science and Mathematics Achievement: Are They Related?" *Sex Roles* 17 (1987): 115–138.

103 Katherine Clarricoates, "Dinosaurs in the Classroom—A Re-examination of Some Aspects of the 'Hidden Curriculum' in Primary Schools," *Women's Studies International Quarterly* 1 (1978): 353–364; Abraham Yogev and Hanna Ayalon, "Learning to Labor or Laboring to Learn? Curricular Stratification in Israeli Vocational High Schools," *International Journal of Educational Development* 11 (1991): 209–219.

104 Jere E. Brophy, "Teacher-Student Interaction," in *Teacher Expectancies*, ed. Jerome B. Dusek, Vernon C. Hall, and William J. Meyer (Hillsdale, NJ: Lawrence Erlbaum, 1985), 303–327; Myra Sadker, David Sadker, and Susan S. Klein, "The Issue of Gender in Elementary and Secondary Education," *Review of Research in Education* 17 (1991): 297–298.

105 Moha Ennaji, *Multilingualism, Cultural Identity, and Education in Morocco* (Boston, MA: Springer, 2005).

106 Said Graiouid, *Communication and Everyday Performance: Public Space and the Public Sphere in Morocco* (Rabat: Publications of the Faculty of Letters and Human Sciences, 2011).

107 Sadiqi, *Moroccan Feminist Discourses*, 105.

108 *Ibid.*, 105.

109 Abdelmajid Benjelloune, *Fi at-Tufula* [*In Childhood*] (Casablanca: Matba'atal-Andalus, 1957), 83.

110 See generally, Henri Lefebvre, *The Production of Space*, translated by Donald Nicholson-Smith (Oxford: Basil Blackwell, 2011), 20; indeed, the French cultural geographer Lefebvre states that urban (modern) space shapes the ways inhabitants read reality and interact with it. According to him, various spatial practices structure the way we think, experience, and live reality. The author also qualifies modern urban space organization in modern Western cities as "abstract" in the sense that it is "mappable" and open to the reader's gaze through various guides and visitors' books. In this context, people easily work out patterns of interaction to "map" their social practices according to the exposed space. Places and people are connected via networks and routes as well as via patterns and interactions. So too are images and reality, as well as work and leisure.

111 Said Graiouid, *Communication and Everyday Performance.*

112 This is also a symptom of the violence perpetrated against women; see Kamal Salhi, "Rethinking Francophone Culture: Africa and the Caribbean between History and Theory," *Research in African Literatures* 35, no. 1 (2004): 9–29.

113 Sadiqi, *Moroccan Feminist Discourses.*

114 Article 503 of the Moroccan penal code states that whoever harasses another person by the virtue of their authority by issuing orders, threats, constraints or any other mean in exchange of sexual favors is guilty of sexual harassment and liable to one to two years of imprisonment and a fine amounting to MAD 5000.

Moreover, Article 40 of the same code gives harassed employees the right to leave their positions and claim legitimate compensation.

115 Sadiqi, *Moroccan Feminist Discourses*, 110.

116 Linguistically, the Arabic word *ijtihad* means "striving, exerting." Classical Muslim Sunni jurists (such as Abu Husays al-Basri, Al-Ghazali, Al-Amidi, and others) transposed this meaning to the realm of Islamic jurisprudence and defined *ijtihad* as the exertion of the maximum "mental energy" in order to first comprehend and then apply *fiqh* (legal theory) with the aim of discovering the "law of God." See generally, Edward Sell, *The Faith in Islamic Law* (Madras: S. P. C. K. Press, 1907); Wael B. Hallaq, "Was the Gate of Ijtihad Closed?" *International Journal of Middle East Studies* 16, no. 1 (1984): 3–41; Shaista P. Ali-Karamali and Fiona Dunne, "The Ijtihad Controversy," *Arab Law Quarterly* 9 (1994): 238–257.

Bibliography

Abouzeid, Leila. *Year of the Elephant: A Moroccan Woman's Journey toward Independence.* Austin: University of Texas at Austin Press, 1989.

Abu Khalil, As'ad. "Gender Boundaries and Sexual Categories in the Arab World." *Feminist Issues* 15, no. 1–2 (1997): 91–104.

Al-Hibri, Azizah. *A Study of Islamic Herstory: Or How Did We Ever Get Into This Mess?* Oxford: Pergamon Press, 1982.

Ali-Karamali, Shaista P., and Fiona Dunne. "The Ijtihad Controversy." *Arab Law Quarterly* 9 (1994): 238–257.

Barlas, Asma. *"Believing Women" in Islam: Unreading Patriarchal Interpretations of the Qur'ān.* Austin: University of Texas Press, 2006.

Benjelloune, Abdelmajid. *Fi at-Tufula* [*In Childhood*]. Casablanca: Matba'atal – Andalus. 1957. Reprinted second edition. Casablanca: Dar Nashr al-Marifa. 2006.

Blau, Peter M. "Critical Remarks on Weber's Theory of Authority." *The American Political Science Review* 57, no. 2 (1963): 305–316.

Bourdieu, Pierre. *Language and Symbolic Power.* Translated by John Thompson. Cambridge, MA: Harvard University Press, 1991.

———. *Outline of a Theory of Practice.* Cambridge: Cambridge University Press, 1977.

———. "The School as a Conservative Force: Scholastic and Cultural Inequalities." In *Contemporary Research in the Sociology of Education*, edited by John Eggleton, 32–46. London: Methuen, 1974.

Brett, Michael, and Elizabeth Fentress. *The Berbers.* Oxford: Blackwell Publishers, 1996.

Brophy, Jere E. "Teacher-Student Interaction." In *Teacher Expectancies*, edited by Jerome B. Dusek, Vernon C. Hall, and William J. Meyer, 303–327. Hillsdale, NJ: Lawrence Erlbaum, 1985.

Burke, Edmund. *Prelude to the Protectorate in Morocco.* Chicago, IL: University of Chicago Press, 1976.

Buskens, L. Léon. "Recent Debates on Family Law Reform in Morocco: Islamic Law as Politics in an Emerging Public Sphere." *Islamic Law and Society* 10, no. 1 (2003): 70–131.

Chafik, Mohamed. "La Poésie Amazighe et la Résistance Armée au Moyen et au Haut Atlas Entre 1912–1934." *Al-Akadimiyyah*, no. 4 (November 1987).

Clarricoates, Katherine. "Dinosaurs in the Classroom—A Re-Examination of Some Aspects of the 'Hidden Curriculum' in Primary Schools." *Women's Studies International Quarterly* 1 (1978): 353–364.

Collins, Randall. *Weberian Sociological Theory*. Cambridge: Cambridge University Press, 1986.

Combs-Schilling, Margaret Elaine. *Sacred Performances: Islam, Sexuality, and Sacrifice*. New York: Columbia University Press, 1989.

Coser, Lewis A. *Masters of Sociological Thought*. New York: Harcourt Brace Jovanovich, 1971.

Eickelman, Dale. *Moroccan Islam, Tradition and Society in a Pilgrimage Center*. Austin and London: University of Texas Press, 1976.

Ennaji, Moha. *Multilingualism, Cultural Identity, and Education in Morocco*. Boston, MA: Springer, 2005.

Esposito, John L., and Natana J. DeLong-Bas. *Women in Muslim Family Law*. New York: Syracuse University Press, 2001.

Foucault, Michel. "Subjectivity and Truth." In *Ethics: Subjectivity and Truth*, edited by Paul Rabinow. New York: The New Press, 1997.

Frawley, Timothy. "Gender Bias in the Classroom: Current Controversies and Implications for Teachers." *Childhood Education* 8, no. 4 (2005): 221.

Geertz, Clifford. *Islam Observed: Religious Development in Morocco and Indonesia*. Chicago, IL: University of Chicago Press, 1968.

Gellner, Ernest. *Saints of the Atlas*. Chicago, IL: University of Chicago Press, 1969.

Graiouid, Said. "A Place on the Terrace: Café Culture and the Public Sphere in Morocco." *The Journal of North African Studies* 12, no. 4 (2011): 531–550.

———. *Communication and Everyday Performance: Public Space and the Public Sphere in Morocco*. Rabat: Publications of the Faculty of Letters and Human Sciences, 2011.

Hallaq, Wael B. "Was the Gate of Ijtihad Closed?" *International Journal of Middle East Studies* 16, no. 1 (1984): 3–41.

Hammoudi, Abdellah. *Master and Disciple*. Chicago, IL: University of Chicago Press, 1997.

Hart, David. M. "The Tribe in Modern Morocco." In *Arabs and Berbers: From Tribe to Nation*, edited by Ernest Gellner and Charles Antoine Micaud, 25–58. Lexington, KY: Heath, 1972.

Hughes, Michael, Carolyn J. Kroehler, and James W. Vander Zanden. *Sociology, the Core*. Fifth Edition. Boston, MA: McGraw Hill, 1999.

Johnson, Allan G. *The Gender Knot: Unraveling Our Patriarchal Legacy*. Philadelphia, PA: Temple University Press, 1997.

Kandiyoti, Deniz. "Bargaining with Patriarchy." *Gender and Society* 2, no. 3 (1988): 274–290.

———. "Identity and Its Discontents: Women and the Nation." *Millennium* 20, no. 3 (1992): 429–443.

Keddie, Nikki. *Modern Iran: Roots and Results of Revolution*. New Haven, CT: Yale University Press, 2003.

———. "Secularism and Its Discontents." *Daedalus* 132, no. 3 (2003): 14–30.

Khaldun, Ibn. *The Muqaddimah: An Introduction to History*. Abridged Edition. Translated and introduced by Franz Rosenthal, edited and abridged by N.J. Dawood, with a new Introduction by Bruce B. Lawrence. Princeton, NJ: Princeton University Press, 1969.

Kozma, Liat. "Moroccan Women's Narratives of Liberation: A Passive Revolution?" *The Journal of North African Studies* 8, no. 1 (2003): 112–130.

Laroui, Abdallah. *The History of the Maghrib: An Interpretive Essay*. Translated by Ralph Manheim. Princeton, NJ: Princeton University Press, 1977.

Larsen, Lena, Ziba Mir-Hosseini, Christian Moe, and Kari Vogt, eds. *Gender and Equality in Muslim Family Law: Justice and Ethics in the Islamic Legal Tradition*. London: I. B. Tauris, 2013.

Lazreg, Marnia. *The Eloquence of Silence: Algerian Women in Question*. London: Routledge, 1994.

Lefebvre, Henri. *The Production of Space*. Translated by Donald Nicholson-Smith. Oxford: Basil Blackwell, 2011.

Lerner, Gerda. *The Creation of Patriarchy*. New York: Oxford University Press, 1986.

Lightman, Marjorie, and Benjamin Lightman. *A to Z of Ancient Greek and Roman Women*. New York: Facts on File, 2008.

Maddy-Weitzman, Bruce. *The Berber Identity Movement and the Challenge to North African States*. Austin: Texas University Press, 2011.

Mernissi, Fatima. *Beyond the Veil, Male-Female Dynamics in Muslim Society*. Cambridge: Schenkman Publishing Company, 1975.

———. *Dreams of Trespass*. Cambridge, MA: Perseus Books, 1994.

Moghadam, Valentine M. *Modernizing Women: Gender and Social Change in the Middle East*. Boulder, CO: Lynne Rienner Publishers, 1993.

Moroccan Penal Code, Section 40, 503. Rabat: Dahir, 1962.

Newcomb, Rachel. *Women of Fez: Ambiguities of Urban Life in Morocco*. Philadelphia: University of Pennsylvania Press, 2009.

Riesebrodt, Martin. "Charisma in Max Weber's *Sociology of Religion*." *Religion* 29 (1999): 1–14.

Sadiqi, Fatima. *Moroccan Feminist Discourses*. New York: Palgrave Macmillan U.S., 2014.

Sadiqi, Fatima, Amira Nowaira, Azza El Khouly, and Moha Ennaji, eds. *Women Writing Africa: The Northern Region*. New York: The Feminist Press, 2009.

———. *Women Writing Africa: The Northern Region (French Version)*. New York: The Feminist Press, 2013.

Sadker, Myra, David Sadker, and Susan S. Klein. "The Issue of Gender in Elementary and Secondary Education." *Review of Research in Education* 17 (1991): 297–298.

Salhi, Kamal. "Rethinking Francophone Culture: Africa and the Caribbean between History and Theory." *Research in African Literatures* 35, no. 1 (2004): 9–29.

Sanders, Jo. "Teaching Gender Equity in Teacher Education." *Education Digest* 68, no. 5 (2003): 25–29.

Sefrioui, Ahmed. *La Boîte à Merveille*. Paris: Le Seuil, 1954.

Sell, Edward. *The Faith in Islamic Law*. Madras: S. P. C. K. Press, 1907.

Streitmatter, Janice L. "Ethnic/Racial and Gender Equity in School Suspensions." *The High School Journal* 68 (1985–1986): 139–143.

Tillion, Germaine. *Le Harem et Les Cousins*. Paris: Editions du Seuil, 1982.

Tracy, Dyanne M. "Toys, Spatial Ability, and Science and Mathematics Achievement: Are They Related?" *Sex Roles* 17 (1987): 115–138.

Wadud, Amina. *Inside the Gender Jihad: Reform in Islam*. Oxford: One World Publishers, 2006.

Weber, Max. "The Three Types of Legitimate Rule." Translated by Hans Gerth. *Berkeley Publications in Society and Institutions* 4, no. 1 (1958): 1–11.

———. "The Three Pure Types of Legitimate Rule." In *The Essential Weber: A Reader*, edited by Sam Whimster, Chapter 7, 133–138. London and New York: Routledge Press, 2003.

Yogev, Abraham, and Hanna Ayalon. "Learning to Labor or Laboring to Learn? Curricular Stratification in Israeli Vocational High Schools." *International Journal of Educational Development* 11 (1991): 209–219.

4 Media representations of Palestinian women

Post-Arab Uprisings

Halla Shoaibi

Introduction

In February 2012, we woke up to a widely shared video on Facebook: a collection of pictures of Palestinian women in protests. The video was originally titled "Palestine: Women First," but was later changed to "*Nesa'iyéh* (a Woman Thing)." The video's background music features the sexy voice of Lebanese singer Yasmin Hamdan, singing, "Where are you? And where is the love?" As Yasmin searches for her lover, the video reveals pictures of Palestinian women protesting against the Israeli occupation and participating in the March 2011 protests demanding unity between Palestinian factions. The caption reads, "I began to photograph the *increasingly* central role played by Palestinian women activists [...] These politically-independent women implement a *strategy of strictly non-violent* protests against Israeli troops."[1] One might think the images, words, and song selection are a contradiction; however, a closer examination of the pictures and the captions beneath them reveal the interrelation between Yasmin's song and the images of these women.

A few months later, I aimed to research the effect of the Arab Uprisings on the Palestinian women's movement after 2011, and the contradictions evidenced in the video. I anticipated that Palestinian women would reflect on and speak about the transformative effect of the uprisings on their activism, and how they altered their views of activism and liberation. However, after numerous talks with active women[2] in popular resistance in the West Bank,[3] my research question shifted. The women spoke largely about the media's obsession with their activism since the start of the Arab Uprisings and the distorted image surrounding their political participation. The women sensed that their agenda and messages were hijacked by foreign media and replaced with images that did not necessarily represent them. They were portrayed as "modern, "Western," and "non-violent": categorizations that they felt distanced them from the overall Palestinian popular resistance and ones they feel are not truly representative of their activism. This characterization is also perceived by some of the interviewed women as politically motivated and part of a larger recreation of the Palestinian image.

This chapter analyzes the media's preoccupation with active women within the larger scheme of the Arab Uprisings, the Palestinian Authority's (PA's) reintroduction of the "non-violent Palestinian," and the NGO-ization of the Palestinian national agenda. The media's emphasis—especially that of Western media—originates from the overall Western focus on the participation of women in the Arab Uprisings, along with the PA's open refusal and, at times, condemnation of armed resistance while deploying nonviolence. The main argument of this chapter is that we must observe the images of protesting women within the shifting variables of class, gender, and politics.

This chapter is largely built on the personal experiences of women who were active in popular resistance against the Israeli occupation in the West Bank after the Arab Uprisings, between 2011 and 2015. This qualitative study is composed of three basic methods: individual interviews, participant observations, and primary and secondary source analyses. The study is based on seven individual interviews conducted with young women who were politically active in the West Bank after the Arab Uprisings. Participants were told the purpose of the study, and the interviews were conducted in Arabic. The women were chosen based on three criteria: their towns, the periods during which they became activists, and the types of protests they attended. All of the interviewed women are active in political and social spheres, and are well known in their local communities.

The women interviewed were from four different cities in Palestine: Ramallah, Nablus, Bethlehem, and Nazareth. All of the women except one participated in protests against both the Israeli occupation and the PA's request for political representation. Two of the interviewed women have been active since the beginning of the Second Intifada in 2000, while four of them began participating in protests between 2003 and 2008. One of the interviewed women became active in 2010. The names present in the study are fictional in order to respect the privacy of the individuals.

Upon interviewing the women regarding their political participation after the Arab Uprisings, many voiced their discontent with the portrayal of women in the media, whether in news articles and photographs, or on social media. For this chapter, I selected a few media articles that most often caused controversy among active women and men when politically active Palestinian women shared the articles on social media. Noticeably, photos and exhibits titled "*Nesa'iyeh*" by Israeli photographer Mati Milstein stirred intense discussions among active women and men. Some of his photographs will be examined in this chapter. Two of the interviewed women were represented in these photographs, while three others who were photographed in this exhibit shared their opinions in informal group settings.

This chapter sheds light on how the media fixated on women's images in popular resistance and protests in an attempt to categorize the protests in Palestine—and in doing so, have created a distorted image of the reality of women's involvement. It proceeds in three sections. Section "The Palestinian women's movement" provides a brief background on the Palestinian women's movement since the late 1920s. Section "Palestinian women in the wake of the Arab Uprisings" discusses how the media portrays Palestinian women's participation after the "Arab Uprising." Section "The Palestinian authority: the recreation of the "nonviolent Palestinian"" then argues that the media's preoccupation with active Palestinian women should be viewed within larger contexts: the Arab Uprisings, the PA's reintroduction of the "nonviolent Palestinian," and the NGO-ization of the Palestinian national agenda. In conclusion, the chapter reflects on how Palestinian women's image was reconstructed by the political and social changes surrounding them. This image demonstrated how women's bodies were used as carriers of a modernized, nonviolent message.

The Palestinian women's movement

Palestinian women's political participation and organization are strongly connected to the history of Palestine and the Palestinian national struggle. The Palestinian women's movement articulated in the 1920s under the British Mandate was strongly intertwined with the national movement and its goals. Yet, although this movement played an important role in organizing demonstrations against British colonial policies and Jewish immigration,[4] most of the women's work was charity based and at times only turned to politicized charity work to assist male fighters.[5] Furthermore, Palestinian women often met with government officials and constricted ties with other international associations when engaging in demonstrations and organizing.

Hence, the Palestinian women's movement originated from a political national liberation background rather than a feminist-identifying movement or a movement related to women's rights.[6] As Fleischmann stated in her introduction to *The Nation and Its "New" Women*,

> Women living under colonial hegemonies could not—still cannot—ignore the fact that social and political inequalities of men and women alike were consolidated, controlled, and maintained by colonial state structures. Crucial to understanding Third World feminists is a "notion of agency which works not through the logic of [gender] identification but through the logic of opposition to colonial structures of domination."[7]

Islah Jad explains how cultural, religious, and political settings shape the outcomes and strategies of groups; one example is the backlash against urban women in the Great Revolt of 1936–1939.[8] Peasants disputed the urban elite women's new ascribed roles during the Mandate and imposed the veil on them—not, as Jad argues, for reasons of "traditionalism" but as a "reflection of class antagonism (resentment) directed against the cultural hegemony of the urban elite, including their women."[9] The peasants described elite women as "less authentic" and "Westernized," resulting in urban women's withdrawal from the public sphere.[10] Additionally, Fleischmann describes a heated debate in 1920s media between writers and intellectuals on whether or not women must be veiled.[11] Those who advocated veiling viewed unveiled women as "Westernized" or closer to the Mandate regime. It seemed a matter of defying Westernization vis-à-vis authentic culture.[12] Indeed, in several times throughout history, and particularly when Palestinians were shifting their discourse of resistance and when differences between classes or ideologies clashed, women were tactically attacked for being "modernized," "Westernized," or not aligned with the Palestinian society or with a particular individual group, class, or political party.

The Palestinian women's movement continued to develop throughout the 1948 *Nakba* ("catastrophe") of the Palestinians, and during the occupation of the West Bank and Gaza in 1967, women were integral in various acts of resistance.[13] Palestinians sustained a popular uprising while living under the conditions of Israeli military rule, shifting and modifying Palestinian social and political structures, including the roles of women. Between 1967 and 1972, women not only delivered food and weapons to Palestinian freedom fighters but were directly involved in the armed struggle by planning armed activities.[14]

During the First Intifada—the Palestinian uprising against the Israeli military occupation in 1987—women were a part of everyday resistance. Women of all ages and from different sectors of society participated in protests and civil disobedience. The end of the First Intifada was marked by the signature of the Oslo Peace Accords. The Palestinian Liberation Organization (PLO) and the Israeli government signed the Declaration of Principles on Interim Self-Government (Oslo I Accords) in 1993,[15] and the Israeli–Palestinian Interim Agreement in 1995 (Oslo II Accords).[16] The PLO recognized Israel's right to exist and, in return, the Israeli government recognized the PLO as the legitimate representative of the Palestinian people.[17] The parties also agreed on the creation of the PA, through which Palestinians would self-rule under the Israeli occupation for a transitional period that would eventually lead to a permanent resolution and a viable Palestinian state based on the 1967 borders.[18] As Jad points out,

> In the historic discourse of the Palestinian national movement women were constructed either as the struggling militant or as the self-sacrificing mother ... the woman 'freedom fighter' with a gun in her hand was an image promoted by different Palestinian factions, especially on the left.

She rightly asks, "What happened to these images of women under the [Palestinian Authority]?"[19]

After Oslo, the PA confined women's activism under its authoritarian and compromised rule, resulting in the demobilization and weakening of grassroots organizations, including the women's movement.[20] Former members of the Palestinian movement mostly became part of the PA's governmental apparatus or part of the NGO-ization process. Palestinian nongovernmental organizations (NGOs), which are internationally funded institutions, automatically intervened with national and international policy making. The growing numbers of these organizations both after the First Intifada and immediately after Oslo became a dominant trend in the evolution of the Palestinian women's movement.[21]

After the failure of the Oslo peace process, the Second Intifada erupted in September 2000 and was largely categorized as violent compared to the first. It is within the aftermath of the Second Intifada and, later, during what became known as the "Arab Uprising," in which this chapter analyzes the images of Palestinian women deployed by the media. This chapter attempts to view these images within the "complex way in which hegemonic ... political, and patriarchal powers, including the mass media, ostracize Palestinian women and reproduce oppressive gender politics."[22]

Palestinian women in the wake of the Arab Uprisings

Once the Arab Uprisings commenced, news agencies and social media activists portrayed the image of Arab women participating and leading protests in their respective revolutions with rejuvenated hope. The women interviewed believed that such images delivered a sense of pride that transcended gender norms and beliefs. Palestinian women viewed all Arab women as citizens of revolutions and as revolutionaries taking their natural roles.

On March 15, 2011, numerous Palestinian youth took to the streets, demanding an end to the political division between Fatah of the West Bank and Hamas of Gaza, and further calling for direct elections to the Palestinian National Council of the PLO. Palestinians were frustrated with the division between political parties that had resulted in the creation of two separate governments in 2007. Palestinian voices also echoed others in the Arab world that demanded political representation and participation in the political process. Protesters felt that Palestinian parties were preoccupied with their internal power struggles, thus diverging the attention from Israeli colonization. They demanded that the PLO hold elections in order to create a unified national resistance strategy.[23]

Palestinian youth also attempted to occupy streets and camp in the middle of Palestinian cities, demanding change with varied results. In Gaza, high numbers of people took to the streets, resulting in direct confrontations with Hamas government and police. Protesters were attacked and imprisoned, which defeated the movement before it began. In the West Bank, the PA's use of intimidation resulted in a decreased number of participants, a strategy that co-opted their protests. Young women and men in Ramallah, Nablus, and Bethlehem camped in the middle of the cities in very small numbers, eventually vacating in late April in political disillusionment; the youth felt that they were unsuccessful in gaining the support of the Palestinian masses, which they felt resulted in an insufficient impact on the PA. Not only did they feel their protests were unproductive, but they felt that there was a need to re-prioritize their goals and disengage themselves from the political parties' interests. This also coincided with Hamas' and Fatah's signing yet another unity agreement[24] that neither party has implemented at the time of this chapter's writing.

Among the Palestinian youth, women have been present, visible, and audible in all the protests. Amal, an activist from Nablus, explained how women's participation in the Arab Uprisings influenced her participation in unity protests on March 15, 2011. Pictures of women leading protests in the Arab world reminded her of images from the First Intifada, encouraging her to head to protest sites in both Nablus and Ramallah. In one incident, Amal was the only woman who insisted on spending the night along with her male comrades at Ramallah's protest site. Other women did not join the overnight demonstrations because of the social condemnation sleeping in public with fellow male protesters would inevitably bring. Nevertheless, during the day, women were leading protests and demanding equal space with men.

During the interviews, the women were questioned on whether the Arab Uprising and March 15 unity protests also encouraged young women to participate in ongoing popular resistance against the Israeli occupation. In response, the study reveals that the answer to this question is somewhat complicated. Although the young women interviewed admitted that the Arab Uprisings affected their participation in the March 15 unity protests, they did not have much to say about how these uprisings affected their participation in ongoing popular resistance against Israeli occupation—that is, except in regard to the usage of social media.

Social media: a tool for Palestinian women in popular resistance?

Undoubtedly, an important influence of the Arab revolutions on Palestinians was the inspiration to use social media for political activism. Palestinian youth utilized it in various ways, including calling for protests, sharing footage of popular resistance activities, and organizing online petitions to raise awareness.[25]

Globally, women make up almost half of Facebook users in the world; yet, in the Arab world, only one-third of the users are women.[26] A study by the Dubai School of Government that explored the connection between women's usage of social media and their political and civic empowerment concluded that the main barriers to women's utilization of social media were "societal and cultural constraints."[27] In a 2009 study, Nadera Shalhoub-Kevorkian analyzed the impact of cyberspace and digital technologies on women in conflict areas. Her study specifically focused on the Occupied Palestinian Territory.[28] She concluded that the Internet has positively affected power dynamics and the roles of women in contested areas. She also found that the Internet can actually "enhance women's opportunities to resist and cope with patriarchal oppression in the domestic sphere as well as with militarization outside the home."[29] Shalhoub-Kevorkian introduced the term "e-resistance" to refer to feminist electronic resistance against both political and patriarchal oppression in conflict zones.[30] One recent example is the Facebook campaign, "Uprising of Women in the Arab World."[31] Beginning in October 2011, and following images of the Arab Uprisings, four Arab women—two Lebanese women, one Palestinian woman, and one Egyptian woman—led this social media campaign. Their campaign's agenda was to advance women's freedom and independence and to "create a platform for solidarity with women activists, who may have felt isolated in their individual struggles all over the region."[32] Noticeably, the largest participation in the campaign came from Palestine.[33] Countless Palestinians sent pictures of themselves wearing the traditional Kufiyah and demanding women's rights, thus uniting both struggles.

Although, in the Arab world, only one-third of social media users are women, Amira, a social media activist, argues that, when women have access to social media, they suddenly stand on "equal" ground with men. It creates a podium whereby the gender of the account holder does not matter, only the quality of the news shared. More importantly, the interviewees attest that it is a space where women can talk on behalf of themselves without formal media serving as an intermediary between them and the masses. In this way, the virtual world facilitates women's access to the streets. As Amira argues, "Women bloggers' voices were heard, and they were able to situate themselves as equal decision makers to men in the virtual world." Having done so, some of the activists argued that it paved the way for them to engage in street protests and politics both in the March 2011 disunity protests and, later, in popular resistance against the Israeli occupation.

Images of the Arab Uprising

In an attempt to categorize ongoing Arab revolutions—including protests in Palestine—as youth and women oriented, foreign media fixated on women's images in popular resistance. This focus created a distorted image of the reality of women's involvement. Journalists, reporters, photographers, and analysts enthusiastically grouped Palestinian women along with the women in Arab revolutions throughout the region. This generalization created what they thought of as the "gender revolution" or the "women's revolution."[34]

Western, Israeli, and Arab photographers alike raced to take pictures of Palestinian women in protests,[35] at times depicting them as "Palestinian Gandhis,"[36] the long-awaited nonviolent Palestinians. There is an ongoing assumption that Palestinians have not succeeded in their liberation or in acquiring a state because men have not yet adopted a nonviolent strategy. However, as some have argued, once Palestinians understand nonviolence, their future will change. Palestinian foreign journalists restlessly insisted on interviewing women rather than men during protests, and in many instances, they attempted to frame women's popular resistance as a separate, more novel model of resistance. Some Palestinian journalists and bloggers fell into the trap of casting women's recent levels of participation in Palestine as "new."[37]

Given the nature of media coverage of Palestinian women in popular resistance against Israel after 2011, one might envision that the Arab Uprisings encouraged Palestinian women to "return" once again to an activist- and community-based framework in their struggle. Media images portrayed Palestinian women in protests against the occupation but simultaneously presented them as "modern," "sexy," and "pacifist."[38] Foreign newspapers and photo exhibits focused on unveiled women and, in some instances, on the particulars of their outfits and bodies. The viewer's attention is thus shifted away from the issues behind the protests to the gender of the protesters.

In such instances, the media did not portray women as part of the communal protesting community but rather as a significant sector unto itself. Such a message offers a misleading suggestion that the current form of popular resistance is specific to a certain sector of women and not to all Palestinian women. The women interviewed in this study argue that this message is much more likely to appeal to Western audiences than to other Palestinians. Not only are the images seeking to satisfy the Western spectator's assumptions of what Palestinian resistance ought to be, but they erroneously employ the women as "carriers" of a nonviolent message of peace in sharp distinction from "violent" Palestinian men.[39]

Through his Facebook page, Israeli photographer Mati Milstein provides a clear example of his project on protesting Palestinian women, titled "*Nesa'iyeh* (A Woman Thing)." Milstein portrays a picture of a man with a Kufiyah wrapped around his head picking up what seems to be a gas canister from the ground, along with a picture of a woman in the same body position and who is also wrapped in a Kufiyah but is picking up flowers instead. The caption reads, "Men & Women: What might they choose to pick up off the ground in the midst of a protest?"[40] Milstein's photo exhibition of Palestinian women featured in an art exhibit in New Mexico in the United States instigated heated debates between youth groups concerning the forms of resistance portrayed in his photographs.[41] Milstein's pictures focus on women's facial expressions, certain aspects of their attire, and, in some cases, he completely removes them from their surroundings.[42]

In analyzing Milstein's artistic decisions, Khawla, a Nazarene who has been politically active since 2000, believes that Milstein is engaging in a form of female objectification. She argues that neither the photographs nor Palestinian women's actions can be situated outside the context of the Palestinian struggle and its history. In these images, not only are women detached from their conflicted surroundings, but they are also detached from the earlier Palestinian women's movement and its achievements. Admittedly, some of the interviewed women assert that, at times, Western media's discourse is so overpowering that Palestinian women themselves fail to demonstrate their existence as an extension of a deeply rooted Palestinian women's movement. Basma believes that "this disconnect ends up reinforcing the media's distorted images."

All of the Palestinian women activists interviewed in the study claimed that the media's interpretation of active women is distorted, incorrect, or exaggerated. One inaccurate piece of deployed information is the claim that there has been an increase in women's participation in protests and activities after 2011. Both Khawla from Nazareth and Shatha from Al-Waljeh, a town northwest of Bethlehem, have been politically active for more than fifteen years, and they indicate that since the start of the Arab revolutions, there has been no real rise in women's overall participation in popular resistance. This conception is in stark contrast to the images of women in the March 15 unity protests.

Khawla, who was regularly active in protests against the Wall in Budrus and other villages during the Second Intifada, believes that women's participation has actually declined after 2011 when compared with early protests against the Wall in 2003. She asserts that women were an essential part of the confrontation against the Wall in local villages; they played vital roles in some of the protests' successes, which she claims is not the case in demonstrations against the occupation that occurred after 2011. Shatha confirms that the Arab revolutions instigated a reverse reaction in Al-Waljeh, one she asserts is of "anticipation" and "waiting." Indeed, popular resistance activities in the village slowed down in an attempt to understand the consequences of the Arab Uprisings. This "anticipation period" further decreased women's participation.

In an interview with Iltizam Morar from Budrus, Morar praises the relationship dynamics between men and women in the protests, and the roles women were able to assume between 2003 and 2005. Iltizam describes the crucial roles women played in weekly protests and in mobilizing for protests since 2003. Not only did they participate in general demonstrations, but they also held women-only protests and meetings. Women were also an integral part of the struggle against the Wall in Budrus. In fact, Iltizam did not have much to say about the effect of the Arab Uprisings on women's participation in Budrus, as women in Budrus were visible since 2003. However, Iltizam admits that women were excluded from "men-only strategy formulating" meetings. As the daughter of the village's popular resistance leader, and as a woman with good English skills (a necessary and highly appreciated skill when meeting with foreigners), Iltizam was privileged to attend such meetings. Nevertheless, she believes that women's participation in protests taking place in other villages were not as predominant as those in Budrus. Iltizam acknowledges that when she participated in protests in other villages, very few local women were present.

Even so, there is a history of Palestinian women's resistance that has been discredited in the wake of Palestinian women's protest images after 2011 and the Arab revolutions. For example, women organized at the grassroots level in villages to resist the Separation Wall. As early as 2003, women in popular resistance formed a local coalition under the name "Women Against the Wall."[43] The coalition was supposed to serve as a women's branch of each male-dominated Popular Committee, which presented a form of community-based organizing and resistance similar to that of the First Palestinian Intifada, and aimed at strengthening women's participation and involvement in decision-making.

In another example, women in Tulkarm established a women's group called "Women's Wall Defense Committee." This group attempted to mobilize women to participate in protests[44] and held several meetings in Salfeet to organize against the Wall in their village.[45] However, it is unclear how successful these women actually were in organizing and campaigning. The intensity of popular resistance activities in these villages varied, as did the participation of the women. In any case, the formation of these coalitions attests to the fact that women were attempting to organize on the grassroots level—a development absent from protests after 2011.

In support of this observation, several women interviewed indicated that the possible increase of women's participation in popular resistance is that of "younger, educated, urban, socially active females in Ramallah." These women, who were mostly unveiled and wearing jeans, t-shirts, and Kufiyahs, were highly deployed by the media. Such images resonate with Western viewers who can relate to the Palestinian who "looks like them"—a picture that does not resemble the violent Palestinian man, nor the Palestinian women "in voluminous dresses involved in domestic activities."[46]

The Palestinian authority: the recreation of the "nonviolent Palestinian"

Since the establishment of the PA in 1994, it has faced trouble focusing on the peacebuilding process. However, by 2000, it was evident that the Oslo Accords had failed, and all other attempts at negotiation were unsuccessful.[47] The situation for Palestinians was only deteriorating, with no foreseeable political solution.[48] On September 29, 2000, following the then-Israeli Prime Minister Ariel Sharon's visit to Al-Aqsa mosque along with 1,000 Israeli soldiers, Palestinian protests erupted. This marked the start of the Second Intifada, which killed thousands of Palestinians and 1,000 Israelis.[49] Palestinians utilized several tools in fighting the Israeli occupation and aggression, including the usage of arms.

In the wake of the Oslo Accords, the new image of Palestinians as carriers of a "peaceful" message suffered a setback after the Second Intifada. Three specific images of the Second Intifada come to mind. The first is of Muhammed Al-Durra, a twelve-year-old boy hiding behind his father as countless Israeli bullets penetrate his body. The second is of Faris Odeh, a fourteen-year-old child throwing stones at an Israeli tank. The final one is a photograph of a young Palestinian man raising his bloody hand after the lynching of two Israeli soldiers in Ramallah. Palestinian scholars Rema Hammami and Salim Tamari indicate that images of the Second Intifada, including that of Muhammed Al-Durra, were "soon superseded by the far more numerous images of the lynching of two Israeli soldiers in Ramallah."[50] This image, along with others, reintroduced the image of the violent Palestinian man.

The rhetoric of nonviolence was reinforced, however, with the appointment of Mahmoud Abbas as Prime Minster of Palestine and, a few years later, as its President.[51] Nonviolent rhetoric can be clearly mapped out when examining the policies and speeches of President Abbas. In an interview in 2013, he stated, "[R]egarding the word 'resistance,' yes, I tell you that I will not utter the words 'armed resistance.' We have tried it, most recently in the Second Intifada, which destroyed everything for us."[52] Instead, President Abbas continuously called for peaceful popular resistance,[53] even financially supporting the Popular Struggle Coordination Committee, which is responsible for coordinating popular resistance activities.[54] Moreover, in 2014, in a speech to 300 Israeli students visiting the PA's headquarters, he claimed that the security coordination with Israel is "sacred" and that it shall continue whether Palestinians and Israelis politically agree or not.[55] Such coordination is seen as a pillar for preventing Palestinian usage of armed resistance in the West Bank.[56]

President Abbas and his government have repeatedly depicted Palestinians as nonviolent and peaceful to the world. The Arab Uprising provided an excellent opportunity to group Palestinians with their fellow nonviolent Arab revolutionists. This depiction directly served the PA's message in attempting to prove to the world that Palestinians are more "civilized" than the infamous "terrorists." The PA and its leaders continuously seek to justify Palestinian resistance and align it with what seems to be a more palatable Western notion of resistance: unarmed, Gandhi-style, and nonviolent. The portrayal of Palestinian women in the Arab Uprising is one way to illustrate a neutral, palatable version of active women's revolution as an empowered nonviolent one.[57]

NGO-ization

The image of these "nonviolent women" is further elaborated through the process of *NGO-ization*. NGO-ization is defined by Islah Jad as a combination of professionalization and projectization.[58] She posits that the establishment of the PA, the hegemony of the donor agenda, and the NGO-ization of local grassroots organizations were all significant factors that resulted in demobilizing more militant and effective organizations—including the women's movement—in Palestine. Jad further criticizes that NGO-ization watered-down "many political positions concerning vital issues related to refugees; Jerusalem, forms of resistance, and the formation of the future state are adopted by the official participants in international conferences without any consultation with the Palestinian population."[59] According to Jad, international donors have hijacked the Palestinian agenda and replaced it with a Western-led approach. Jad asserts that this has resulted in a dichotomy between the leadership and its people.[60]

Like most others, Palestinian NGOs are defined as mediators that communicated "peace process[es]," thus intervening in national and international policy processes. These NGOs became a continuing reflection of how the Palestinian elites compromised their agendas to adhere to international proposals. It is apparent that the women's standpoint has shifted from earlier activism to a world of internationally funded institutions. Evidently, NGOs provided a platform for Palestinian women to continue their activism, as their activism took a different approach, transforming their political agenda. After the First Intifada and immediately after the Oslo Accords, a growing numbers of NGOs became a dominant trend in the evolution of the Palestinian women's movement.[61] The creation of a nonresistant society post-Oslo helped overwhelmed Palestinians with a general feeling of incapability and hopelessness. The issue of losing track of a Palestinian personal national agenda is evidently not one specific to the Palestinian women's movement but is a feature of the Palestinian national movement in general.

Sociologist Ala Alazzeh maps out the role of NGOs in promoting nonviolence as an ideology and explains how NGO-ization "functioned as a force of re-politicization through the construction of a new paradigm of 'non-violence' to narrate the Palestinian history of struggle."[62] Alazzeh argues that NGOs assisted in perceptions of the Palestinian struggle within the binary of violence and nonviolence, thus moving away from the overall colonial struggle structure. Such binary vision is part and parcel of the shift from national liberation to a state-building phase, in which most NGOs altered their agendas to adopt a more globalized apolitical agenda.[63] This transformed role of Palestinian civil society hinted at a false narrative for women's activism in Palestine and created a gateway for the media to shape the image of female activists as "sexy" and "new," thus isolating it from the Palestinian women's movement and its history.

Within the context of "gendering" the Arab Uprisings, the PA's emphasis on the nonviolent Palestinian and the emergence of an apolitical civil society, women's bodies were deployed as important actors of nonviolence. Images of women leading nonviolent protests depicted them as "modernized," "Westernized," and peaceful, and became important icons in the newly structured phase.

Conclusion

While watching the Arab Uprisings unfold, it was natural for Palestinians to reflect on their own local context. Amid the revolutions, Western media fixated on the women of the Arab world as pioneers of the uprisings at a time of national and gender awakening of the masses. Palestinian women in popular resistance also dominated the media's attention as the news focused on Palestine. Media images portrayed the women as leaders of nuanced "nonviolent resistance"—but at the same time detaching them from the surrounding context and the earlier women's movement. With the NGO-ization of Palestinian civil society, and the eagerness of the PA to deploy a resistance message approved by the Western world, women's bodies were used as carriers of this modernized, nonviolent message.

In this context, it was, at first, hard to contextualize Yasmin Hamdan's three-minute love song within the Palestinian national struggle and emancipation; however, later on, the choice of the song vis-à-vis the images of protesting Palestinian women made sense. Yasmin, an icon for alternative music, provides the background for an alternative reality: along with kohled eyes under a Kufiyah face wrap, a ring adorned with Arabic calligraphy, colorful tennis shoes, white sunglasses, and some bold, defiant images, her voice assisted in recreating the new Palestinian.

Notes

1 Emphasis mine.
2 For the purposes of this chapter, the term "active women" refers to women who frequently participate in and lead political and social activities.
3 Mazin B. Qumsiyeh, *Popular Resistance in Palestine: A History of Hope and Empowerment* (London: Pluto Press, 2011), defines popular resistance on page 11:

> Muqawama sha'biya, the term commonly used in Palestine, is roughly translated as popular resistance. The word sha'biya has its roots in sha'b (people) and is understood by many Palestinians to refer to the kinds of resistance practiced by large numbers of the population, as opposed to more narrow-armed resistances (muqawama musallaha). On the other hand, we do have in common use thawra sha'biya, or people's revolution .... In English, it is more accurate to use nonviolent resistance to differentiate it from violent resistance; but the term translated literally into Arabic would be a very poor (and rather negative) description of the complex and empowering acts of popular resistance practiced in Palestine that cannot count as armed resistance. But because of the limitations of language, we shall use the term "popular resistance" in this book.

4 Ellen L. Fleischman, "The Emergence of the Palestinian Women's Movement, 1929–39," *Journal of Palestine Studies* 19, no. 3 (2000): 18–20.
5 Islah Jad, "Women at the Cross-Roads: The Palestinian Women's Movement between Nationalism, Secularism and Islamism" (PhD diss., School of Oriental and African Studies University of London, 2004), 77; Ellen Fleischmann, *The Nation and Its "New" Women: The Palestinian Women's Movement, 1920–1948* (London: University of California Press, 2003), 95–115.
6 Jad, "Women at the Cross-Roads," 79.
7 Fleischmann, *The Nation and Its "New" Women*, 7.
8 Islah Jad, "Re-reading the Mandate: Palestinian Women and the Double Jeopardy of Colonialism," *Review of Women Studies, Birzeit University* 3 (2005): 8–29.
9 Jad, "Re-reading the Mandate," 21.
10 *Ibid.*
11 Fleischmann, *The Nation and Its "New" Women*, 63–80.
12 *Ibid.*
13 Jad "Women at the Cross-Roads," 85.
14 Hamida Kazi, "Palestinian Women and the National Liberation Movement: A Social Perspective," in *Women in the Middle East*, edited by The Khamsin Collective (London: Zed Press, 1987), 26–39, www.matzpen.org/english/1987-07-10/palestinian-women-and-the-national-liberation-movement-a-social-perspective-hamida-kazi/.
15 Declaration of Principles on Interim Self-Government Arrangement, Isr.-PLO, September 13, 1993, 32 I.L.M. 1525.
16 The Israeli-Palestinian Interim Agreement on the West Bank and the Gaza Strip, Isr.-PLO, August 27, 1995, 36 I.L.M. 551.
17 Letters between Yasser Arafat, Chairman, The Palestine Liberation Organization, and Yitzhak Rabin, Prime Minister of Israel, *in Israeli-PLO Mutual Recognition, 13–14 Letters and Speeches*, 107, September 10, 1993, http://mfa.gov.il/mfa/foreignpolicy/mfadocuments/yearbook9/pages/107%20israel-plo%20mutual%20recognition-%20letters%20and%20spe.aspx.
18 *Ibid.*; President of the PLO, Yasser Arafat, sent a letter to Rabin recognizing the right of Israel to exist in peace, and, more importantly, "renounce[ing] the use of terrorism and other acts of violence and [assuming] responsibility over all PLO elements and personnel in order to assure their compliance, prevent violations and discipline violators."
19 Jad, "Women at the Cross-Roads," 120–125.
20 *Ibid.*
21 Eileen Kuttab, "Palestinian Women's Organizations: Global Cooption & Local Contradictions," *Review of Women's Studies* 5, (2009): 70–71.
22 Nadera Shalhoub-Kevorkian, *Militarization and Violence against Women in Conflict Zones in the Middle East* (London, Cambridge University Press, 2009), 2.
23 See Linah Alsaafin, "Imperfect Revolution: Palestine's 15 March Movement One Year On," *The Electronic Intifada*, March 13, 2012, https://electronicintifada.net/content/imperfect-revolution-palestines-15-march-movement-one-year/11092; Harriet Sherwood, "Young Palestinians Call for Protests on 15 March," *The Guardian*, February 24, 2011, www.theguardian.com/world/2011/feb/24/palestinian-young-people-protests.
24 Conal Urquhart and Harriet Sherwood, "Palestine Rivals Fatah and Hamas on Verge of Historic Deal," *The Guardian*, April 27, 2011, www.theguardian.com/world/2011/apr/27/palestine-rivals-fatah-hamas-deal.
25 See, for example, Facebook pages "Tamimi Press" at www.facebook.com/Tamimipresspage, and "Palestinians for Dignity," www.facebook.com/palestiniansfordignity?ref=ts&fref=ts.
26 Salem and Mourtada, "The Role of Social Media in Arab Women's Empowerment," *Arab Social Media Report* 1, no. 3 (November 2011): www.researchgate.net/publication/230709416_The_Role_of_Social_Media_in_Arab_Women%27s_Empowerment.

27 *Ibid.*
28 Nadera Shalhoub-Kevorkian, "E-Resistance among Palestinian Women: Coping in Conflict-Ridden Areas," *Social Service Review* 85, no. 2 (June 2011): 179–204.
29 Shalhoub-Kevorkian, "E-Resistance among Palestinian Women," 181.
30 *Ibid.*, 180.
31 "The Uprising of Women in the Arab World," *Facebook* post, accessed on October 29, 2012, www.facebook.com/intifadat.almar2.
32 Sara Abbas, "Revolution is Female: The Uprising of Women in the Arab World," December 2, 2012, www.opendemocracy.net/5050/sara-abbas/revolution-is-female-uprising-of-women-in-arab-world.
33 Katherine Jane O'Neill, "More Arab Females Join Women's Rights Movement to Demand Equality," *Al Arabiya*, October 10, 2012, http://english.alarabiya.net/articles/2012/10/09/242742.html.
34 Carla Power, "Silent No More: The Women of the Arab Revolutions," *Time*, March 24, 2011, http://content.time.com/time/world/article/0,8599,2059435,00.html; Emine Saner, "What Will the Changes of the Arab Spring Mean for Women? Journalist Nabila Ramdani is Wary of What will Happen Next, but Rana Kabbani is Rapturously Optimistic [Interview]," *The Guardian*, December 16, 2011, www.theguardian.com/commentisfree/2011/dec/16/the-conversation-women-arab-spring; "Women and the Arab Awakening: Now is the Time," *The Economist*, October 15, 2011, www.economist.com/node/21532256; Sheera Frenkel, "After the Revolution, Arab Women Seek More Rights," *National Public Radio*, August 6, 2011, www.npr.org/2011/08/06/137482442/after-the-revolution-arab-women-seek-more-rights.
35 Lazar Simeonov, "Women Protesting in Ramallah," *Demotix*, March 15, 2011, www.demotix.com/news/643133/women-protesting-ramallah; Mati Milstein, "*Nesa'iyeh* (a Woman Thing)," *Vimeo* video, 03:22, December 7, 2011, https://vimeo.com/33312186.
36 Mati Milstein, "There are Already Palestinian Gandhis—They're Women [Interview by Yasmina Mrabet]," *Peace and Collaboration Development Network*, January 23, 2012, www.peacexpeace.org/2012/01/there-are-already-palestinian-gandhis-theyre-women/.
37 See for example, Maath Musleh, "Women Activism in Palestine," *Uprooted Palestinians*, April 16, 2012, http://uprootedpalestinians.blogspot.co.il/2012/04/from-disappointment-of-first-intifada.html: "But the year of 2011 certainly took the role of women in the Palestinian struggle to a new level. For the first time, women decided to act equal rather than seek permission for an equal role."
38 Deema Alsafin, "Her Resistance is the Large Beauty," *Thekfemonument*, accessed on July 29, 2013, http://thekfcmonument.wordpress.com/2012/06/29/her-resistance-is-the-larger-beauty/; Sami Kishawi, "'*Nesa'iyeh*' and Its Objectification of Women in the Face of Resistance," *Sixteen Minutes to Palestine*, June 30, 2012, https://smpalestine.com/2012/06/30/nesaiyeh-and-its-objectification-of-women-in-the-face-of-resistance/.
39 See comparisons between women and men throwing stones: Emily Harris, "Palestinian Girls Look for Ways to Protest, Without Stones," *National Public Radio*, May 30, 2013, www.npr.org/sections/parallels/2013/05/30/181928768/Palestinian-Girls-Look-For-Ways-To-Protest-Without-Stones.
40 Mati Milstein, "*Nesa'iyeh* (a Woman Thing)/Photographic Exhibition," *Facebook* post, accessed on July 27, 2013, www.facebook.com/photo.php?fbid=241790195904804&set=a.208633409220483.51904.208046755945815&type=3&theater.
41 *Ibid.*
42 The author makes no note regarding the artistic value of the pictures.
43 Sophie Richter-Devroe, "Defending Their Land, Protecting Their Men: Palestinian Women's Popular Resistance after the Second Intifada," *International Feminist Journal of Politics* 14, no. 2 (April 2012): 181–201.

44 International Women's Peace Service, "Palestinian Women Mobilizing to Resist Israel's Apartheid Wall," *The Electronic Intifada*, September 17, 2003, https://electronicintifada.net/content/palestinian-women-mobilising-resist-israels-apartheid-wall/1341.
45 Fatima Khaldi, "Women against the Wall," *The Electronic Intifada*, July 16, 2004, https://electronicintifada.net/content/women-against-wall/5163.
46 Tori Lee, "Palestinian Gandhis?" *The New Mexico Jewish Link*, August 2012, www.facebook.com/PalestineWomenFirst/photos/a.264656020284888.64024.208046755945815/342939969123159/?type=3&theater.
47 Akram Hanieh, "The Camp David Papers," *Journal of Palestine Studies* 30, no. 2 (Winter 2001): 75–97.
48 See Rema Hammami and Salim Tamari, "The Second Uprising: End or New Beginning?" *Journal of Palestine Studies* 30, no. 2 (2001): 5–25; Jeremy Pressman, "The Second Intifada: Background and Causes of the Israeli-Palestinian Conflict," *Journal of Conflict Studies* 23, no. 2 (Fall 2003), https://journals.lib.unb.ca/index.php/jcs/article/view/220/378.
49 See "Fatalities before Operation 'Cast Lead,'" *B'Tselem*, accessed on May 2, 2014, www.btselem.org/statistics/fatalities/before-cast-lead/by-date-of-event; U.N. Secretariat, Office for the Coordination of Humanitarian Affairs, *Israeli-Palestinian Fatalities Since 2000—Key Trends*, last modified August 31, 2007, http://unispal.un.org/UNISPAL.NSF/0/BE07C80CDA457946852573480050O272; "Intifada Toll 2000–2005," *BBC News*, accessed on September 17, 2017, http://news.bbc.co.uk/2/hi/middle_east/3694350.stm.
50 Hammami, "The Second Uprising," 15.
51 For more on nonviolence, see Ala Alazzeh, "Non-Violent Popular Resistance in the West Bank: The Case of the Popular Struggle Committees," *International Institute for Nonviolent Action* (February 2011): 18–19.
52 Jean Aziz, "Abu Mazen: I Will Not Utter the Words 'Armed Resistance,'" *Al-Monitor*, July 5, 2013, www.al-monitor.com/pulse/originals/2013/07/palestine-abbas-oppose-armed-resistance-israel.html.
53 Sufian Abu Zaida, "Changing the Status Quo: What Directions for Palestinians? Peaceful Popular Resistance: Is it an Option?" *Palestinian Center for Policy and Survey Research*, May 2016, www.pcpsr.org/sites/default/files/Sufian%20Abu%20Zaida%20print%20English.pdf.
54 Michael J. Carpenter, "Unarmed and Participatory: Palestinian Popular Struggle and Civil Resistance Theory," (Doctoral diss., University of Victoria, 2017), 177.
55 Falafelcafe, "RAW FOOTAGE—Muhammad Al Durrah Incident," *YouTube* video, 3:12, May 22, 2013, www.youtube.com/watch?v=arRgkXDLwlM; Isabel Kershner, "Abbas, Talking to Israeli Students about Peace, Finds a Receptive Audience," *The New York Times*, February 16, 2014, www.nytimes.com/2014/02/17/world/middleeast/abbas-talking-to-israeli-students-about-peace-finds-a-receptive-audience.html?mcubz=1.
56 Hani Al-Masri, "Changing the Status Quo: What Directions for Palestinians? Is It Possible to Suspend Security Coordination?" *Palestinian Center for Policy and Survey Research*, May 2016, www.pcpsr.org/sites/default/files/Hani%20Masri%20print%20English.pdf.
57 See Ala Alazzeh, "Locating Nonviolence: The People, the Past and Resistance in Palestinian Political Activism," (Doctoral diss., Rice University, 2014).
58 Islah Jad, "NGOs: Between Buzzwords and Social Movements," *Development in Practice* 17, no. 4/5 (August 2007): 622.
59 *Ibid*., 626.
60 *Ibid*., 625.
61 Kuttab, "Palestinian Women's Organizations," 70.
62 Alazzeh, "Locating Nonviolence," 18.
63 See Tariq Dana, "The Structural Transformation of Palestinian Civil Society: Key Paradigm Shifts," *Middle East Critique* 24, no. 2 (2015): 191–210.

Bibliography

Abbas, Sara. "Revolution Is Female: The Uprising of Women in the Arab World." December 2, 2012. www.opendemocracy.net/5050/sara-abbas/revolution-is-female-uprising-of-women-in-arab-world.

Abu Zaida, Sufian. "Changing the Status Quo: What Directions for Palestinians? Peaceful Popular Resistance: Is it an Option?" *Palestinian Center for Policy and Survey Research*, May 2016. www.pcpsr.org/sites/default/files/Sufian%20Abu%20Zaida%20print%20English.pdf.

Alazzeh, Ala. "Locating Nonviolence: The People, the Past and Resistance in Palestinian Political Activism." Doctoral dissertation, Rice University, 2014.

———. "Non-Violent Popular Resistance in the West Bank: The Case of the Popular Struggle Committees." *International Institute for Nonviolent Action*, February 2011, 18–19.

———. "Nonviolent Popular Resistance in the West Bank: The Case of Popular Struggle Committees." Accessed October 6, 2018. https://novact.org/2013/10/nonviolent-popular-resistance-in-the-west-bank-the-case-of-popular-struggle-committes/.

Al-Masri, Hani. "Changing the Status Quo: What Directions for Palestinians? Is It Possible to Suspend Security Coordination?" *Palestinian Center for Policy and Survey Research*, May 2016. www.pcpsr.org/sites/default/files/Hani%20Masri%20print%20English.pdf.

Alsaafin, Deema. "Her Resistance is the Large Beauty." *Thekfcmonument.* Accessed July 29, 2013. http://thekfcmonument.wordpress.com/2012/06/29/her-resistance-is-the-larger-beauty.

Alsaafin, Linah. "Imperfect Revolution: Palestine's 15 March Movement One year On." *The Electronic Intifada*, March 13, 2012. https://electronicintifada.net/content/imperfect-revolution-palestines-15-march-movement-one-year/11092.

Aziz, Jean. "Abu Mazen: I Will Not Utter the Words 'Armed Resistance.'" *Al-Monitor*, July 5, 2013. www.al-monitor.com/pulse/originals/2013/07/palestine-abbas-oppose-armed-resistance-israel.html.

Carpenter, Michael J. "Unarmed and Participatory: Palestinian Popular Struggle and Civil Resistance Theory." Doctoral dissertation, University of Victoria, 2017.

Dana, Tariq. "The Structural Transformation of Palestinian Civil Society: Key Paradigm Shifts." *Middle East Critique* 24, no. 2 (2015): 191–210.

Falafelcafe. *RAW FOOTAGE—Muhammad Al Durrah Incident.* YouTube video, 3:12. May 22, 2013. www.youtube.com/watch?v=arRgkXDLwlM.

Falasteeni. *Abbas: Al-tanseeq Al-amni Mukadas w Sayastamir Sawa' 'Iktelafna fi Al-seyaseh 'aw 'Itefakna.* YouTube video, 0:12. May 29, 2014. www.youtube.com/watch?v=DFrCcj588MI.

"Fatah and Hamas Sign Reconciliation Deal." *Aljazeera.* Accessed July 29, 2013. www.aljazeera.com/news/middleeast/2011/04/2011427152119845721.html.

"Fatalities before Operation 'Cast Lead.'" *B'Tselem.* Accessed May 2, 2014. www.btselem.org/statistics/fatalities/before-cast-lead/by-date-of-event.

Fleischmann, Ellen L. "The Emergence of the Palestinian Women's Movement, 1929-39." *Journal of Palestine Studies* 29, no. 3 (2000): 16–32. doi:10.2307/2676453.

Frenkel, Sheera. "After the Revolution, Arab Women Seek More Rights." *National Public Radio*, August 6, 2011. www.npr.org/2011/08/06/137482442/after-the-revolution-arab-women-seek-more-rights.

Hammami, Rema, and Salim Tamari. "The Second Uprising: End or New Beginning?" *Journal of Palestine Studies* 30, no. 2 (2001): 5–25.

Hanieh, Akram. "The Camp David Papers." *Journal of Palestine Studies* 30, no. 2 (Winter 2001): 75–97.

Harris, Emily. "Palestinian Girls Look for Ways to Protest, Without Stones." *National Public Radio*, May 30, 2013. www.npr.org/sections/parallels/2013/05/30/181928768/Palestinian-Girls-Look-For-Ways-To-Protest-Without-Stones.

International Women's Peace Service. "Palestinian Women Mobilizing to Resist Israel's Apartheid Wall." *The Electronic Intifada*, September 17, 2003. https://electronicintifada.net/content/palestinian-women-mobilising-resist-israels-apartheid-wall/1341.

"Intifada Toll 2000–2005." *BBC News*. Accessed September 17, 2017. http://news.bbc.co.uk/2/hi/middle_east/3694350.stm.

Jad, Islah. "NGOs: Between Buzzwords and Social Movements." *Development in Practice* 17, no. 4/5 (August 2007): 622–629.

———. "Re-Reading the Mandate: Palestinian Women and the Double Jeopardy of Colonialism." *Review of Women Studies* 3 (2005): 8–29.

———. "Women at the Cross-Roads: The Palestinian Women's Movement between Nationalism, Secularism and Islamism." Doctoral dissertation, School of Oriental and African Studies, University of London, 2004.

Jad, Islah. *Women at the Cross-Roads: The Palestinian Women's Movement Between Nationalism, Secularism and Islamism*. University of London, 2004.

Johnson, Penny, and Eileen Kuttab. "Where Have All the Women (and Men) Gone? Reflections on Gender and the Second Palestinian Intifada." *Feminist Review* no. 69 (Winter 2001): 21–43.

Kazi, Hamida. "Palestinian Women and the National Liberation Movement: A Social Perspective." In *Women in the Middle East*, edited by The Khamsin Collective. London: Zed Press, 26–39, 1987.

Kershner, Isabel. "Abbas, Talking to Israeli Students About Peace, Finds a Receptive Audience." *The New York Times*, February 16, 2014. www.nytimes.com/2014/02/17/world/middleeast/abbas-talking-to-israeli-students-about-peace-finds-a-receptive-audience.html?mcubz=1.

Khaldi, Fatima. "Women against the Wall." *The Electronic Intifada*, July 16, 2004. https://electronicintifada.net/content/women-against-wall/5163.

Kishawi, Sami. "'*Nesa'iyeh*' and its Objectification of Women in the Face of Resistance." *Sixteen Minutes to Palestine*, June 30, 2012. https://smpalestine.com/2012/06/30/nesaiyeh-and-its-objectification-of-women-in-the-face-of-resistance/.

Kuttab, Eileen. "Palestinian Women's Organizations: Global Cooption & Local Contradictions." *Review of Women's Studies* 5 (2009): 21–43.

Lee, Tori. "Palestinian Gandhis?" *The New Mexico Jewish Link*, August 2012. www.facebook.com/PalestineWomenFirst/photos/a.264656020284888.64024.208046755945815/342939969123159/?type=3&theater.

Milstein, Mati. "*Nesa'iyeh* (a Woman Thing)." *Vimeo* video, 3:22. December 7, 2011. https://vimeo.com/33312186.

———. "*Nesa'iyeh* (a Woman Thing)/Photographic Exhibition." *Facebook Post*. Accessed July 27, 2013. www.facebook.com/photo.php?fbid=241790195904804&set=a.208633409220483.51904.208046755945815&type=3&theater.

———. "There are Already Palestinian Gandhis—They're Women [Interview by Yasmina Mrabet]." *Peace and Collaboration Development Network*, January 23, 2012. www.peacexpeace.org/2012/01/there-are-already-palestinian-gandhis-theyre-women/.

Musleh, Maath. "Women Activism in Palestine." *Uprooted Palestinians*, April 16, 2012. http://uprootedpalestinians.blogspot.co.il/2012/04/from-disappointment-of-first-intifada.html.

O'Neill, Katherine Jane. "More Arab Females Join Women's Rights Movement to Demand Equality." *Al Arabiya*, October 10, 2012. http://english.alarabiya.net/articles/2012/10/09/242742.html.

Palestine Today. "Altoum . . . Althikra al 12 li'istishad algeneral Faris Odeh." Accessed September 14, 2017. https://paltoday.ps/ar/post/150939/اليوم-الذكرى-الـ-12-لاستشهاد-الجنرال-فارس-عودة.

Power, Carla. "Silent No More: The Women of the Arab Revolutions." *Time*, March 24, 2011. http://content.time.com/time/world/article/0,8599,2059435,00.html.

Pressman, Jeremy. "The Second Intifada: Background and Causes of the Israeli-Palestinian Conflict." *Journal of Conflict Studies* 23, no. 2 (Fall 2003). https://journals.lib.unb.ca/index.php/jcs/article/view/220/378.

Qumsiyeh, Mazin B. *Popular Resistance in Palestine: A History of Hope and Empowerment*. London: Pluto Press, 2011.

Richter-Devroe, Sophie. "Defending Their Land, Protecting Their Men: Palestinian Women's Popular Resistance after the Second Intifada." *International Feminist Journal of Politics* 14, no. 2 (April 2012): 181–201.

Sabbagh, Suha. *Palestinian Women of Gaza and the West Bank*. Bloomington: Indiana University Press, 1998.

Salem, Fadi, and Racha Mourtada. "The Role of Social Media in Arab Women's Empowerment." *Arab Social Media Report* 1, no. 3 (November 2011). www.researchgate.net/publication/230709416_The_Role_of_Social_Media_in_Arab_Women%27s_Empowerment.

Saner, Emine. "What Will the Changes of the Arab Spring Mean for Women? Journalist Nabila Ramdani Is Wary of What Will Happen Next, But Rana Kabbani Is Rapturously Optimistic [Interview]." *The Guardian*, December 16, 2011. www.theguardian.com/commentisfree/2011/dec/16/the-conversation-women-arab-spring.

Shalhoub-Kevorkian, Nadera. "E-Resistance among Palestinian Women: Coping in Conflict-Ridden Areas." *Social Service Review* 85, no. 2 (June 2011): 179–204.

Shalhoub-Kevorkian, Nadera. *Militarization and Violence against Women in Conflict Zones in the Middle East: A Palestinian Case-Study*. Cambridge Studies in Law and Society. Cambridge ; Cambridge University Press, 2009.

———. *Militarization and Violence against Women in Conflict Zones in the Middle East*. London: Cambridge University Press, 2009.

Sherwood, Harriet. "Young Palestinians Call for Protests on 15 March." *The Guardian*, February 24, 2011. www.theguardian.com/world/2011/feb/24/palestinian-young-people-protests.

Simeonov, Lazar. "Women Protesting in Ramallah." *Demotix*, March 15, 2011. www.demotix.com/news/643133/women-protesting-ramallah.

U.N. Secretariat, Office for the Coordination of Humanitarian Affairs. "Israeli-Palestinian Fatalities Since 2000—Key Trends." Last modified August 31, 2007. http://unispal.un.org/UNISPAL.NSF/0/BE07C80CDA457946852573480050O272.

Urquhart, Conal, and Harriet Sherwood. "Palestine Rivals Fatah and Hamas on Verge of Historic Deal." *The Guardian*, April 27, 2011. www.theguardian.com/world/2011/apr/27/palestine-rivals-fatah-hamas-deal.

"Women and the Arab Awakening: Now is the Time." *The Economist*, October 15, 2011. www.economist.com/node/21532256.

Part III

The Arab diaspora

gender, human rights, and migration

5 Theorizing sexual violence against men in the Middle East and North African region as gender-related persecution under refugee and asylum law

Valorie K. Vojdik

Introduction

While international law has recognized that sexual violence against women during war may constitute gender-related persecution, sexual violence against men has been virtually invisible, both in the Middle East and North African (MENA) region and around the globe. During the Syrian conflict, for example, media reports primarily focused on the rape of women and girls, mostly ignoring the widespread rape of Syrian men and boys in detention by Syrian forces.[1] Recently, the United Nations High Commissioner for Refugees (UNHCR) has begun to recognize that men and boys are also victims of sexual violence and gender-based persecution.[2] Drawing on examples from Syria and the MENA region, this chapter argues that feminists and human rights advocates should similarly broaden the theoretical framework of refugee and asylum law[3] to recognize and conceptualize claims of male refugees as gender-related persecution.

Both the 1951 UN Convention Relating to the Status of Refugees (1951 Refugee Convention or Refugee Convention) and the U.S. Immigration and Naturalization Act (INA) provide protection to refugees, defining refugee as a person with well-founded fear of persecution on several enumerated grounds that do not include sex or gender. Following the mass rape of women during armed conflicts in the 1990s, feminist scholars and human rights activists mobilized to persuade courts to recognize gender-related violence against women as a form of persecution that may qualify for asylum protection.[4] In so doing, feminist advocates have tended to theorize gender-related persecution in sex-specific terms, conceptualized as harm to women perpetrated by men.

While the international community has begun to recognize gender-related claims of women as grounds for human rights protection, it has largely ignored gender-related claims of men and boys.[5] Like women, men and boys are subjected to conflict-related sexual violence and torture by the government and military forces that is gender-related and may constitute grounds for asylum protection. The erasure of men and boy refugees from accounts of gender-based persecution not only denies them the ability to be protected as refugees but also undermines feminist efforts to eradicate the subordination of women.

Treating gender-based persecution as a sex-specific phenomenon tends to essentialize the categories of male and female, reinforcing gender stereotypes that assume that women are victims and men are perpetrators.[6] This in turn obscures the role of gender as a social process or institution of distinction and domination that regulates both men and women.

Focusing on international standards and asylum jurisprudence in the United States, this chapter critiques the failure to recognize gender persecution against men and boys. United Nations Security Council Resolution 2106 recognized in 2016 that men and boys are also victims of sexual violence during conflict, which can constitute a war crime, crime against humanity, and constitutive act of genocide.[7] Concentrating on the MENA region, this chapter argues that sexual violence against men during conflict similarly may constitute gender-related persecution and grounds for refugee protection. Specifically, it argues that feminists should expand the theoretical framework of asylum law to incorporate and theorize men's experiences of gender violence and persecution.

This chapter begins with a discussion of the movement to recognize gender-related persecution of women as grounds for protection and asylum. The next section examines relevant guidance from the UNCHR and the United States examining asylum claims by women, arguing that the documents recognize that men may also suffer gender-related forms of persecution but miss the opportunity to adequately theorize such harms. The final section then examines reports of sexual violence against Syrian men in detention to illustrate the need to broaden the feminist framework to recognize and consider gender-related persecution of men under the Refugee Convention in the United States and internationally.

Theorizing gender-related persecution

Feminist scholars and human rights activists have long advocated for the recognition of gender-related persecution as a ground for asylum for women. Neither the 1951 Refugee Convention nor the U.S. INA specifically enumerates gender as a ground for persecution in their definitions of refugee. The 1951 Refugee Convention and its 1967 Protocol defines a refugee as an individual with a "well-founded fear of being persecuted for reasons of race, religion, nationality, membership of a particular social group or political opinion."[8] The Refugee Convention does not explicitly include sex or gender as one of the five grounds of persecution for which a person may claim refugee protection.[9]

Section 208 of the INA similarly fails to include sex and gender as protected grounds. It defines a refugee as

> a person who is unwilling or unable to return to her country of origin or last habitual residence because of persecution or a well-founded fear of persecution on account of race, religion, nationality, membership in a particular social group or political opinion.[10]

These categories are called "protected grounds."[11] To establish a claim for refugee status in the United States, an applicant must establish that (1) she has been persecuted in the past or that she has a well-founded fear that she will be persecuted in the future, (2) that the persecution she fears is at the hands of the government or an individual or entity the government either cannot or will not control, and (3) that the persecution is "on account of" one of the five enumerated grounds.[12] The terms "fear of persecution"[13] and "particular social group" are not defined in the statute.[14]

As Karen Musalo argues, "[h]istorically, the violation of women's rights was not seen as an issue of concern within the international human rights framework."[15] Seeking to extend the protection of asylum to female refugees, feminist scholars have criticized refugee law as being rooted in the experiences of men.[16] Under this critique, refugee law reflects a male paradigm that privileges the experiences of male refugees and excludes those of women.[17] Refugee law, feminists have argued, has focused on state and public forms of persecution considered more common to men and not forms of private violence experienced by women.[18] As a result, persecution historically has been understood to constitute beatings, torture, and political imprisonment. In contrast, feminist scholars argue that female refugees often flee persecution within the private sphere, including domestic violence, rape, and female genital cutting, which human rights and asylum jurisprudence historically have conceptualized as private harms that occur within the home.[19] These forms of persecution that women experience have been distinguished from violence committed by the state against persons (men) because of their political views, race, religion, or nationality.[20] Refugee and asylum law thus "failed to recognize the political nature of seeming private acts and harm to women."[21] Feminist advocates and scholars similarly argued that human rights and refugee law historically failed to consider rape and sexual violence against women in conflict as forms of persecution.[22] As a result, feminist scholars have argued that refugee law failed to protect women from many forms of gender-related persecution.

Beginning in 1985, UNHCR began to issue guidance interpreting the Refugee Convention to protect women from gender-based persecution.[23] The Executive Committee of UNHCR issued Conclusion 39 on Refugee Women and International Protection, interpreting Article IA(2) of the Refugee Convention to recognize that "women asylum-seekers who face harsh or inhuman treatment due to their having transgressed the social mores of the society in which they live may be considered as a 'particular social group'" within the meaning of the Convention.[24] In 2002, UNHCR issued more comprehensive gender guidelines, "Guidelines on International Protection No. 1: Gender-Related Persecution within the Context of Article IA(2) of the 1951 Convention and/or Its 1967 Protocol Relating to the Status of Refugees," specifically to ensure proper consideration to refugee claims by women.[25] The UNHCR Guidelines acknowledged that the Refugee Convention covers gender-related claims.[26] Echoing claims by feminist activists and advocates, the Guidelines explain that refugee claims have been interpreted through a framework of male experiences, which has failed to recognize many claims "of women and homosexuals."[27] Although gender is not specifically included in the refugee definition, gender-related claims have proceeded under the protected category of social group.[28] The social group category, like other protected categories, is based on immutable characteristics that an asylum seeker cannot change or that is fundamental to their identity or consciousness.[29] Claims of gender-related persecution are recognized under the Refugee Convention because gender can "influence, or dictate" the type of persecution or harm suffered and "the reasons for this treatment."[30]

The UNHCR Guidelines define gender as referring to "the relationship between women and men based on socially or culturally constructed and defined identities, status, roles and responsibilities that are assigned to one sex or another, while sex is a biological determination."[31] While "gender-related persecution" has no legal meaning *per se*, the Guidelines state that it is "used to encompass the range of different claims in which gender is a relevant consideration in the determination of refugee status."[32] The Guidelines, for example, explain that

> rape and other forms of gender-related violence, such as dowry-related violence, female genital mutilation, domestic violence, and trafficking, are acts which inflict severe pain and suffering—both mental and physical—and which have been used as forms of persecution, whether perpetrated by State or private actors.[33]

Gender-related persecution also includes persecution arising from the enforcement of laws such as those based on traditional or customary practices or which discriminate on the basis of sex or gender. Even where a state prohibits persecutory practices (such as female genital cutting), it may fail to protect women and/or tolerate or condone the violation, which also can constitute persecution.[34] Severe punishment for women who violate a law and thereby transgress social norms could also amount to persecution, even if the law is one of general applicability.[35] Discrimination based on sexual orientation, moreover, may also constitute persecution because "the claimant has refused to adhere to socially or culturally defined roles or expectations of behaviour attributed to his or her sex."[36] The Guidelines recognize the intersectional nature of gender-related persecution, explaining that gender can intersect with other Convention grounds such as race, nationality, religion, and political belief.[37]

While the UNHCR Guidelines state that both men and women may bring gender-related claims,[38] they analyze only examples of persecution of women. Paragraph 3, for example, states that "[g]ender-related claims have typically encompassed, although are by no means limited to, acts of sexual violence, family/domestic violence, coerced family planning, female genital mutilation, punishment for transgression of social mores, and discrimination against homosexuals." While the list is nonexhaustive, most of the examples discussed in the Guidelines are either specific to women (e.g., dowry-related violence and female genital mutilation) or assumed to be specific to women (e.g., domestic violence and sexual violence).

The UNHCR Guidelines similarly recognize that gender intersects with other enumerated grounds of persecution, yet analyze such claims as specific to women.[39] With respect to race, for example, the UNHCR explained that a persecutor may seek to destroy the ethnic identity of a racial group "by killing, maiming or incarcerating the men, while the women may be viewed as propagating the ethnic or racial identity and persecuted in a different way, such as through sexual violence or control of reproduction."[40] Similarly, the Guidelines explain that persecution on the basis of nationality may "take a gender-specific form, most commonly that of sexual violence directed against women and girls."[41] This analysis, as discussed below, relies on essentialized notions of sex and gender that incorrectly assume that women are victims and men are perpetrators.[42]

Seeking to redress the exclusion of women from the reach of refugee and asylum law, feminist advocates in the United States have sought to persuade courts to recognize gender-related violence and persecution of women under asylum law. Nancy Kelly, a clinical instructor in Harvard's Immigration Clinic and attorney for the Women's Refugee Project,[43] participated in the drafting of U.S. guidelines on asylum and gender claims. Kelly explained that the feminist campaign to recognize gender-related persecution was fueled by the international human rights movement, which sought to recognize gender-specific human rights violations directed at women because of their gender, including wartime rape, sexual abuse of women in detention, and the failure of states to protect women from private violence.[44] The systematic and mass rape of women during the Bosnian conflict, she argued, exemplified the need for "gender-specific protocols in asylum law."[45]

In collaboration with the Women's Refugee Project and other nongovernmental organizations, in 1995, the Immigration and Naturalization Service (INS) of the United States issued nonbinding guidance for asylum officers in considering claims for asylum by women, in a memorandum titled "Considerations for Asylum Officers Adjudicating Asylum Claims from Women" (U.S. Guidance).[46] The U.S. Guidance focuses on claims by women, providing examples of gendered harms that could constitute persecution, including "sexual abuse, rape, infanticide, genital mutilation, forced marriage, slavery, domestic violence and forced abortion."[47] It explains that certain forms of mistreatment are "primarily directed" at women and girls, including rape, mass rape (such as in Bosnia), and genital mutilation.[48] Rape of women, it concludes, is a particular kind of harm that "is unique to women or that befalls women more commonly than men" and may result in social stigmatization and social ostracism of female survivors by their communities.[49] These forms of mistreatment may constitute evidence of past persecution on the basis of one or more of the protected grounds. The U.S. Guidance recognizes that women can assert gender-related asylum claims based on other protected grounds, such as their political opinion, religion, or membership in a particular social group.[50] Like the UNHCR Guidelines, however, the U.S. Guidance analyzes gender-related persecution that is specific to women.

Considering sexual violence and gender-based persecution of men and boys

Despite the shortcomings of the UNHCR Guidelines and the U.S. Guidance, both are arguably broad enough to encompass claims of gender-related persecution against men and boys—both in the MENA region and around the globe—who have experienced sexual violence during conflict. Men also experience other forms of gender-related persecution that may trigger asylum protection, including persecution for failing to conform to gender norms and persecution on the basis of their sexual orientation and/or gender identity. Given the space constraints of this project, this chapter focuses on sexual violence against men and boys as a basis for claims of gender-related persecution.

Sexual violence against men is a broad category of physical and mental abuse that includes rape, including anal or oral penetration with the penis or other objects; castration, which can result in sterilization and infertility; genital violence, such as blunt force trauma to the penis or scrotum; and forced circumcision.[51] It also includes forced incest, where men or boys are forced to have sex with family members (brothers, fathers, daughters, sisters, or other relatives) or nonrelatives (male or female detainees or members of their community). Sometimes, the sexual violence involves humiliation or the violation of sexual or social norms, such as forced nudity, where men are forced to strip naked, often in public; forced masturbation; and other forms of sexual humiliation.[52] Much of the abuse occurs in detention, where it often is characterized as torture rather than sexual violence or rape. The effects of the violence are enormous and severe, causing male survivors to feel extreme shame, guilt, hopelessness, anger, and suicidal ideations.[53]

As Article B(9) of the UNHCR Guidelines explain, "international human rights and international criminal law clearly identify certain acts as violations of [Refugee Convention] laws, such as sexual violence, and support their characterization as serious abuses, amounting to persecution."[54] While the earlier guidance from UNHCR and the United States defined sexual violence during war as specific to women, the United Nations and international law recently has recognized that men are also victims of sexual violence during conflict.[55] The gendered nature, meaning, and harm of this form of violence demonstrates how persecution against men and boys may be defined within the meaning of the Refugee Convention and under U.S. asylum law.

MENA-specific gender-related persecution of men and boys in conflict

Reports of rape and sexual violation of male civilians, detainees, and combatants recently have surfaced in dozens of conflicts in nations, including in the MENA region, such as Syria, Iraq, Libya, and Egypt.[56] The Syrian conflict, for example, illustrates use of sexual violence against men and boys in detention that, while recognized by some as torture or human rights violations, also may constitute gender-related violence and possible grounds for claims of gender-related persecution. As in other conflicts in the MENA region and around the world, the use of sexual violence functions as a means of power and domination over particular groups of men. As the UNHCR Guidelines recognize, the violence appears to intersect with other grounds of persecution, such as political opinion, religion, and national origin, as well as membership in particular social groups.[57]

During the Syrian conflict, reports of conflict-related rape and sexual violence against men and boys in Syria have been well publicized.[58] While much of the media publicity has focused on the rape of women and girls, men and boys have also been victims of widespread gender-related persecution by the Syrian forces. A study published by the UNHCR in 2017, "'We Keep it in Our Heart': Sexual Violence Against Men and Boys in the Syria Crisis," concluded that men and boys in Syria are subjected to sexual violence and torture by multiple parties to the conflict, often in detention centers.[59] The study notes that sexual violence was used in Syria prior to the conflict as a form of persecution and political violence.[60] Early in the conflict, reports of rape of men and boys in detention centers surfaced. Reports of sexual violence against men have included

> electric shocks to and beatings of the genitals particularly while in a stress position, rape including gang rape and rape with objects such as sticks, coke bottles, hoses, drills, and metals skewers, forced sex with family members, cigarette burns to the genitals and anus, tying of the genitals, injury to and mutilation of the penis and testes, and castration (resulting in death).[61]

The study states that survivors may face social ostracization, shaming, and persecution, and may be perceived as gay. Quoting an adult male survivor, "He will no longer be seen as a man."[62]

The UNHCR study found that multiple parties to the conflict perpetrated the violence.[63] Human Rights Watch (HRW), however, reported in 2012 that Syrian government forces used sexual violence to torture both men and women in detention.[64] While HRW did not have evidence that high-level Syrian officials commanded troops to commit the violence, it received information that government officials did not take action to investigate or punish offenders. Under the Refugee Convention and the Convention against Torture, a government's unwillingness or inability to control non-state actors or acquiesce in torture obligates signatories to these Conventions to not return an individual back to their home country.[65] The abuse reportedly occurred in military intelligence branches in Damascus, Jisr al-Shughur, Idlib, and Homs, as well as political security and air force intelligence branches and the Idlib Central Prison.

Sexual violence against Syrian men and boys, unfortunately, is not an aberration. For example, U.S. military troops in Iraq sexually abused Iraqi detainees at the Abu Ghraib Prison, including inter alia keeping Muslim male detainees naked for several days, forcing them to masturbate themselves in front of others, arranging and photographing their naked bodies in sexually explicit positions, threatening them with rape, and sodomizing a detainee with a chemical light.[66] The recent conflict in Libya has been marked by sexual violence against men and boys by the state and/or armed groups. UNHCR reported in 2016 that it had received credible reports that armed groups were committing sexual violence against women, girls, and boys with impunity.[67] Palestinian men and boys have reported being subjected to sexual violence by Israeli police and security authorities while in Israeli military custody; the allegations included threats of sexual assault, genital violence, forced nudity, and sexual humiliation.[68] UNICEF reported in 2013 that the Israeli military detention system engaged in widespread, systematic, and institutionalized ill-treatment of Palestinian children in custody, the great majority of whom are boys. Allegations of abuse included threats of sexual assault against the detainees or their families.[69]

These reports of sexual violence illustrate the importance of recognizing and categorizing such allegations as complaints of conflict-related gender violence. Historically, the international community has ignored sexual abuse of men, or when it has recognized the abuse, categorized it as "abuse" or "torture," which obscures the sexual and gender meaning and consequences of the act.[70] Reframing such abuse as conflict-related sexual and gender-related violence is critical to understand its gendered nature and meaning. Because sexual violence against men is underreported, there is an urgent need for further investigation to assess the nature and extent of these allegations.[71] As a practical matter, human rights and health professionals need training to help recognize and document reports of male sexual violence, particularly because males are often reluctant to report the abuse.[72]

On a theoretical level, examining the violence experienced by men and boys in the MENA region through the lens of conflict-related gender violence helps reveal the gendered use of power, particularly the intersection of gender with race, nationality, religion, and other forms of collective identity. Sexual violence is a gendered form of violence directed at men who are defined not only by their sex or gender but also by their age, national and ethnic identity, religion, and perhaps their political opinion. Focusing on the gendered nature of the alleged persecution explains the gendered nature of the harm experienced by individual males, as well as the larger collective to which they belong. The sexualized nature of such violence, for example, may violate social taboos and notions of honor among the male victims, which may result in humiliation and social stigma of the individual men as well as the larger ethnic, national, racial, or other collective group that they embody.[73] That, in fact, may be the intended consequence.

These reports of sexual violence refute the assumption that conflict-related sexual violence is specific to women. Like sexual violence against women, sexual violence against men in conflict results in serious physical and emotional harm, including loss of sexual function, infertility, anxiety, and depression.[74] Male victims suffer great social stigma and shame because of the gendered nature and meaning of the abuse.[75] Conflict-related sexual violence against men symbolically masculinizes the perpetrator as dominant and aggressive, while symbolically constructing the victim as weak and powerless, challenging his gender identity as a man.[76] The social stigma and humiliation that results means that it is vastly underreported, as male victims are often unable or unwilling to seek protection and assistance.[77] Many countries do not have criminal statutes that prohibit rape of men, and in seventy countries, homosexuality is a crime, which deters men and boys from reporting these crimes for fear they will be presumed to be homosexual and in violation of the law.[78] Male survivors who report may face social ostracism. The UNHCR report on Syria, for example, explains that "[m]ale survivors whose sexual victimisation [sic] becomes known to the community experience debilitating social stigma and marginalization," including "ostracisation [sic], shaming, persecution, and even death threats, and [they] may be perceived as gay."[79]

Sexual violence against men also illustrates how gender-related violence intersects with ethnicity, race, national identities, and other collective identities to harm particular men and particular groups and communities.[80] Like the rape of women, the sexual violation of men represents the humiliation and subordination of the ethnic or racial group to which he belongs.[81] It thus functions as a gendered means to attack both the individual man and the larger ethnic, racial, religious, or political collective to which he belongs. As Dubraka Žarkov explained, the castration of a single man of "an ethnically defined enemy is symbolic appropriation of the masculinity of the entire group."[82] The reports of sexual abuse and torture of boys and men in detention, for example, symbolize the subordination of an entire group of people to which they belong. The rape of both men and women during conflict by the government or other groups serves to terrorize and displace the population. The sexual violation of male detainees not only results in physical and mental harm to the individual male victim but also serves to punish and deter political expression and protest.

Because men and boys are also subjected to gender-related persecution, such as rape and sexual violence, feminist and human rights theorists need to begin to recognize that such persecution may give rise to a claim for protection under the Refugee Convention and in U.S. asylum jurisprudence. Any claims for asylum, of course, would have to satisfy the necessary elements in the Refugee Convention or U.S. asylum law to qualify for refugee protection. Recognizing the need to broaden feminist theories of gender-based persecution, however, is a critical first step.

Incorporating men and boys as victims of gender-related violence or persecution does not undermine the gendered nature of persecution against women. Rather, it helps deepen the understanding of the ways in which gender functions to construct and enforce dominance by particular social groups and to subordinate both women and many men. Theorizing male experiences as gender-related persecution, therefore, helps better recognize and understand the relationship between gender and power. Sexual violence against men and women are not separate or distinct but interrelated. Recognizing the men may suffer gender-related persecution also helps reveal the multiple ways in which gender intersects with other bases of persecution such as race, national identity, and other forms of collective identity. Shifting from a sex-specific theory of gender persecution that tends to essentialize sex and gender, therefore, encourages a more complete understanding of gender as a social process of domination, a necessary step in dismantling larger systems of gender oppression that harm both women and many men.

Conclusion

Reports from the Syrian conflict corroborate the growing recognition that conflict-related sexual violence is not unique to women. International law has begun to recognize that men and boys are also victims and that such violence may constitute violations of international law. Feminists have led the struggle to broaden the reach of refugee and asylum law to recognize gender-related persecution of women as a ground for protection—a struggle that continues. Broadening the theoretical framework to recognize gender-related persecution of men and boys deepens our understanding of gendered power and harm, and offers a means to protect all survivors and victims, regardless of sex, gender, sexual orientation, and/or gender identity. It also helps focus attention on the intersection of gender with other forms of persecution based on nationality, religion, political opinion, and other forms of collective identity.

Notes

1 See, for example, Amanda Erickson, "I Screamed But No None Came,' the Horrifying Sexual Violence Facing Syria's Women and Girls," *The Washington Post*, March 16, 2018, www.washingtonpost.com/news/worldviews/wp/2018/03/16/i-screamed-but-no-one-came-the-horrifying-sexual-violence-facing-syrias-girls/?utm_term=.985834cdb5a0; Human Rights Watch, "Syria: Sexual Assault in Detention," June 15, 2012, www.hrw.org/news/2012/06/15/syria-sexual-assault-detention.

2 United Nations High Commissioner for Refugees Evaluation and Policy Unit, "Comparative Analysis of Gender Related Persecution in National Asylum Legislation and Practice in Europe," May 2004, www.unhcr.org/40c071354.pdf.

3 The author utilizes the term refugee law to connote defining an individual who has obtained refugee status; whereas asylum law refers to an individual seeking to obtain refugee status and the legal standards associated with obtaining the status.

4 See, for example, Valorie K. Vojdik, "Sexual Violence against Men and Boys in Conflict," *Nevada Law Journal* 14 (2014): 923–952; Lara Stemple, "Male Rape and Human Rights," *Hasting Law Journal* 60 (2009): 605–647, 605, 612; Miranda Alison, "Wartime Sexual Violence: Women's Human Rights and Questions of Masculinity," *Review of International Studies* 33, no. 1 (2007): 75–90; C. Charli Carpenter, "Recognizing Gender-Based Violence against Civilian Men and Boys in Conflict Situations," *Security Dialogue* 37, no. 1 (2006): 83–103.

5 *Ibid.*

6 Stemple, "Male Rape and Human Rights"; Sandesh Sivakumaran, "Sexual Violence against Men in Armed Conflict," *European Journal of International Law* 18 (2007): 253–276, 264–265.

7 United Nations S.C. Res. 2106, U.N. Doc. S/RES/2106 (June 24, 2013).

8 United Nations Convention relating to the Status of Refugees, opened for signature July 28, 1951, Art. 1(A)(2), 19 U.S.T. 6259, 189 U.N.T.S. 137; United Nations Protocol relating to the Status of Refugees, opened for signature January 31, 1967, 19 U.S.T. 6223606 U.N.T.S. 267 ("U.N. Refugee Convention" or "Refugee Convention").

9 *Ibid.*

10 8 U.S.C. §§ 1101(a)(42); 1231(b)(3).

11 *Matter of Acosta*, 19 I. & N. Dec. 211 (BIA)(1985).

12 *Ibid.*

13 *Ibid.*, 233.

14 *Ibid.*, 232–233.

15 Karen Musalo, "Personal Violence, Public Matter: Evolving Standards in Gender-Based Asylum Law," *Harvard International Review* 36, no. 2 (2014): 45–48, 46.
16 Karla McKanders, "Morocco at the Crossroads: The Intersection of Race, Gender and Refugee Status," in *Women and Social Change in North America: What Counts As Revolutionary?* edited by Doris H. Gray and Nadia Sonneveld (New York: Cambridge University Press, 2018), 189–214, 196.
17 Musalo, "Personal Violence, Public Matter;" Nancy Kelly, "Gender-Related Persecution: Assessing the Asylum Claims of Women," *Cornell International Journal of Law* 26 (1993): 625–674, 630–633, http://lawdigitalcommons.bc.edu/cgi/viewcontent.cgi?article=1284&context=iclr.
18 See, for example, Deborah Anker, "Refugee Status and Violence against Women in the 'Domestic' Sphere: The Non-State Actor Question," *Georgetown Immigration Law Journal* 15 (2001): 391–402, 391–392.
19 See, for example, Karen Musalo and Stephen Knight, "Steps Forward and Steps Back: Uneven Progress in the Law of Social Group and Gender-Based Claims in the United States," *International Journal of Refugee Law* 13 (2001): 51–70, 51–52; Heaven Crawley, "Engendering the State In Refugee Women's Claims for Asylum," in *States of Conflict: Gender, Violence, and Resistance*, 87–104, 96–100.
20 *Ibid.*
21 Kelly, "Gender-Related Persecution," 628.
22 See, for example, Crawley, "Engendering the State," 92–94; Rhonda Copelon, "Surfacing Gender: Reconceptualizing Crimes against Women in Times of War," in *Violence: A Reader*, edited by Caroline Bestemen (New York: NYU, 2002), 193–207; Rhonda Copelon, "Gendered War Crimes: Reconceptualizing Rape in Time of War," in *Women's Rights, Human Rights: International Feminist Perspectives*, edited by Julia Peters and Andrea Wolper (New York: Routledge, 1995), 197–214; Charlotte Bunch, "Women's Rights as Human Rights: Toward a Re-vision of Human Rights," *Human Rights Quarterly* 12 (1990): 486–498; 496–498 (explaining feminist critique and approaches to recognizing women in human rights and refugee law).
23 See Musalo, "Personal Violence, Public Matter," 49.
24 EXCOM, Conclusion on Refugee Women and International Protection, EXCOM Conclusion No. 39 (XXXVI), October 18, 1985.
25 UNHCR, *Guidelines on International Protection No. 1: Gender-related Persecution within the Context of Article 1A(2) of the 1951 Convention and/or its 1967 Prototcol Relating to the Status of Refugees*, UN Doc. HCR/GIP/02/01 (May 7, 2002).
26 *Ibid.*, para. 6.
27 *Ibid.*
28 McKanders, Morocco at Crossroads, 169.
29 *Matter of R-A-*, 22 I. & N. Dec. 906, 912 (BIA 1999), vacated, 22 I. & N. Dec. 906 (A.G. 2001).
30 UNHCR, *Guidelines*, 3.
31 *Ibid.*, para. 3
32 *Ibid.*, para. 1.
33 *Ibid.*, para. 9.
34 *Ibid.*, para. 11.
35 *Ibid.*, para. 12.
36 *Ibid.*, para. 16.
37 *Ibid.*
38 *Ibid.*, para. 3.
39 *Ibid.*
40 *Ibid.*, 24.
41 *Ibid.*, 27.
42 Vojdik, "Sexual Violence against Men and Boys in Conflict," 923; Rosemary Grey and Laura J. Shepherd, "'Stop Rape Now?': Masculinity, Responsibility, and Conflict-Related Sexual Violence," *Men & Masculinities* 16, no. 1 (2013): 115–135, 120.

43 Kelly, "Gender-Related Persecution," 630–633.
44 *Ibid.*
45 *Ibid.*
46 U.S. Immigration and Naturalization Service, *Considerations for Asylum Officers Adjudicating Asylum Claims from Women* (1995), www.state.gov/s/l/65633.htm. The Office of the Immigration and Naturalization Service no longer exists; asylum officers are now trained through the Department of Homeland Security.
47 *Ibid.*
48 *Ibid.*
49 *Ibid.*
50 *Ibid.*
51 Monica Adhiambo Onyango and Karen Hampanda, "Social Constructions of Masculinity and Male Survivors of Wartime Sexual Violence: An Analytical Review," *International Journal of Sexual Health* 23 (2011): 239–240, 237.
52 *Ibid.*
53 Pauline Oosterhoff et al., "Sexual Torture of Men in Croatia and Other Conflict Situations: An Open Secret," *Reproductive Health Matters* 12, no. 23 (2004): 68–77, 74; R. Charli Carpenter, "Recognizing Gender-Based Violence against Civilian Men and Boys in Conflict Situations," 95.
54 UNHCR, Guidelines, art. B(9).
55 U.N., Report of the Secretary-General Pursuant to Security Council Resolution 1820 (2008), U.N. Doc. S/2009/362 (August 20, 2009), para. 6.
56 UNHCR, "'We Keep it in Our Heart' – Sexual Violence Against Men and Boys in the Syria Crisis," October 2017, https://data2.unhcr.org/en/documents/download/60864; U.N. Human Rights Council, "Investigation by the Office of the United Nations High Commissioner for Human Rights on Libya: Detailed Findings," A/HRC/31/CRP3 (February 23, 2016); Weisburt, "Sexual Torture of Palestinian Men by Israeli Authorities," *Reproductive Health Matters* 23 (2015): 71–84, www.tandfonline.com/doi/full/10.1016/j.rhm.2015.11.019; Sivakumaran, "Sexual Violence against Men in Armed Conflict."
57 UNHCR, "Gender Guidelines."
58 UNHCR, "We Keep It in Our Heart."
59 *Ibid.*
60 *Ibid.*, 23.
61 *Ibid.*, 25.
62 *Ibid.*, 37.
63 *Ibid.*, 5.
64 Human Rights Watch, "Syria: Sexual Assault in Detention."
65 UNHCR, "Summary Conclusion- Gender Related Persecution," Global Consultants on International Protection San Remo Expert Roundtable September 6–8, 2001, no. 6.
66 Maj. Gen. Antonio M. Taguba, U.S. Dep't of Defense, Article 15–16 Investigation of the 800th Military Police Brigade (2004): 15–17, www.npr.org/iraq/2004/prison_abuse_report.pdf.
67 UNHCR, Investigation by the Office of UNHCR on Libya, para. 182.
68 Weisburt, "Sexual Torture of Palestinian Men"; UNICEF, Children in Israeli Military Detention.
69 UNICEF, Children in Israeli Military Detention, 1, 11.
70 Sandesh Sivakumaran, "Sexual Violence against Men"; Weishut, "Sexual Torture of Palestinian Men," 78–79.
71 See Weishut, Sexual Torture of Palestinian Men, 84.
72 *Ibid.*
73 *Ibid.*, 78–79.
74 Oosterhoff et al., "Sexual Torture of Men," 74.

75 Onyango and Hampanda, "Social Constructions of Masculinity and Male Survivors of Wartime Sexual Violence," 241

("[M]en who become helpless and are overpowered by other males may be judged to have failed in their masculine duty. Therefore, compared with female survivors, males become more stigmatized, ashamed with their situation, and less likely to report the incident or seek help.")

76 See Alison, "Wartime Sexual Violence," 81; Carpenter, "Recognizing Gender-Based Violence against Civilian Men and Boys in Conflict," 94; Sivakamaran, "Sexual Violence against Men in Armed Conflict," 265–272.

77 UNHCR, "Summary Conclusions Gender Persecution."

78 See, for example, Gillian Mezey and Michael King, "The Effects of Sexual Assault on Men: A Survey of Twenty-Two Victims," in *Confronting Rape and Sexual Assault*, edited by Mary E. Odem and Jody Clay-Warner (Lanham, MD: Rowman and Littlefield, 1998) 83, 88; Emily Dugan, "More Than 70 Countries Make Being Gay a Crime," Independent, August 2010, www.independent.co.uk/news/world/politics/more-than-70-countries-make-being-gay-a-crime-2040850.html.

79 UNHCR, "We Keep it in Our Heart," 37.

80 Vojdik, "Sexual Violence Against Men and Boys," 946; Carpenter, "Recognizing Gender-Based Violence against Civilian Men and Boys in Conflict," 86–87; Dubravka Žarkov, "The Body of the Other Man: Sexual Violence and the Construction of Masculinity, Sexuality and Ethnicity in Croatian Media," in *Victims, Perpetrators or Actors?: Gender, Armed Conflict and Political Violence*, edited by Caroline O. N. Moser and Fiona C. Clark (London and New York: Zed Books, 2001), 69, 78. See also, Kimberlé W. Crenshaw, "Mapping the Margins: Intersectionality, Identity Politics, and Violence against Women of Color," *Stanford Law Review* 43 (1991): 1241; Rashida Manjoo, "Report of the Special Rapporteur on Violence against Women, Its Causes and Consequences," *United Nations General Assembly Human Rights Council*, May 2, 2011, www2.ohchr.org/english/bodies/hrcouncil/docs/17session/A-HRC-17-26.pdf (recognizing the applicability of intersectionality theory and intersectional discrimination into UN resolutions and "acknowledged that discrimination is understood as having multiple forms that combine to heighten the vulnerability of some women and girls to violence").

81 *Ibid.*

82 Žarkov, "The Body of the Other Man," 78.

Bibliography

Alison, Miranda. "Wartime Sexual Violence: Women's Human Rights and Questions of Masculinity." *Review of International Studies* 33, no. 1 (2007): 75–90.

Anker, Deborah. "Refugee Status and Violence Against Women in the 'Domestic' Sphere: The Non-State Actor Question." *Georgetown Immigration Law Journal* 15 (2001): 391–402.

B'Tselem. Abuse and Torture in Interrogations of Dozens of Palestinian Minors in the Israel Police Etzion Facility, August 21, 2013, updated December 28, 2014. www.btselem.org/download/201308_etzion_eng.pdf.

Bunch, Charlotte. "Women's Rights as Human Rights: Toward a Re-Vision of Human Rights." *Human Rights Quarterly* 12, no. 4 (1990): 486-98.

Carpenter, C. Charli. "Recognizing Gender-Based Violence Against Civilian Men and Boys in Conflict Situations." *Security Dialogue* 37, no. 1 (2006): 83–103.

Copelon, Rhonda. "Gendered War Crimes: Reconceptualizing Rape in Time of War." In *Women's Rights, Human Rights: International Feminist Perspectives*, edited by Julia Peters and Andrea Wolper, 197–214. New York: Routledge, 1995.

———. "Surfacing Gender: Reconceptualizing Crimes against Women in Times of War." In *Violence: A Reader*, edited by Caroline Bestemen, 193–207. New York: NYU, 2002.

Crawley, Heaven. "Engendering the State in Refugee Women's Claims for Asylum." In *States of Conflict: Gender, Violence, and Resistance*, edited by Ruth Jacobson and Jennifer Marchbank, 87–104, London: ZedBooks, 2000.

Crenshaw, Kimberlé W. "Mapping the Margins: Intersectionality, Identity Politics, and Violence against Women of Color." *Stanford Law Review* 43, no. 6 (1991): 1241–1299.

Dugan, Emily. "More Than 70 Countries Make Being Gay a Crime." *Independent*, August 2010. www.independent.co.uk/news/world/politics/more-than-70-countries-make-being-gay-a-crime-2040850.html.

Erickson, Amanda. "'I Screamed, but No One Came': The Horrifying Sexual Violence Facing Syria's Women and Girls." *The Washington Post*, 2018.

EXCOM. "Conclusion on Refugee Women and International Protection." Vol. 39 EXCOM Conclusion (XXXVI), October 18, 1985.

Grey, Rosemary, and Shepherd, Laura J. "'Stop Rape Now?': Masculinity, Responsibility, and Conflict-Related Sexual Violence." *Men & Masculinities* 16, no. 1 (2013): 115–135.

Human Rights Watch. "Syria: Sexual Assault in Detention," June 15, 2012. www.hrw.org/news/2012/06/15/syria-sexual-assault-detention.

Kelly, Nancy. "Gender-Related Persecution: Assessing the Asylum Claims of Women." *Cornell International Journal of Law* 26: (1993) 625–674. http://lawdigitalcommons.bc.edu/cgi/viewcontent.cgi?article=1284&context=iclr.

Manjoo, Rashida. "Report of the Special Rapporteur on Violence against Women, Its Causes and Consequences." *United Nations General Assembly Human Rights Council*, May 2, 2011. www2.ohchr.org/english/bodies/hrcouncil/docs/17session/A-HRC-17-26.pdf.

Matter of Acosta, 19 I. & N. Dec. 211 (BIA) (1985).

Matter of R-A-, 22 I. & N. Dec. 906 (BIA 1999), vacated, 22 I. & N. Dec. 906 (A.G. 2001).

McKanders, Karla. "Morocco at the Crossroads: The Intersection of Race, Gender and Refugee Status." In *Women and Social Change in North Africa: What Counts as Revolutionary?* edited by Doris H. Gray and Nadia Sonneveld, 189–214, 196. New York: Cambridge University Press, 2018.

Mezey, Gillian, and King, Michael. "The Effects of Sexual Assault on Men: A Survey of Twenty-Two Victims." In *Confronting Rape and Sexual Assault*, edited by Mary E. Odem and Jody Clay-Warner. Lanham, MD: Rowman and Littlefield, 1998.

Musalo, Karen. "Personal Violence, Public Matter: Evolving Standards in Gender-Based Asylum Law." *Harvard International Review* 36, no. 2 (2014): 45.

Musalo, Karen, and Stephen Knight. "Steps Forward and Steps Back: Uneven Progress in the Law of Social Group and Gender-Based Claims in the United States." *International Journal of Refugee Law* 13 (2001): 51–70.

Onyango, Monica Adhiambo, and Karen Hampanda. "Social Constructions of Masculinity and Male Survivors of Wartime Sexual Violence: An Analytical Review." *International Journal of Sexual Health* 23 (2011): 239–240.

Oosterhoff, Pauline, Zwanikken, Prisca, and Ketting, Evert. "Sexual Torture of Men in Croatia and Other Conflict Situations: An Open Secret." *Reproductive Health Matters* 12, no. 23 (2004): 68–77.

Sivakumaran, Sandesh. "Sexual Violence against Men in Armed Conflict." *European Journal of International Law* 18 (2007): 253–276.

Stemple, Lara. "Male Rape and Human Rights." *Hastings Law Journal* 60 (2009): 605–647.

Maj. Gen. Taguba, Antonio M. U.S. Dep't of Defense, Article 15–16 Investigation of the 800th Military Police Brigade, 2004. www.npr.org/iraq/2004/prison_abuse_report.pdf.

U.N. Report of the Secretary-General Pursuant to Security Council Resolution 1820. U.N. Doc. S/2009/362, August 20, 2009.

———. Human Rights Council. "Investigation by the Office of the United Nations High Commissioner for Human Rights on Libya: Detailed Findings." UN Doc. A/HRC/31/CRP3, February 23, 2016.

UNHCR. Evaluation and Policy Unit. "Comparative Analysis of Gender Related Persecution in National Asylum Legislation and Practice in Europe," May 2004. www.unhcr.org/40c071354.pdf.

———. "Guidelines on International Protection No. 1: Gender-Related Persecution Within the Context of Article IA(2) of the 1951 Convention and/or Its 1967 Protocol Relating to the Status of Refugees." UN Doc. HCR/GIP/02/01, May 7, 2002.

———. "Summary Conclusion – Gender Related Persecution." Global Consultants on International Protection San Remo Expert Roundtable. No. 6, September 2001.

———. "'We Keep it in Our Heart' – Sexual Violence against Men and Boys in the Syria Crisis," October 2017. https://data2.unhcr.org/en/documents/download/60864.

UNICEF. "Children in Israeli Military Detention, Observations and Recommendations," February 2013. www.unicef.org/oPt/UNICEF_oPt_Children_in_Israeli_Military_Detention_Observations_and_Recommendations_-_6_March_2013.pdf.

———. "Children in Israeli Military Detention: Observations and Recommendations," Bulletin, No. 2, February 2015. www.unicef.org/oPt/Children_in_Israeli_Military_Detention_-_Observations_and_Recommendations_-_Bulletin_No._2_-_February_2015.pdf.

United States Department of Justice. "Considerations for Asylum Officers Adjudicating Asylum Claims from Women," 1995. www.state.gov/s/l/65633.htm.

Vojdik, Valorie K. "Sexual Violence against Men and Boys in Conflict." *Nevada Law Journal* 14 (2014): 923–952.

Weishut, Daniel J. N. "Sexual torture of Palestinian Men by Israeli Authorities." *Reproductive Health Matters* 23 (2015): 71–84. www.tandfonline.com/doi/full/10.1016/j.rhm.2015.11.019.

Žarkov, Dubravka. "The Body of the Other Man: Sexual Violence and the Construction of Masculinity, Sexuality and Ethnicity in Croatian Media." In *Victims, Perpetrators or Actors?: in Gender, Armed Conflict and Political Violence*, edited by Caroline O. N. Moser and Fiona C. Clark. London and New York: Zed Books, 2001: 69–82.

6 Gender, Islamophobia, and refugee exceptionalism

Karla M. McKanders

Introduction

Muslim men are perceived as opponents to Western democracy and social progress, and have become symbolic of a rigid gender oppressing regime.[1] This chapter critically analyzes how gender interfaces with xenophobic and Islamophobic bias to exclude young males from Muslim-majority countries from third country refugee resettlement programs under the 1951 Refugee Convention (Convention). The power of the Refugee Convention has been tested over the past few years as signatories have invoked their power as sovereigns to implement the Convention consistent with their countries' national security interests. Over the years, sovereignty and security arguments have been increasingly evoked to curtail legitimate refugee resettlement. This trend has caused the application of the Refugee Convention to become an immigration control mechanism that undermines the ability to obtain the durable solution of third country resettlement for refugees.[2]

Throughout history, and specifically during times of war and conflict, there is a tension between the admission of refugees and the fear that individuals from oppositional countries will exploit refugee protections to harm the host country. The contemporary example of this issue is the exclusion of young males from Muslim-majority countries from Convention protection—that is, third country resettlement.[3] Instead of warranting Convention protection, this demographic is stereotyped as threatening terrorists from whom countries *need* protection. Furthermore, single males from Muslim-majority countries are further stigmatized as individuals who are a threat to a country's national security without evaluating the person's individual circumstances to assess his qualifications as either a Convention refugee and/or a danger to the country. This results in the fungibility of individuals from Muslim-majority countries which, as scholar Leti Volpp states, "make[s] it impossible to screen individually loyal citizens from enemy aliens."[4]

This chapter explores how the narratives around Islamophobia, masculinity, and gender norms affect if a person is classified as vulnerable and in need of third country refugee resettlement. Most scholarship has focused on refugee women's and Muslim women's experiences of subordination and discrimination—this chapter fills this gap. Increasingly, young single men from Muslim-majority countries are portrayed as perpetrators of violence who are not worthy of protection, whereas women, children, and sexual minorities, including gay males, are portrayed as victims in need of protection. In this chapter, I argue that the exclusion of males from Muslim-majority countries is constructed through narratives which facilitate the development of policies and the legally constructed priority categories of vulnerability that conform to gendered norms, which results in the exclusion of this population from Convention protections.

This chapter contains three sections. Section "Refugee convention as migration control" defines the contemporary issues and the narratives that have been disseminated in which single males from Muslim-majority countries have been stereotyped and preemptively excluded from third country resettlement. Section "Constructing refugee vulnerability" provides the historical and legal backdrop necessary to understand that state's interests are intertwined in the "refugee" definition and how vulnerability is legally conceptualized. To accomplish this goal, this section describes the history of religious sanctuary in contrast to the pre-Nansen refugee construct and state-centric conceptions of refugees (from which the present-day concepts of refugee vulnerability are derived). To place the comparison in context, this section examines how the United Nations High Commissioner for Refugees (UNHCR), Germany, Canada, and the United States have constructed priority categories based on vulnerability for third country resettlement. These countries are relevant because they have played prominent roles in contemporary international debates over the resettlement of young males from Muslim-majority countries.

Section "Gender, Islamophobia, and refugee vulnerability" analyzes how single male refugees from Muslim-majority countries have been denied refugee resettlement based on their inability to establish eligibility for the priority categories, which are based on vulnerability, because they are portrayed as (1) terrorist threats to the state and (2) threats to Muslim women, who resettling states need to protect. This section demonstrates how gender interfaces with xenophobic and Islamophobic bias in the application of the Convention and how narratives develop which result in the discriminatory application of the Convention.[5] The conclusion offers an analysis of how the exclusion of young single males from Muslim-majority countries highlights how Islamophobic and gender narratives are deeply intertwined in informing policy decisions on which populations are prioritized in obtaining Convention protection.

Refugee convention as migration control

There is often a dichotomy between the deserving and undeserving immigrants that influences the depiction of refugees and affects the application of priority categories, which are based on vulnerability assessments. This dichotomy highlights the tension of a Kantian perspective of refugee rights as universal rights and obligations[6] in contrast to a utilitarian, pragmatic model which considers both the rights of refugees and the rights of states.[7] Within the vulnerability construct, assumptions about who is perceived as vulnerable often determines the choice of charity afforded to individuals within a country's legal and immigration systems.[8] The deserving immigrant is a victim of his circumstances, whereas the undeserving immigrant is one who is perceived as actively transgressing societal norms and is not worthy of Convention protection.[9] Media, presidents, legislatures, and politicians create the narratives that impact policies towards different immigrant populations, thus furthering the dichotomy of deserving and undeserving immigrants.[10] The narratives undermine the Convention's goal of ensuring recognition of the human right to seek refuge when there is a fundamental break in the relationship between the state and the individual that could result in persecution.[11]

In 2015, the world experienced an unprecedented increase in refugee flows from the Middle East and North African regions. The increase was a result of the height of the Civil War in Syria and the proliferation of the Islamic State of Iraq and the Levant ("ISIL" or, in Arabic, "Daesh"). The Syrian conflict caused the displacement of more than 11 million refugees.[12] Prior to the conflict, Syria had an open borders policy that permitted Iraqi refugees to resettle there.[13] In 2010, UNHCR reported that, of the 1.3 million refugees in Syria, 1 million were from Iraq.[14]

In September 2, 2015, the image of Alan Kurdi, a three-year-old Syrian boy of Kurdish descent, made global headlines after he drowned in the Mediterranean Sea. Canada had allegedly denied the Kurdi family's asylum application, which forced them to flee by sea.[15] Contrastingly, in 2015, Germany responded to the refugee crisis by opening its borders to asylum seekers. In 2015, German Chancellor Angela Merkel became an advocate for refugees, urging other European Union members to similarly welcome asylum seekers.[16]

In the wake of Germany's acceptance of asylum seekers and the graphic images of fleeing refugees, on Friday, November 13, 2015, a series of terrorist attacks occurred in Paris, France, and the city's northern suburb, Saint-Denis. Next to the body of one of the assailants was a Syrian passport.[17] These attacks sparked a worldwide debate regarding the security risks around acceptance of asylum seekers and the resettlement of refugees.

Shortly after the Paris attacks, on November 23, 2015, the Canadian government stated that it would "accept only whole families, lone women or children in its mass resettlement of Syrian refugees while unaccompanied men—considered a security risk—will be turned away."[18] However, on November 24, 2015, Prime Minister Justin Trudeau and the Canadian government stated that single gay men—a group often targeted by the Islamic state militant group ISIS—would still be welcomed.[19]

In 2015, President Obama experienced extreme pushback to his declaration to resettle 10,000 Syrian refugees for the fiscal year 2016.[20] In December 2015, Texas sued the Obama administration over the resettlement of refugees. In an attempt to terminate refugee resettlement to the state, Texas filed the lawsuit under the United States Refugee Act of 1980.[21] The complaint alleged that the United States government failed to consult Texas in placing resettled refugees in the state.[22] Simultaneously, thirty U.S. governors issued statements in opposition to refugee resettlement.[23]

In 2016, then-presidential candidate Donald Trump called for a total and complete shutdown of Muslims entering the United States until "our country's representatives can figure out what is going on."[24] As the presidential candidate, Donald Trump repeated claims that the Syrian refugees the United States was accepting were "strong young men" who would carry out terrorist attacks.[25] He stated,

- ... You look at the migration, it's young, strong men. We cannot take a chance that the people coming over here are going to be ISIS-affiliated.[26]
- ... I'm saying, Where are the women? Where are the children? We're taking in people we have no idea who they are ....[27]
- This could be the great Trojan horse of all time ... I said to myself, "Wow. They're all men." You look at it. There are so few women and there are so few children. And not only are they men, they're young men. And they're strong as can be—they're tough-looking cookies. I say, "What's going on here?"[28]

In furtherance of his campaign promise, at the beginning of 2017, President Trump issued multiple executive orders halting the U.S. Refugee Resettlement Program, citing national security reasons.[29]

In September 2017, the President issued a proclamation titled "Enhancing Vetting Capabilities and Processes for Detecting Attempted Entry into the United States by Terrorists or Other Public-Safety Threats" (Proclamation).[30] Section 2 of the Proclamation suspended the entry of certain nationals from Chad, Iran, Libya, North Korea, Syria, Venezuela, Yemen, and Somalia based on the perceived threat posed by each country and the measures used to prevent the spread of terrorism from these countries.[31] On June 26, 2018, the U.S. Supreme Court upheld the travel ban finding Trump's campaign and contemporaneous statements vowing to ban Muslims irrelevant to his purported national security justifications.[32] The Court stated that a sovereign state's ability to control immigration and protect its country warranted a deferential review.[33]

In the summer of 2018, the image of Merkel as creating the ideal safe haven for refugees also began to crumble as allegations surfaced of widespread fraud in Germany's system for processing asylum seekers.[34] Specifically, a German asylum officer faced allegations that she granted asylum to some 1,200 migrants in exchange for bribes, between 2013 and 2016.[35] These allegations tainted Germany's reputation as the prototype for resettling refugees and processing asylum seekers.

The narratives promulgated by legislatures, media, prime ministers, and presidents impact the application of the Convention. Refugee populations who fit within the stereotypes of these narratives are perceived as security threats undeserving of resettlement. The manner in which resettlement programs are implemented fails to fully assess whether an individual should be classified as vulnerable and in need of third country resettlement based on the fungibility of all members of a particular group—single males from Muslim-majority countries.[36] Through these narratives, individual nations set policies and states make decisions on how to apply the Refugee Convention.

There is extensive scholarly literature depicting "refugees and asylum seekers as innocent victims and, simultaneously, as invaders and threat [sic] to the physical, economic, and cultural well-being of the respective host country."[37] This dichotomy has been exacerbated in recent narratives, depicting all single males from Muslim-majority countries as a threat to the countries in which they are placed.[38] The narratives are so pervasive that they impede the ability to engage in a comprehensive assessment about whether an individual is in need of resettlement (i.e., vulnerable) or is an actual security risk to the host country.

Constructing refugee vulnerability

This section provides the historical and legal backdrop for understanding the construction of "vulnerability" in the Refugee Convention and its applications to third country resettlement. To accomplish this goal, this section juxtaposes religious sanctuary with the Nansen refugee and contemporary applications of vulnerability and third country resettlement. To place the comparison in context, this section examines how UNHCR, Germany, Canada, and the United States construct priorities based on vulnerability for third country resettlement. While determinations of vulnerability are typically presented as legally objective and neutral decisions, they are in fact deeply subjective and political.[39]

The foundations of state-centric refugee regimes

The development of the contemporary international refugee protection regime sheds light on how vulnerability in relation to refugees is conceptualized today and why males from Muslim-majority countries are excluded from protection. Before 1920, leading up to World War I, refugee protection was not strictly delineated. Protection operated in a manner that recognized humanitarian and human rights norms of refugees to move freely between countries.[40] While most scholars mark the beginning of refugee protection at the start of the modern nation-state,[41] religious norms have also provided underlying principles for extending protection to exiles.[42]

In Judeo-Christian religious traditions, the concept of sanctuary was provided by

> churches, which offered places of refuge for those accused of crimes and were susceptible to revengeful attacks by their victims. The occurrence of retaliatory attacks on accused persons coincided with the lack of legal protection afforded to them during those historical periods. "The religious origins of sanctuary imply a certain level of ethics and compassion towards individuals who are displaced from their home countries."[43]

Similarly, the concept of *hijrah* in Islam provided the right to refuge in any Muslim state.[44] "The refugee regime itself was based on the almost entirely *laissez-faire* attitude of nations toward the fugitives who crossed their borders."[45] There was no distinction between the immigrant and refugee. They were both treated equally.[46] Sanctuary was not conceived of as an international affair or an issue of government concern.[47]

The contemporary international refugee law regime began with Fridtjof Nansen's creation of international instruments and refugee travel documents, which became known as Nansen passports.[48] This framework was premised on the categorization of groups under an exclusion and inclusion model that is aligned with a nation-state's interest. The initial refugee protections were categorical, with a focus on repatriation.[49] For example, in 1917, the Russian Revolution caused a mass exodus.[50] In response, the League of Nations implemented a categorical approach to refugee protections, extending refugee travel documents to Armenians in 1924, and to Turks, Assyrians, Syrians, Assyro-Chaldeans, and Kurds in 1928.[51] This highly categorical approach was geared toward protecting ethnic and national groups, and religious minorities who were persecuted and unable to return to their countries of origin.[52] The 1931 Great Depression marked a further constraint on refugee protection, as receiving nations became increasingly concerned with the financial obligations of welcoming refugees.[53]

The regime that emerged relies heavily on state interests, in contrast to past religious sanctuary protections that were, in theory, premised on a refugee's right to a safe haven. With religious sanctuary, refuge was given to both criminals and individuals subject to retaliatory attacks in their home countries.[54] In contrast, refugee law scholar James Hathaway posits that since World War II (WWII), state interest has been the greatest factor shaping international refugee policy.[55] The universal protection of refugees became filtered through the lens of a nation-state's interest, where international law, politics, economics, and ideology influence who qualifies as a refugee. This concept of the refugee was also premised on state actors persecuting its own citizens.[56]

Refugee law scholars have critiqued the refugee regime that has emerged post-WWII as being incongruent with humanitarian and human rights principles that underlie protection.[57] The varied presumptions about which migrants constitute refugees hinder the nondiscriminatory implementation and global consensus of who qualifies as a refugee under the Convention.[58]

Contemporary systems for processing refugees are premised on a state's interest, which has resulted in a system where state politics govern protection.[59] According to Hathaway, "Current refugee law can be thought of as a compromise between the sovereign prerogative of states to control immigration and the reality of coerced movements of persons at risk."[60] Understanding the history, aspirations and the creation of the contemporary international refugee law provide the foundation for understanding how vulnerability is framed and why, under the post-WWII system, young single males from Muslim-majority countries are excluded from protections.

The vulnerability assessment in the refugee resettlement process

Refugee resettlement is one of the UNHCR's durable solutions to refugee flows. A durable solution is one that assists refugees to live safely while rebuilding their lives.[61] Resettlement is the transfer of refugees from an asylum country (typically a refugee camp) to a third state that, under its legal provisions, has agreed to admit the refugee for permanent resettlement in an effort to find a durable solution.[62] This section describes the legal criteria in which UNHCR, Germany, Canada, and the United States apply to assess vulnerability for resettlement. These countries were selected because of the pervasive contemporary issues and intranational debates on both refugee resettlement and the resettlement of males from Muslim-majority countries.

An individual is first designated as meeting the criteria of a refugee through UNHCR's refugee status determination (RSD) process; they then may await resettlement while being provided aid in the form of housing at a refugee camp or aid within the country where they are currently residing.[63] Resettlement is an alternative to traveling to a country's border and demanding asylum there.[64] Individuals who demand asylum at or within a country are identified as "asylum seekers." Increasingly, asylum seekers have begun to place themselves in deadly circumstances in attempts to reach safety.[65]

Although there are approximately thirty-seven countries that have refugee resettlement programs,[66] refugee resettlement is typically a very limited remedy. Out of the 25.4 million refugees and 3.1 million asylum seekers worldwide,[67] less than 1% benefit from third country resettlement.[68] Refugee resettlement is typically reserved for the "most vulnerable" refugees. Individual countries set admission quotas to safely bring particularly vulnerable individuals to their countries.[69] According to UNHCR, "During 2015, UNHCR referred 134,000 refugees for resettlement—a twenty-nine percent increase from 2014, and the highest such number in about two decades."[70] In 2015, "Syrians constituted the single largest nationality submitted, with 53,300 individuals referred."[71] UNHCR and resettlement countries have developed priority categories around the construct of vulnerability in order to select the most vulnerable refugees for resettlement. UNHCR and countries with resettlement programs have also developed factors to assess when an individual is most "vulnerable" to qualify for resettlement.

UNHCR construction of vulnerability for refugee resettlement

UNHCR prioritizes seven categories of vulnerable refugees for resettlement.[72] The categories include the following:

1 Legal and/or Physical Protection Needs of the refugee in the country of refuge (this includes a threat of refoulement);
2 Survivors of Torture and/or Violence, where repatriation or the conditions of asylum could result in further traumatization and/or heightened risk or where appropriate treatment is not available;

3 Medical Needs, particularly life-saving treatment that is unavailable in the country of refuge;
4 Women and Girls at Risk, who have protection problems particular to their gender;
5 Family Reunification, when resettlement is the only means to reunite refugee family members who, owing to refugee flight or displacement, are separated by borders or entire continents;
6 Children and Adolescents at Risk, where a best-interest determination supports resettlement;
7 Lack of Foreseeable Alternative Durable Solutions, which is generally relevant only when other solutions are not feasible in the foreseeable future, when resettlement can be used strategically, and/or when it can open possibilities for comprehensive solutions.[73]

Once UNHCR makes an assessment of an individual's vulnerability through establishing qualification via one of the categories, refugees must then wait to have their case submitted to a country with a resettlement program.[74] In addition to UNHCR's criteria, individual countries have their own priority categories.[75] Based on a country's own assessment and priority categories, it will set admission quotas to bring individuals who are particularly vulnerable safely to their country.[76]

In 2017, UNHCR resettled a total of 65,074 refugees—38,345 were men and 36,825 were women.[77] Of that total, within the age range of 18–59, 17,254 (approximately 22%) were males and 17,631 (approximately 24%) were females.[78] In the age range of 0–17 years old, 18,260 (approximately 28%) were males and 20,247 (approximately 24%) were females.[79] If we examine the data on the settlement of Syrian refugees, in 2017, UNCHR resettled 17,823 female Syrian refugees and 19,509 males; in the 18–59 age range, 8,159 were men, and women totaled 8,154.[80]

Vulnerability prioritized in Canada

The Canadian government sets a target each year for the resettlement of refugees,[81] with the Department of Immigration, Refugees and Citizenship administering Canada's resettlement program.[82] Canada has three general categories of refugee resettlement programs: the Humanitarian-protected Persons Abroad Class (HPC), the Urgent Protection Program (UPP), and the Private Sponsors Refugee Program.[83] In general, a resettled refugee must meet the Refugee Convention definition to qualify for resettlement or meet the criteria of the HPC.[84]

Canada's UPP protects persons who qualify for resettlement who are in "need of urgent protection through resettlement due to immediate threats to their life, liberty or physical safety. Medical emergencies do not qualify for the UPP."[85] Canadian visa officers assess vulnerability by evaluating individuals whose circumstances give rise to "a heightened risk to his/her physical safety or well-being."[86] In addition, medical or family conditions may result in a heightened vulnerability assessment.[87] When UNHCR designates a case as "urgent," Canadian visa officers will consider the case for expedited processing within 1–4 months.[88]

Canada also has a special category for refugees who have medical needs or are survivors of violence or torture, as well as for *women at risk, children,* and the elderly.[89] The "Canadian Women-at-Risk Program provides protection and assistance to refugee women who are in critical situations," which includes "women without the normal protection of a family who find themselves in precarious situations and who are in a place where local authorities cannot ensure their safety."[90]

In 2016, Canada's target for resettling refugees from the Middle East and North Africa was 35,000.[91] From January 2015 to March 2017, Canada resettled a total number of 74,840 refugees: 38,790 were male and 36,035 were female.[92] Out of the 43,725 resettled Syrian refugees, 30,460 were total dependents and/or spouses.[93] Spouses totaled 8,245, whereas dependents totaled 22,215.[94] In January 2017, of the 1,300 Syrian families that were resettled, most consisted of eight or more people, and another 1,200 were families of seven or more.[95] The impact of the application of Canada's vulnerability factors, coupled with priorities as articulated by the Canadian government, resulted in the majority of individuals resettled being large families, with very few unattached single males. In 2016, Canadian Citizenship and Immigration did not reply when asked how many single males had been admitted.[96]

Vulnerability prioritized in Germany

In 2015 and 2016, Germany experienced an increase of asylum seekers (i.e., individuals who seek classification as a refugee at the border) as opposed to resettled refugees. In fact, "Three-quarters of first-time asylum applicants in 2015 were male, and 68% of them were under the age of 33. Roughly half of them were married. The most common native languages [were] Arabic, Albanian and Dari/Farsi."[97]

Germany's refugee resettlement program is relatively new, as it only began in 2012.[98] Before 2012, Germany only had an ad hoc resettlement program.[99] Germany's Federal Ministry of the Interior, the Federal Office for Migration and Refugees (BAMF), and the Federal Foreign Office are responsible for implementing its resettlement program. Section 23(4) of Germany's Residence Act provides that "the Federal government, in consultation with individual states, can instruct the Refugee office to admit to Germany certain groups of foreigners who are granted temporary or permanent residence permits upon arrival."[100] Under Germany's resettlement program, UNHCR must first designate the individual as a refugee in order to qualify for resettlement.[101] Next, the Federal Ministry of Interior develops the admission criteria for the resettlement program.[102] The criteria include

> preservation of family unity (if the family members are staying in the country from which the person is to be admitted), family or other ties in Germany conducive to integration, the "integration potential," determined by level of school and occupational training, work experience, language skills, religious affiliation, age, [and] *degree of vulnerability.*[103]

Germany also gives special attention to the following categories of refugees: survivors of violence and/or torture, medical cases, ***women and girls at risk, children*** and adolescents at risk, and unaccompanied minors.[104] In addition, "A sub-quota of up to 5% is reserved for persons in critical medical condition; there are no specific sub-quota for the other groups."[105]

In response to the conflict in Syria, Germany expanded its resettlement program to create the temporary Syrian Humanitarian Admissions Program.[106] Under this program, between 2013 and 2015, 20,000 Syrians were permitted to enter Germany directly from Syria's neighboring countries, or from Egypt or Libya.[107] Germany also has a private resettlement program that permits "primarily German and Syrian citizens who have been living in Germany for more than a year and who wish to bring Syrian relatives seeking protection into the country."[108]

In 2011, Germany implemented a pilot program to annually resettle 300 "particularly vulnerable" refugees who would be admitted from third countries.[109] The German government data indicated, "Taking account of the national quota, in 2016 and 2017, Germany will resettle 1,600 persons in total and 800 persons per year within the framework of an EU resettlement pilot programme."[110] Germany implemented a "one-time admission of 1,600 of a total of 20,000 refugees to be resettled throughout the EU in 2016 and 2017." [111] The goal of the one-time admission program was to reduce irregular migration by providing legal forms of protection.[112] Through irregular migration, individuals request asylum when they arrive at a country's border. In 2017, through its refugee resettlement program, Germany resettled 3,005 refugees; this included 1,890 females and 1,762 males.[113]

Vulnerability prioritized in the United States

In the United States, the president, in consultation with congressional committees, sets the maximum annual number for refugee admissions.[114] The United States' Immigration and Nationality Act states that "admissions ... shall be allocated among refugees of special humanitarian concern to the United States." [115] The U.S. Department of State's Bureau of Population, Refugees, and Migration (PRM) handles the resettlement program through the U.S. Refugee Admissions Program.[116] Prospective refugees may be referred to the U.S. program by the UNHCR, a U.S. embassy, or a designated nongovernmental organization (NGO); in some cases, they can access the national refugee program directly.[117] PRM works with NGOs, international organizations, or U.S. embassy contractors who manage a Resettlement Support Center (RSC) to assist in refugee resettlement.[118] The RSCs assist applicants in completing documentary requirements and scheduling refugee eligibility interviews with the Department of Homeland Security's (DHS) U.S. Citizenship and Immigration Services (USCIS), which adjudicates refugee applications and makes decisions about eligibility for refugee status. The USCIS officer must determine whether the applicant is qualified under one of the refugee processing priorities, meets the INA definition of a refugee, is not firmly resettled in another country, and is admissible to the United States under U.S. immigration laws.

Refugees are categorized into three different priority categories:

Priority 1 (P-1) covers refugees for whom resettlement seems to be the appropriate durable solution, who are referred to the U.S. refugee program by UNHCR, a U.S. embassy, or a designated NGO.

Priority 2 (P-2) covers groups of *special humanitarian* concern to the United States. It includes specific groups that may be defined by their nationalities, clans, ethnicities, or other characteristics. P-2 cases can access the U.S. refugee program directly.

Priority 3 (P-3) covers family reunification cases. This priority is limited to designated nationalities. Refugee applications under P-3 are based on an affidavit of relationship filed by an eligible relative in the United States. P-3 cases can access the U.S. refugee program directly.[119]

Refugee applicants must clear all required security checks before their applications can receive final approval.[120] Individuals are first resettled based on where they have family; otherwise, they are resettled according to the community's resources and the refugee's needs.[121]

Since 2000, the Bureau of PRM expressed a commitment to fund gender-based violence prevention, particularly violence targeted at women and girls during disasters and conflicts.[122] The partnership and priority categories between both PRM and UNHCR may result in UNHCR referring more women and children for resettlement in the United States. While the President and Congress establish priorities, PRM "has led in proposing admissions ceilings and processing priorities."[123]

The refugee admission numbers reveal that under the U.S. Refugee Admissions Program in 2016, 78% of the more than 8,000 Syrian refugees admitted to the country were women or children.[124] Some 58% were children, with a roughly even split between girls and boys.[125] In 2015, half of the Syrian refugees brought to the United States were also children, with only 2.5% of them over age sixty, and only 2% "single males of combat age."[126]

Recently, Convention signatories excluded bona fide refugees based on a presumption of dangerousness and nonvulnerability of males from Muslim-majority countries. The Canadian Prime Minister's statement and the President of the United States demonstrate how narratives can develop into policies that facilitate the discriminatory exclusion of certain categories of refugees. The broad policy statements of the leaders directly affect the decision to admit a refugee. This results in excluding broad categories of individuals without a full evaluation as to whether the individual qualifies as a refugee, fits within vulnerability priority categories, or has committed (or will commit) acts that render him or her ineligible for Convention protection. In reference to the exclusion of young single refugee males from Muslim-majority countries, the rhetoric from politicians and resulting policies and laws reinforce gendered norms and stereotypes that lead to the exclusion of this demographic of refugees.[127]

Gender, Islamophobia, and refugee vulnerability

The narratives against males from Muslim-majority countries and the ways in which countries have applied vulnerability assessments have resulted in the exclusion of this segment of refugees from resettlement. In this section, I argue that gender interfaces with xenophobic and Islamophobic bias and results in the discriminatory application of vulnerability to assess eligibility for refugee resettlement to the exclusion of Muslim males. This section relies on intersectionality[128] and hegemonic masculinity theories[129] to understand the underlying ideologies that lead to exclusion of this demographic from protection. Individuals who are conceptualized as compatible with the "currently accepted" masculinity or femininity norms (i.e., those who are perceived as being marginalized or persecuted) are provided Convention protection. This narrative creates two problems that result in the exclusion of young single refugee males from Muslim-majority countries: (1) the narrative of the Muslim male who is a threat to Muslim women in need protection; and, (2) the narrative of the victimless male refugee who is the perpetrating criminalized Other and a national security risk.

Victimless male refugees from Muslim-majority countries

When assessing vulnerability and refugee resettlement, women are often portrayed as victims from the Global South and are summarily grouped together with children.[130] As Megan Denise Smith, a U.N. International Office of Migration officer and researcher, has noted, "[F]itting women into the 2002 Guidelines on Gender-Related Persecution has only been achieved by painting a monolithic picture of women as passive, dependent, vulnerable victims and thus peripheral to international politics and without agency."[131] At the other end of the spectrum is the Muslim male refugee Other, who is portrayed as the violator of social norms, and whose conformance to "immigrant stereotypes" enables his invisible status and fosters marginalization and lessened protections under the law.[132] The young single Muslim male is portrayed as being of combat age, violent, and ready to act against Western countries at any cost.

This narrative creates a monolithic picture that deprives refugee women of agency and reinforces their marginalization.[133] It cultivates a "paternalistic narrative of the state, as saviour [sic] to protect 'women and children.'"[134] This frame is based on "Orientalism's binary juxtaposition of a 'traditional' East with a 'modern' West-the theoretical engine of colonialism was premised in part on perceptions of non-Western women as oppressed subjects."[135] A clear example is President Trump's first iteration of the travel ban, which halted immigration from the Muslim-majority countries of Iran, Iraq, Libya, Somalia, Sudan, Syria, and Yemen, as well as the U.S. refugee resettlement program.[136] The first iteration of the travel ban promulgated the protection-of-women-from-the-persecution-of-Muslim-men narrative. The order stated that

> In addition, the United States should not admit those who engage in acts of bigotry or hatred (including 'honor' killings, other forms of violence against women, or the persecution of those who practice religions different from their own) or those who would oppress Americans of any race, gender, or sexual orientation.[137]

The protection of women from Muslim males who inflict honor killings or other forms of violence against women reinforces the flattened narrative that women are in need of protection, while Muslim men are the perpetrators of violence *from which the women need protection.* Legal Scholar Leti Volpp states, "[h]istorically, the status of women in need of uplift was a source of justification for Western colonization of regions of the world—'white men saving brown women from brown men.'"[138] The aftermath of September 11 witnessed the redeployment of the idea of protection of Muslim women from Muslim males.[139] "One of the stated justifications for American intervention in Afghanistan—made by both President George Bush and First Lady Laura Bush—was that Afghan women needed to be saved from the Taliban and Islamic barbarism."[140] After September 11, "At home and abroad, it seems that everyone from Laura Bush on down has taken up the plight of Muslim women."[141] The idea that Muslim women need to be "liberated into the 'progressive' social customs of the West"[142] justifies the marginalization of Muslim men and provides a justification for the invasion of Arab nations.

This creates a dichotomy between the vulnerability and victimhood of refugee women and the refugee male, who becomes the perpetrating, criminalized Other. Muslim women become victims who suffer from their minority cultures.[143] This dichotomy was fully present post-September 11 in the Bush administration's framing of the narrative of Middle Eastern men:[144]

> [...] The Bush administration's post-September 11 rhetoric was focused on the abuses of the Taliban and Saddam Hussein regimes and expressed support for women's human rights, it actually served to justify American intervention in the name of masculine protection by framing the United States as a liberator of Afghani and Iraqi women and children.[145]

Within this monolithic narrative, individuals are positioned in relation to masculine norms which dictate their ability to obtain benefits for inclusion as refugees. For men, fitting within the monolithic narrative constitutes

> largely unattainable or unachievable realities. Therefore, even at a prima facie level the assumption that emerges immediately is that, rather than practicing the hegemonic form of masculinity, men alternatively 'position themselves in relation to it' to gain whatever advantages may flow from it.[146]

As such, vulnerability-based resettlement policies can reinforce masculinity norms in admitting immigrant populations that conform to dominant conceptions of western masculinities while excluding marginalized ones.[147] These dualistic narratives

> [i]nstead of treating asylum seekers as complex, multifaceted fellow humans, their subjectivity is *flattened*, reduced to a singular dimension. The consequence of this reduction is that receiving states recognize *no moral obligation*, but conceive of asylum as a form of *charity*. It is offered *unilaterally* and at the *discretion of the state*.[148]

There is also another nuanced level to the applicability of hegemonic masculinity in relation to the exclusion of males from Muslim-majority countries. The gendered conceptualization of the male who is empowered to find a job and provide for himself is not regarded as a victim in need of protection. At the same time, however, in a cultural context, masculinity is upheld, and men are constrained from showing their vulnerability, which makes it even harder to fit into this "weak" narrative as individuals deserving of protection.

This flattened portrayal of vulnerability causes forms of gender-based violence in which refugee males from Muslim-majority countries may be overlooked, resulting in their marginalization, and similarly narrowly constructs Muslim women as victims without any agency. Gender-based violence includes violence targeted at women or men because of their genders and/or their socially constructed gender roles.[149] Both men and women can be, and often are, victims and perpetrators of gender-based violence.[150] During conflicts, even though the international community has struggled to document forms of gender-based violence against men, both men and boys experience sex-selective massacre, forced recruitment, and sexual violence.[151] All of these factors make them eligible for protection under the Convention. In addition, more often than women, young children, or the elderly, military-age men, and adolescent boys are forcibly recruited to join armed conflicts and militias against their will.[152] This is the impetus that often motivates men to flee. As human security analyst R. Charli Carpenter states, "There is a general understanding that women are more likely than men to be displaced or sexually assaulted, and that men are more likely than women to be massacred, detained, or recruited."[153]

Viewing vulnerability from a dichotomous frame also fails to account for the intersecting levels of identity in the framing of women refugees from Muslim-majority countries.[154] The colonialism trope that stereotypes women as victims in need of saving masks the role that Muslim women can and have played in terrorist activities. As immigration scholar Muneer Ahmad states, "[t]he veil in the American context is reduced to a symbol of foreignness and clandestine terror."[155] "[T]he hijab does not just signify foreignness; it represents an ambiguously defined geographic part of the world that is antagonistic to democracy and American values: the Muslim world."[156] Again, the prevailing narrative around Muslim females who engage in terrorism also portrays women through the same frame of manipulation by the Muslim male.[157] "The process of brainwashing seems to require male influence, particularly that of a husband, boyfriend or lover, as if convert Muslim women married only strangers with secret agendas for their new-to-Islam wives."[158] The image of Muslim female fighters is often justified and reinforced through the image of the Muslim woman in need of saving.

In the application of the refugee resettlement vulnerability provisions, particular attention must be given to the ways in which gender norms result in a one-dimensional, flattened characterization of both women and men from Muslim-majority countries. This characterization results in the exclusion of male populations through the dualistic view that women are victims and men are perpetrators unworthy of protection. According to Carpenter, "Much of the 'human security' discourse in international institutions is based upon a highly gendered understanding of who is to be secured, characterized by the exclusion of civilian males as subjects of 'protection' or as victims of 'gender-based violence'."[159]

Islamophobia, terrorism, and vulnerability

The construction of the single, young refugee man from Muslim-majority countries as the terrorist Other escalated after the events of September 11, 2001:[160] "Stereotypes of the dark-skinned, bearded, Muslim male as representative of the primary threat to national security consume[d] the (predominantly male) government's anxious attempts to prevent the next terrorist attack."[161] This stereotype has led to the exclusion of males from Muslim-majority countries regardless of their actual religion or if they are even from an Arab country from refugee resettlement.[162] Post September 11, individuals from Muslim-majority nations have been excluded as refugees without considering if they are vulnerable to persecution.[163] In 2002, public policy analyst Monette Zard predicted that "the broad application of the Exclusion Clauses [in the Convention] could come dangerously close to attributing guilt purely on the basis of association and are clearly at odds with the necessarily individual character of the exclusion procedure."[164] She warned of the ability of the broad application of these provisions to undermine the humanitarian refugee regime.[165] In addition, European Scholar Brad Blitz stated that "[F]ollowing 9/11, there has been a reconfiguration of refugee policy and a reconnecting of humanitarian and security interests which has enabled a discourse antithetical to the universal right to asylum."[166] Scholar Leti Volpp posited that post 9/11 "the American public [was] being instructed that looking 'Middle Eastern, Arab, or Muslim' equals 'potential terrorist.'"[167]

This reconfiguration became more firmly entrenched after the incidents involving immigrants in Paris, Brussels, Cologne, and Nice, and are used to justify blanketed exclusion of refugees from the Middle East as potential terror threats.[168] For example, Former United States Federal Bureau of Investigation Director James Comey stated, "So, there's going to be a diaspora out of Syria at some point and we are determined not to let lines be drawn from Syria today to a future 9/11."[169]

In theorizing the Muslim male Other, there is systematic failure to conceptualize individual deviant actors; instead, one person's actions become representations for an entire group.[170] Various scholars have conducted statistical analyses, to combat the group versus deviant actor frame, the results of which rebut the presumption of the terrorist Muslim male perpetrator. For example, a CATO institute study focused on whether foreign-born people from the Muslim-majority countries excluded from Trump's travel ban (Iran, Iraq, Syria, Libya, Yemen, Sudan, and Somalia) had committed or were convicted of attempting to commit a terrorist attack on the United States' soil from 1975 through 2015.[171] The study found that

> 17 foreign-born folks from those nations [Iran, Iraq, Syria, Libya, Yemen, Sudan, and Somalia] were convicted of carrying out or attempting to carry out a terrorist attack on U.S. soil and they killed zero people. Zero Libyans or Syrians intended to carry out an attack on U.S. soil during this time.[172]

The study also found that the majority of terrorist attacks in the West were by homegrown groups or individuals with no significant ties to any foreign terrorist organization.[173]

In another study by Scholar Marc Sageman, in surveying the 25 million Muslims who reside in Western countries, less than one in one million Muslims a year could be considered a terrorist.[174] Furthermore, "the number of people moving to join Syria's civil war would appear as a barely visible black thread in the wide, wide arrow pointing out from the country: 20,000 people going in against 4 million headed out."[175] Military-aged males are actually the majority of individuals fleeing the conflict.[176] "It makes good sense that so many young men are leaving countries like Afghanistan, Iraq, and Syria: their demographic is often at greater risk of being conscripted into fighting groups or being killed rather than captured by such groups."[177]

We must also take into consideration how the narratives of the terrorist male from Muslim-majority countries mask the exception that has been carved out for the resettlement of gay males and sexual minorities. Prime Minister Justin Trudeau's November 24, 2015, comments evince the carving out gay exception to Islamophobia where gay Muslim males are acceptable candidates for refugee resettlement.[178] Placed in context, "Canada has the highest acceptance rates for sexual minorities of any receiving country in the world."[179] Accordingly, "Canada's cultivated international image as a protector of those persecuted by their home states because of their sexual orientation." [180] In addition, the Trump travel ban included a clause to protect sexual minorities from persecution in Muslim-majority countries.[181]

To place the gay male and sexual minority exception to the ban on refugee resettlement of males from Muslim-majority countries in context, it is important to consider scholar Jasbir K. Puar's homonationalism theory.[182] Puar posits that homonationalism (i.e., homonormative nationalism) occurs when a nation engages in sexual exceptionalism to justify its xenophobia policies against Islamic nations based on its image as an egalitarian Western nation accepting of sexual minorities.[183] In this context, "[s]exual minority refugees are therefore encouraged to seek protection in Canada while simultaneously being framed as a potential threat to the health of the Canadian public."[184] Similar to the frame discussed above where the exclusion of male refugees is justified by Western countries utilizing colonial narratives on saving victimized Muslim women, sexual minority refugees, in this case sexual minorities from Muslim-majority countries, are also framed as a "universal victimized group in need of freedom—both from an oppressor and freedom to express their sexuality—that can only be provided by the Canadian state."[185] "[R]efugees represent the transition and supposed evolution between the barbaric sexualities of their country of origin, and the liberated sexualities of their desired (Western) destination."[186]

According to Puar, homonationalism facilitates Western states' attempts to frame themselves as "exceptional, progressive and modern in comparison with barbaric, traditional, and backwards non-Western states, Western states are able to adorn themselves with yet another justification for a foreign policy program based on invasion and Westernization."[187] In relation to refugee resettlement, this dynamic is exacerbated at the intersection of sexuality and race, class, religion, gender, and ethnicity[188] where narratives of the progressive protective Western state result in the resettlement of sexual minorities to the exclusion of single, young males from Muslim-majority countries regardless of their level of vulnerability. The narratives that are propagated have resulted in stereotyped, Islamophobic images of Muslim Arab males as the perpetrators of violence, instead of viewing them as individual victims and survivors of the Syrian conflict.[189]

Conclusion

Males who conform to gender norms from Muslim-majority countries are *excluded from* the protections of the Refugee Convention. The exclusion of young single refugee males from Muslim-majority countries reflects the current reality in which narratives become institutions that frame how vulnerability is constructed and who benefits from the protections of the Refugee Convention.[190] This contemporary issue reveals how the application of a binary exclusion and inclusion construct of vulnerability that informs refugee resettlement policies minimalizes the right to be free from persecution principles that underlie the Refugee Convention. The legal categories of vulnerability and informal policy statements have become hardened legal constructs that result in the exclusion of young Muslim refugee males who are profiled as warranting exclusion based on preconceived notions of criminality and the terrorist Other. Underlying their exclusion inherently contains more theoretical conceptions that "the boundaries of the nation continue to be constructed through excluding certain groups."[191]

These narratives are utilized in conjunction with state-centric conceptions of vulnerability, which feigns an egalitarian state that protects sexual minorities to the exclusion of young single refugee males from Muslim-majority countries. Broad profiling and exclusion of males from Muslim-majority countries is contrary to human rights underpinnings of the Refugee Convention.[192] In general, signatories to the Refugee Convention are bound by the *non-refoulement* provisions of Article 33(1). As Article 33(1) stipulates,

> No Contracting State shall expel or return ("refouler") a refugee in any manner whatsoever to the frontiers of territories where his [or her] life or freedom would be threatened on account of his [or her] race, religion, nationality, membership of a particular social group or political opinion.[193]

Additionally, under Article 3, Convention signatories are obligated to apply provisions "without discrimination as to sex, age, disability, sexuality, or other prohibited grounds of discrimination."[194] The current application of the vulnerability criteria further gender normed narratives that exclude young males from Muslim-majority countries while elevating the claims of women and sexual minorities to bolster Western countries' justifications for their foreign policy objectives.

Notes

1 Sherene H. Razack, *Casting Out: The Eviction of Muslims From Western Law & Politics* (Toronto: University of Toronto Press, 2008), 16.

2 Refugee Convention, Foreword (on Durable Solutions). See also, International Covenant on Civil and Political Rights (ICCPR), Dec. 16, 1966, 999 U.N.T.S. 171, Art. 12 (states, "1. Everyone lawfully within the territory of a State shall, within that territory, have the right to liberty of movement and freedom to choose his residence. 2. Everyone shall be free to leave any country, including his own. 3. The above-mentioned rights shall not be subject to any restrictions except those which are provided by law, are necessary to protect national security, public order (ordre public), public health or morals or the rights and freedoms of others and are consistent with the other rights recognized in the present Covenant. 4. No one shall be arbitrarily deprived of the right to enter his own country").

3 The term "men from Muslim-majority countries" is used in this chapter. This demographic includes men who may be secular or otherwise do not identify as Muslim, but who are perceived as Muslim because of their race, nationality, religious heritage, language, dress, or political affiliations. See generally, Leti Volpp, "The Citizen and the Terrorist," *UCLA LAW REVIEW* 49 (2002): 1575–1600, 1580 (reflecting on post 9/11 targeting of individuals both citizens and non-citizens "based solely upon perceptions of their racial, religious, or ethnic Identity" connected with individuals appearing to be "Middle Eastern, Arab, or Muslim").

4 *Ibid.*, 1591.

5 Refugee Convention, Art. 3 (states, "The Contracting States shall apply the provisions of this Convention to refugees without discrimination as to race, religion or country of origin").

6 Universal Declaration of Human Rights (UDHR), Article 14 (stating, "(1) Everyone has the right to seek and to enjoy in other countries asylum from persecution; and (2) This right may not be invoked in the case of prosecutions genuinely arising from non-political crimes or from acts contrary to the purposes and principles of the United Nations"); Michael Barutckski and Astri Suhrke, "Lessons from Kosovo Refugee Crisis: Innovations in Protection and Burden-sharing," *Journal of Refugee Studies* 14, no. 2 (2001): 111; See also, ICCPR, Art. 12; ICCPR Preamble (states, "Recognizing that, in accordance with the Universal Declaration of Human Rights, the ideal of free human beings enjoying civil and political freedom and freedom from fear and want can only be achieved if conditions are created whereby everyone may enjoy his civil and political rights, as well as his economic, social and cultural rights").

7 Barutckski "Lessons from Kosovo," 111.

8 Karla McKanders, "America's Disposable Youth: Undocumented Delinquent Juveniles," *Howard Law Journal* 59, no. 1 (2015): 212, http://dx.doi.org/10.2139/ssrn.2725561.
9 *Ibid.*
10 *Ibid.*
11 UDHR, Article; See generally, Refugee Convention, Art. 33.
12 Lucy Rodgers et al., "Syria: The Story of the Conflict," *BBC News*, March 11, 2016, www.bbc.com/news/world-middle-east-26116868.
13 *Ibid.*
14 *Ibid.*
15 "Canada Denies Alan Kurdi's Family Applied for Asylum," *BBC News*, September 3, 2015, www.bbc.com/news/world-us-canada-34142695.
16 Wesley Dockery, "Two Years since Germany Opened Its Borders to Refugees: A Chronology," *Deutsche Welle*, April 9, 2017, http://dw.com/en/two-years-since-germany-opened-its-borders-to-refugees-a-chronology/a-40327634; see also, Valeria Gomez, Karla Mari McKanders, "Refugee Reception and Perception: U.S. Detention Camps and German Welcome Centers," *Fordham International Law Journal* 40, no. 2 (2017): 523.
17 Tajha Chappellet-Lanier, "What's Next for Migrants After Paris?" *The Atlantic*, November 14, 2015, www.theatlantic.com/international/archive/2015/11/migrant-crisis-paris-attacks/416067/.
18 "Canada to Turn Away Single Men as Part of Syrian Refugee Resettlement Plan," *The Guardian*, November 23, 2015, www.theguardian.com/world/2015/nov/23/canada-syrian-refugee-resettlement-plan-no-single-men.
19 Dipo Faloyin, "Canada Will Welcome 25,000 Refugees, but No Single Straight Men," *Newsweek*, November 14, 2015, www.newsweek.com/canada-will-welcome-25000-refugees-no-single-straight-men-398045.
20 Obama White House, "Statement by National Security Advisor Susan E. Rice on Syrian Refugee Admissions," *Office of the Press Secretary*, August 29, 2016, https://obamawhitehouse.archives.gov/the-press-office/2016/08/29/statement-national-security-advisor-susan-e-rice-syrian-refugee.
21 *Texas Health & Human Servs. Comm'n v. United States*, 166 F. Supp. 3d 706 (N.D. Tex. 2016).
22 *Ibid.* (citing Refugee Act that provides as follows: the Director and the Federal agency administering (a program of initial resettlement) shall consult regularly (not less often than quarterly) with State and local governments and private nonprofit voluntary agencies concerning the sponsorship process and the intended distribution of refugees among the States and localities before their placement in those States and localities; 8 U.S.C. § 1522(a)(2)(A)).
23 Ashley Fantz and Ben Brumfield, "More Than Half the Nation's Governors Say Syrian Refugees Not Welcome," *CNN*, November 19, 2015, http://edition.cnn.com/2015/11/16/world/paris-attacks-syrian-refugees-backlash/.
24 Jeremy Diamond, "Donald Trump: Ban all Muslim travel to U.S," *CNN*, December 8, 2015, www.cnn.com/2015/12/07/politics/donald-trump-muslim-ban-immigration/index.html.
25 Maya Rhodan, "Are the Syrian Refugees All 'Young, Strong, Men'?" *Time*, November 20, 2015, http://time.com/4122186/syrian-refugees-donald-trump-young-men/.
26 *Ibid.*
27 *Ibid.*
28 *Ibid.*
29 President Trump Exec. Order No. 13,767, 82 Fed. Reg. 8,793 (January 25, 2017), Border Security and Immigration Enforcement Improvements; President Trump Exec. Order No. 13,769, 82 Fed. Reg. 8,977 (January 27, 2017), Protecting the

Nation from Foreign Terrorist Entry into the United States; President Trump Exec. Order No. 13,780, 82 Fed. Reg. 13,209 (March 6, 2017), Protecting the Nation from Foreign Terrorist Entry into the United States.

30 White House, "Presidential Proclamation Enhancing Vetting Capabilities and Processes for Detecting Attempted Entry Into the United States by Terrorists or Other Public-Safety Threats," National Security and Defense, September 24, 2017, www.whitehouse.gov/presidential-actions/presidential-proclamation-enhancing-vetting-capabilities-processes-detecting-attempted-entry-united-states-terrorists-public-safety-threats/ (the proclamation carves out an exception, stating, "This proclamation shall not apply to an individual who has been granted asylum by the United States, to a refugee who has already been admitted to the United States, or to an individual granted withholding of removal or protection under the Convention Against Torture. Nothing in this proclamation shall be construed to limit the ability of an individual to seek asylum, refugee status, withholding of removal, or protection under the Convention Against Torture, consistent with the laws of the United States").

31 *Ibid.*

32 *Trump v. Hawaii*, No. 17-965, 2018 WL 3116337 (U.S. June 26, 2018).

33 *Ibid.*

34 Deutsche Welle, Angela Merkel knew of problems at BAMF refugee agency: report, June 3, 2018, www.dw.com/en/angela-merkel-knew-of-problems-at-bamf-refugee-agency-report/a-44057515, accessed on June 6, 2018.

35 *Ibid.*

36 Volpp, "The Citizen and the Terrorist," 1591.

37 Esther Greussing and Hajo G. Boomgaarden, "Shifting the Refugee Narrative? An Automated Frame Analysis of Europe's 2015 Refugee Crisis," *Journal of Ethnic and Migration Studies* 43, no. 11 (2017): 1751, https://doi.org/10.1080/1369183X.2017.1282813.

38 *Ibid.*

39 Lewis Turner, "Who Will Resettle Single Syrian Men?" *Forced Migration Review* 54 (February 2017): 30, www.fmreview.org/sites/fmr/files/FMRdownloads/en/resettlement/turner.pdf.

40 James C. Hathaway, "The Evolution of Refugee Status in International Law: 1920–1950," *The International and Comparative Quarterly* 33, no. 2 (April 1984): 348, www.jstor.org/stable/759064.

41 *Ibid.*

42 Karen Musalo, Jennifer More, and Richard A. Boswell, *Refugee Law and Policy: A Comparative and International Approach*, 4th ed. (North Carolina: Carolina Academic Press, 2011): 5–8; Silas W. Allard, "Reimagining Asylum: Religious Narratives and Moral Obligations to the Asylum Seeker," *Refuge* 29, no. 1 (2013): 121, https://refuge.journals.yorku.ca/index.php/refuge/article/view/37521 (discussing reframing refugee narratives "by interrogating alternative narratives grounded in the Hebrew Bible story of the Exodus and the Qu'ranic story of the Hijra"); Peter Admirand, "The Ethics of Displacement and Migration in the Abrahamic Faiths: Enlightening Believers and Aiding Public Policy," *Journal of Ethnic and Migration Studies* 40, no. 4 (2014): 671, https://doi.org/10.1080/1369183X.2013.847360; Ahmed Abou-El-Wafa, "The Right to Asylum between Islamic Shari'ah and International Refugee Law: A Comparative Study," *UNHCR*, 2009, www.unhcr.org/4a9645646.pdf (stating that principles in Islamic law regarding refugee assistance and protection remain largely ignored in academic and political discourse and certain challenges need to be discussed); UNHCR, "Islam and Refugees," published December 13, 2012, www.unhcr.org/50ab90399.pdf.

43 *Ibid.*, 38.

44 United Nations High Commissioner for Refugees (UNHCR), "Islam and Refugees" ("This *hijrah*, or migration, came to symbolize the movement of Muslims from lands of oppression to those of Islam. Moreover, the hospitable treatment of Muhammed by the people of Medina embodies the Islamic model of refugee protection contained in the Qur'an." Thus, individuals not only have the right to seek and be granted asylum in any Muslim state, but "it is the duty of Muslims to accept and protect these refugees for as long as they seek protection." Here, it is interesting to note that "in comparison to modern refugee law, *hijrah* offers a broader definition of refugees and gives individuals, rather than states, the right to the determination of asylum").

45 Laura Barnett, "Global Governance and the Evolution of the International Refugee Regime," *International Journal of Refugee Law* 14, no. 2 (April 2002): 240, https://doi.org/10.1093/ijrl/14.2_and_3.238.

46 *Ibid.*

47 *Ibid.*

48 Paul Weis, "The Development of Refugee Law," *Michigan Yearbook of International Legal Studies* 3, no. 27 (1982): 28, https://repository.law.umich.edu/cgi/view content.cgi?article=1860&context=mjil.

49 *Ibid.*

50 Barnett, "Global Governance," 241.

51 *Ibid.*, 242.

52 Jill I. Goldenziel, "The Curse of the Nation-State: Refugees, Migration, and Security in International Law," *Arizona State Law Journal* 48 (2016): 601, https://ssrn.com/abstract=2684903.

53 Barnett, "Global Governance," 243.

54 James C. Hathaway, "A Reconsideration of the Underlying Premise of Refugee Law," *Harvard International Law Journal* 31, no. 1 (Spring 1990): 133, www.taylorfrancis.com/books/9781351562218/chapters/10.4324%2F9781315092478-12 (asserting that "pursuit by states of their own well-being has been the greatest factor shaping the international legal response to refugees since World War II Current refugee law can be thought of as a compromise between the sovereign, prerogative of states to control immigration and the reality of coerced movements of persons at risk"); Hathaway, "The Evolution of Refugee Status in International Law: 1920–1950," *The International and Comparative Quarterly* 33, no. 2 (April 1984): 349, www.jstor.org/stable/759064 (stating that this period was marked "by carefully establishing the hallmarks of refugeehood, it was hoped that assistance could be afforded to those in the greatest need without risking the serious domestic political problems likely to result from continued open immigration").

55 Hathaway, "A Reconsideration of the Underlying Premise," 133.

56 Andrew Schoenholtz, "The New Refugees and the Old Treaty: Persecutors and Persecuted in the Twenty First Century," *Chicago International Law Journal* 16 (Summer 2015): 81.

57 Goldenziel, "The Curse of the Nation-State," 579 (arguing that states have always revised international law regarding displaced people to protect their own security interests and changing circumstances of displacement); Hathaway, "A Reconsideration of the Underlying Premise of Refugee Law," 130 ("If conceived of in humanitarian terms, refugee law would be a politically neutral response to the needs of suffering persons who have in some way been forced to leave their homes"); see also, Schoenholtz, "The New Refugees."

58 Jane Freedman, *Gendering the International Asylum and Refugee Debate*, 2nd ed. (London: Palgrave Macmillan, 2015), 4 (stating, "for some there is a clear difference between an asylum seeker and an economic migrant, one fleeing persecution and the other leaving their country of origin 'voluntarily' for economic motives.

This distinction is often made in a form that is not neutral, classifying the two groups of migrants within a particular political schema with the real asylum seeker or genuine refugee as a 'good' migrant, a poor victim of persecution or oppression worthy of support and protection, and the economic migrant a 'bad' [...].").

59 Barnett, "Global Governance," 239 ("Today the refugee regime is struggling to respond to gender and race distributional issues").

60 Hathaway, "A Reconsideration of the Underlying Premise of Refugee Law," 133.

61 UNHCR, "Resettlement Solutions," accessed on March 13, 2018, www.unhcr.org/en-us/resettlement.html.

62 *Ibid.*

63 *Ibid.* See also, "Canada Denies Alan Kurdi's Family Applied for Asylum," *BBC News*.

64 *Ibid.*

65 Janne Grote et al., "Resettlement and Humanitarian Admission Programmes in Germany: Focus-Study by the German National Contact Point for the European Migration Network (EMN)," *Federal Office for Migration and Refugees*, October 10, 2016, 5, www.bamf.de/SharedDocs/Anlagen/EN/Publikationen/EMN/Studien/wp68-emn-resettlement-humanitaere-aufnahme.pdf?__blob=publicationFile.

66 UNHCR, "Resettlement Solutions" (The number of countries offering resettlement programs has grown significantly in recent years, from fourteen resettlement countries in 2005 to thirty-seven resettlement countries worldwide in 2016 (Argentina, Australia, Austria, Belarus, Belgium, Brazil, Bulgaria, Canada, Chile, Croatia, Czech Republic, Denmark, Estonia, Finland, France, Germany, Hungary, Iceland, Ireland, Italy, Japan, Republic of Korea, Latvia, Liechtenstein, Lithuania, Luxembourg, the Netherlands, New Zealand, Norway, Portugal, Romania, Spain, Sweden, Switzerland, the United Kingdom, the United States, and Uruguay). Despite this increase, needs for resettlement continue to vastly exceed the number of available places.).

67 UNHCR, Statistical Yearbook 2016, published in 2017, www.unhcr.org/en-us/statistics/country/5a8ee0387/unhcr-statistical-yearbook-2016-16th-edition.html.

68 UNHCR, "Resettlement Solutions."

69 Grote, "Resettlement and Humanitarian Admission Programmes," 5.

70 UNHCR, "Global Trends Forced Displacement in 2015," accessed on March 13, 2018, www.unhcr.org/576408cd7.pdf.

71 *Ibid.*

72 UNHCR, "UNHCR Resettlement Submission Categories," in *Resettlement Handbook and Country Chapters*, December 2016, 243, www.unhcr.org/en-us/protection/resettlement/4a2ccf4c6/unhcr-resettlement-handbook-country-chapters.html.

73 *Ibid.*

74 *Ibid.*

75 *Ibid.*

76 Grote et al., "Resettlement and Humanitarian Admission Programmes in Germany," 5.

77 UNHCR, "Resettlement Data," accessed on March 8, 2018, www.unhcr.org/en-us/resettlement-data.html.

78 *Ibid.*

79 *Ibid.*

80 UNHCR, "Resettlement Data Finder: Syria," accessed on March 13, 2018, http://rsq.unhcr.org/en/#zeF0.

81 *Ibid.*

82 UNHCR, "Canada," in *UNHCR Resettlement Handbook*, last modified October 2016, www.unhcr.org/3c5e55594.html.

83 *Ibid.*

84 *Ibid.*
85 *Ibid.*
86 *Ibid.*, 9.
87 *Ibid.*
88 *Ibid.*
89 *Ibid.*, 8–10 (emphasis added).
90 *Ibid.*, 9–10.
91 *Ibid.*, 6.
92 Government of Canada, “Resettled Refugees—Monthly Immigration and Refugee Citizenship of Canada (IRCC) Updates,” accessed on March 31, 2018, http://open.canada.ca/data/en/dataset/4a1b260a-7ac4-4985-80a0-603bfe4aec11?_ga=2.187603808.995677009.1494444890-1096638679.1492789911.
93 *Ibid.*
94 Government of Canada, “Admissions of Syrian Refugees by Province/Territory of Intended Destination, Family Status and Immigration Category,” accessed on March 13, 2018, http://open.canada.ca/data/en/dataset/01c85d28-2a81-4295-9c06-4af792a7c209?_ga=2.89053395.995677009.1494444890-1096638679.1492789911.
95 Joe Freison, “Syrian Exodus to Canada: One Year Later, a Look at Who the Refugees Are and Where They Went,” *The Globe and Mail*, December 1, 2016, www.theglobeandmail.com/news/national/syrian-refugees-in-canada-by-the-numbers/article33120934/.
96 *Ibid.*
97 Anna-Katharina Rich, “First-time Asylum Applicants in Germany in 2015: Social Structure, Level of Qualifications and Employment, 3rd ed.,” *Federal Office for Migration and Refugees*, May 2016, www.bamf.de/SharedDocs/Anlagen/EN/Publikationen/Kurzanalysen/kurzanalyse3_sozial-komponenten.pdf?—blob=publicationFile.
98 UNHCR, “Germany,” in *UNHCR Resettlement Handbook*, last modified April 2016, www.unhcr.org/5162b3bc9.html.
99 *Ibid.*, 2.
100 *Ibid.*, 3.
101 *Ibid.*, 3.
102 Grote et al., “Resettlement and Humanitarian Admission Programmes,” 24.
103 *Ibid.*, 24 (emphasis added).
104 *Ibid.*, 24–25.
105 *Ibid.*
106 *Ibid.*, 5.
107 *Ibid.*
108 *Ibid.*, 6.
109 *Ibid.*, 5.
110 *Ibid.*
111 *Ibid.*, 13.
112 *Ibid.*
113 UNHCR, “Resettlement Data on Germany Finder.”
114 United States, Immigration and Nationality Act (INA), 8 United States Code § 207.
115 Andorra Bruno, “Syrian Refugee Admissions and Resettlement in the United States: In Brief,” *Congressional Research Service*, September 16, 2016, 1, https://fas.org/sgp/crs/homesec/R44277.pdf, (citing INA § 207(a)(3)).
116 *Ibid.*, 3.
117 *Ibid.*
118 *Ibid.*
119 *Ibid.* (emphasis added).
120 *Ibid.*

121 *Ibid.*
122 U.S. Department of State, "Addressing Gender-Based Violence in Emergencies," accessed on March 13, 2018, www.state.gov/j/prm/policyissues/issues/c62377.htm.
123 U.S. Citizenship and Immigration Services, "The United States Refugee Admissions Program (USRAP) Consultation & Worldwide Processing Priorities," last modified May 5, 2016, www.uscis.gov/humanitarian/refugees-asylum/refugees/united-states-refugee-admissions-program-usrap-consultation-worldwide-processing-priorities.
124 Refugee Processing Center, "Demographical Profile of Refugee Arrivals Fiscal Year Syria as of 31-December 2016," http://ireports.wrapsnet.org/Interactive-Reporting/EnumType/Report?ItemPath=/rpt_WebArrivalsReports/MX%20-%20Arrivals%20for%20a%20Demographic%20Profile; Jie Zong and Jeanne Batalova, "Syrian Refugees in the United States," *Migration Policy Institute*, January 12, 2017, www.migrationpolicy.org/article/syrian-refugees-united-states; Anne C. Richard, Leon Rodriguez, and Robert Carey, "Transcript of USCIS-DOS-HHS Press Call on Syrian Refugee Processing [moderated by Shin Inouye]," *U.S. Citizenship and Immigration Services*, August 5, 2016, www.uscis.gov/news/news-releases/transcript-uscis-dos-hhs-press-call-syrian-refugee-processing.
125 Refugee Processing Center, "Demographical Profile of Refugee Arrivals"; Jared Goyette, "It's Now Clear that Most of the Syrian Refugees Coming to the United States are Women and Children," *Public Radio International*, August 8, 2016, www.pri.org/stories/2016-08-08/it-s-now-clear-most-syrian-refugees-coming-united-states-are-women-and-children.
126 Rhodan, "Are the Syrian Refugees All 'Young, Strong, Men'?"
127 See generally, U.S. President's Executive Orders, endnote 30.
128 Rashida Manjoo, "Report of the Special Rapporteur on Violence against Women, Its Causes and Consequences," *United Nations General Assembly Human Rights Council*, May 2, 2011, www2.ohchr.org/english/bodies/hrcouncil/docs/17session/A-HRC-17-26.pdf. Intersectionality Theory rejects the notion that issues surrounding discrimination should be categorized as singular issues. The theory requires individuals to view issues through a multidimensional lens, simultaneously taking into account gender, sex, race, and national origin. The U.N. began incorporating intersectional discrimination into resolutions and "acknowledged that discrimination is understood as having multiple forms that combine to heighten the vulnerability of some women and girls to violence." Education level, marital status, economic status, access to justice, race, religion, education level, social status, and sexual orientation present differences among women, and these differences will make some women more likely to be subjected to discrimination and/or violence.
129 R.W. Connell, *Masculinities*, 78 (stating, "Hegemony relates to cultural dominance in the society as a whole," and hegemonic masculinity involves the certain type of maleness that is "currently accepted" by society); *ibid.*, 77 (As R.W. Connell outlines, an example of hegemonic masculinity may be the corporate type of masculinity, which consists of high-level business or government officials, or it could be film actors, but it does not necessarily involve the men with the most power. The same principles are true when defining hegemonic femininity. Hegemonic masculinity and femininity influences how individuals are treated).
130 Megan Denise Smith, "Rethinking Gender in the International Refugee Regime," *Forced Migration Review* 53, (October 2016): 65, www.fmreview.org/community-protection/smith.html.
131 *Ibid.*, 65.
132 McKanders, "America's Disposable Youth: Undocumented Delinquent Juveniles," 212.
133 *Ibid.*, 66.
134 *Ibid.*

135 Leti Volpp, "Feminism versus Multiculturalism," *Columbia Law Review* 101, no. 5 (June, 2001): 1181–1218, 1195.
136 President Trump Exec. Order No. 13,769, 82 Fed. Reg. 8,977 (January 25, 2017), Protecting the Nation from Foreign Terrorist Entry into the United States.
137 *Ibid.*
138 Volpp, "The Citizen and the Terrorist," 1587.
139 *Ibid.*
140 *Ibid.*
141 *Ibid.*, 345.
142 Volpp, "Feminism versus Multiculturalism," 1198.
143 *Ibid.*, 1201.
144 Eric M. Blanchard, "Rethinking International Security: Masculinity in World Politics," *Brown Journal of World Affairs* 21, no. 1 (Fall/Winter 2014): 61 (footnote 59), www.questia.com/magazine/1P3-3594226401/rethinking-international-security-masculinity-in; Taylor Markey, "Westernized Women: The Construction of Muslim Women's Dissent in U.S. Asylum Law," *UCLA Law Review* 64 (2017): 1302, www.uclalawreview.org/wp-content/uploads/securepdfs/2017/09/Markey-Article-64-5.pdf (stating, "For example, in the post-9/11 context, the supposed oppression of women in Muslim society was invoked as a justification for U.S. military intervention in Afghanistan. As the U.S. invasion ramped up, media imagery of female Muslim victims of the Taliban did as well. Laura Bush claimed in her 2001 radio address to the nation that 'the fight against terrorism is also a fight for the rights and dignity of women.' Her husband also expressed this sentiment, urging the United States to stay in Afghanistan after his presidency ended because he felt that the country could not 'stand by and watch women's rights be abused'").
145 Blanchard, "Rethinking International Security," 61 (footnote 59); Markey, "Westernized Women?" 1302.
146 Richard Howson, "Re-Thinking Aspiration and Hegemonic Masculinity in Transnational Context," *Masculinities and Social Change* 3, no. 1 (February 2014): 20–21, http://ro.uow.edu.au/lhapapers/1346/.
147 Jamie R. Abrams, "Enforcing Masculinities at the Borders," *Nevada Law Journal* 13 (Winter 2013): 564, 565, http://scholars.law.unlv.edu/cgi/viewcontent.cgi?article=1474&context=nlj.
148 Silas W. Allard, "Reimagining Asylum," 122–123 (emphasis added).
149 R. Charli Carpenter, "Recognizing Gender-Based Violence Against Civilian Men and Boys in Conflict Situations," *Security Dialogue* 37, no. 1 (March 2006): 83, http://journals.sagepub.com/doi/abs/10.1177/0967010606064139.
150 *Ibid.*, 83–84.
151 *Ibid.*, 84 ("Men are more vulnerable to getting killed. That's a pretty big deal. Getting sick, getting raped, getting attacked are all pretty bad things but dead is dead and they are much more vulnerable to getting killed than women," Program Officer, U.S. Office of Disaster Assistance, July 2002).
152 *Ibid.*, 88, citing Charlotte Lindsey, *Women Facing War* (Geneva: International Committee of the Red Cross, 2001); "Human Security Report 2005," *Liu Institute for Global Issues*, October 17, 2005, https://liu.arts.ubc.ca/research/2005-human-security-report-war-peace-21st-century/; Inter-Agency Standing Committee, "Policy Statement for the Integration of a Gender Perspective in Humanitarian Assistance," May 31, 1999, https://interagencystandingcommittee.org/gender-and-humanitarian-action-0/documents-public/policy-statement-integration-gender-perspective.
153 Carpenter, "Recognizing Gender-Based Violence," 98.
154 Kimberlé W. Crenshaw, "Mapping the Margins: Intersectionality, Identity Politics, and Violence against Women of Color," *Stanford Law Review* 43, (1991): 1241.
155 Ahmad, "Homeland Insecurities," 345.

156 Saher Selod. "Citizenship Denied: The Racialization of Muslim American Men and Women Post-9/11," *Critical Sociology* (2014): 8.
157 Eren Arruna Cervantes, "Mothers, Brainwashed Wives and Tomboys: Muslim Women in Armed Conflict," Muslimah Media Watch, June 27, 2013, www.patheos.com/blogs/mmw/2013/06/mothers-brainwashed-wives-and-tomboys-muslim-women-in-armed-conflict/.
158 *Ibid.*
159 Carpenter, "Recognizing Gender-Based Violence," 85.
160 Sahar F. Aziz, "Sticks and Stones, the Words That Hurt: Entrenched Stereotypes Eight Years After 9/11," *New York City Law Review* 13, no. 33 (2009): 33, https://scholarship.law.tamu.edu/cgi/viewcontent.cgi?article=1187&context=facscholar (stating, "In the case of Muslims, Arabs, and South Asians, the September 11, 2001 terrorist attacks not only caused an upsurge in hatred, violence, and discrimination, but also entrenched preexisting negative stereotypes").
161 Sahar F. Aziz, "From the Oppressed to the Terrorist: Muslim-American Women in the Crosshairs of Intersectionality," *Hastings Race & Poverty Law Journal* 9 (2012): 194–195, https://scholarship.law.tamu.edu/cgi/viewcontent.cgi?referer=https://www.google.com/&httpsredir=1&article=1099&context=facscholar.
162 Muneer Ahmad, "Homeland Insecurities: Racial Violence the Day after September 11," *Race/Ethnicity: Multidisciplinary Global Contexts* 4, no. 3 (Summer 2011): 340–341, www.jstor.org/stable/10.2979/racethmulglocon.4.3.337 (stating, "non-Arabs such as Indians, Pakistanis, and other South Asians have been affected [by September 11th], as have non-Muslims such as Indian Sikhs and Hindus and Arab Christians. [...] This violence depends on a fungibility of 'Middle Eastern–looking' or 'Muslim-looking' people with the individuals who committed the September 11 attacks and leaves Arabs, Muslims, and South Asians enormously vulnerable").
163 Infra page 25—*Section on Convention's Exclusion Provisions*; see generally, Monette Zard, "Exclusion, Terrorism and the Refugee Convention," 32 (stating, "In the aftermath of 11 September, this trend (bypassing status determination once exclusion is alleged) is likely to intensify").
164 *Ibid.*, 32.
165 *Ibid.*
166 Brad Blitz, "Another Story: What Public Opinion Data Tell Us about Refugee and Humanitarian Policy," *Journal on Migration and Human Security* 5, no. 2 (2017): 381, https://doi.org/10.14240/jmhs.v5i2.89.
167 Volpp, "The Citizen and the Terrorist," 1582.
168 *Ibid.*, 385.
169 Daniel Byman et al., "Be Afraid. Be A Little Afraid: The Threat of Terrorism from Western Foreign Fighters in Syria and Iraq," *Brookings Institute*, November 2014, www.brookings.edu/wp-content/uploads/2016/06/Be-Afraid-web.pdf (citing Sari Horowitz and Adam Goldman, "FBI Director: Number of Americans Traveling to Fight in Syria Increasing," *Washington Post*, May 2, 2014, www.washingtonpost.com/world/national-security/fbi-director-number-of-americans-traveling-to-fight-in-syriaincreasing/2014/05/02/6fa3d84e-d222-11e3-937f-d3026234b51c_story.html.).
170 Volpp, "The Citizen and the Terrorist," 1585.
171 Alex Nowrasteh, "Guide to Trump's Executive Order to Limit Migration for 'National Security' Reasons," *Cato at Liberty*, January 26, 2017, www.cato.org/blog/guide-trumps-executive-order-limit-migration-national-security-reasons.
172 *Ibid.*
173 Marc Sageman, *Misunderstanding Terrorism* (Philadelphia: University of Pennsylvania Press, 2017): 32–33.

174 *Ibid.*, 57.
175 Karl Vick, "The Syrian Refugee Crisis Shows Far More Young People Want to Flee War than Fight It," *Time*, September 22, 2015, http://time.com/4042813/syria-refugee-civil-war-isis/.
176 *Ibid.*
177 Valerie Hudson, "Europe's Man Problem," *Politico*, January 5, 2016, www.politico.com/magazine/story/2016/01/europe-refugees-migrant-crisis-men-213500.
178 Faloyin, "Canada Will Welcome 25,000 Refugees, but No Single Straight Men."
179 Megan Gaucher and Alexa DeGagne, "Guilty until Proven Prosecuted: The Canadian State's Assessment of Sexual Minority Refugee Claimants and the Invisibility of the non-Western Sexual Non-Citizen," *Social Politics: International Studies in Gender, State and Society* 23, no. 3 (Fall 2016): 459.
180 *Ibid.*, 462.
181 President Trump Exec. Order No. 13,769, 82 Fed. Reg. 8,977 (January 25, 2017), Protecting the Nation from Foreign Terrorist Entry into the United States.
182 Jasbir K. Puar, Terrorist Assemblages: Homonationalism in Queer Times, Duke University Press, December 2017. *See also*, Gaucher, "Guilty until Proven Prosecuted," 459 (explaining homonationalism's applicability to the resettlement of Canadian refugees who are sexual minorities).
183 Puar, "Terrorist Assemblages," 38–39.
184 Gaucher, "Guilty Until Proven Prosecuted," 463.
185 *Ibid.*, 463–464.
186 *Ibid.*, 462.
187 *Ibid.*
188 *Ibid.*
189 Turner, "Who will Resettle Single Syrian Men?" 29.
190 James C. Hathaway et al., "Making International Refugee Law Relevant Again: A Proposal for Collectivized and Solution-Oriented Protection," *Harvard Human Rights Journal* 10 (1997): 117, https://repository.law.umich.edu/cgi/viewcontent.cgi?referer=https://www.google.com/&httpsredir=1&article=2621&context=articles ("We can no longer insist on either the routine, permanent integration of all refugees, nor expect all governments, whatever their circumstances, simply to receive and provide quality protection to all refugees who arrive at their territory").
191 Volpp, "The Citizen and the Terrorist," 1595.
192 Zard, "Exclusion, Terrorism and the Refugee Convention," 32.
193 Refugee Convention, Article 33(1).
194 *Ibid.*, Article 3.

Bibliography

Abou-El-Wafa, Ahmed. "The Right to Asylum between Islamic Shari'ah and International Refugee Law: A Comparative Study." UNHCR, 2009. www.unhcr.org/4a9645646.pdf.

Abrams, Jamie R. "Enforcing Masculinities at the Borders." *Nevada Law Journal* 13 (Winter 2013): 564–584. http://scholars.law.unlv.edu/cgi/viewcontent.cgi?article=1474&context=nlj.

Admirand, Peter. "The Ethics of Displacement and Migration in the Abrahamic Faiths: Enlightening Believers and Aiding Public Policy." *Journal of Ethnic and Migration Studies* 40, no. 4 (2014): 671–687. https://doi.org/10.1080/1369183X.2013.847360.

Ahmad, Muneer. "Homeland Insecurities: Racial Violence the Day after September 11." *Race/Ethnicity: Multidisciplinary Global Contexts* 4, no. 3 (Summer 2011): 337–350. www.jstor.org/stable/10.2979/racethmulglocon.4.3.337.

Allard, Silas W. "Reimagining Asylum: Religious Narratives and Moral Obligations to the Asylum Seeker." *Refuge* 29, no. 1 (2013): 122–129. https://refuge.journals.yorku.ca/index.php/refuge/article/view/37521.

Aziz, Sahar F. "From the Oppressed to the Terrorist: Muslim-American Women in the Crosshairs of Intersectionality." *Hastings Race & Poverty Law Journal* 9 (Summer 2012): 191–264. https://scholarship.law.tamu.edu/cgi/viewcontent.cgi?referer=https://www.google.com/&httpsredir=1&article=1099&context=facscholar.

———. "Sticks and Stones, the Words That Hurt: Entrenched Stereotypes Eight Years After 9/11." *New York City Law Review* 13, no. 33 (2009): 33–72. https://scholarship.law.tamu.edu/cgi/viewcontent.cgi?article=1187&context=facscholar.

Barnett, Laura. "Global Governance and the Evolution of the International Refugee Regime." *International Journal of Refugee Law* 14, no. 2 (April 2002): 238–262. https://doi.org/10.1093/ijrl/14.2_and_3.238.

Barutckski, Michael, and Astri Suhrke. "Lessons from Kosovo Refugee Crisis: Innovations in Protection and Burden-sharing." *Journal of Refugee Studies* 14, no. 2 (2001): 96–111.

Blanchard, Eric M. "Rethinking International Security: Masculinity in World Politics." *Brown Journal of World Affairs* 21, no. 1 (Fall/Winter 2014): 61–79. www.questia.com/magazine/1P3-3594226401/rethinking-international-security-masculinity-in.

Blitz, Brad. "Another Story: What Public Opinion Data Tell Us About Refugee and Humanitarian Policy." *Journal on Migration and Human Security* 5, no. 2 (2017): 379–400. https://doi.org/10.14240/jmhs.v5i2.89.

Bruno, Andorra. "Syrian Refugee Admissions and Resettlement in the United States: In Brief." *Congressional Research Service*, September 16, 2016. https://fas.org/sgp/crs/homesec/R44277.pdf.

Byman, Daniel, and Jeremy Shapiro. "Be Afraid. Be A Little Afraid: The Threat of Terrorism from Western Foreign Fighters in Syria and Iraq." Brookings Institute, November 2014. www.brookings.edu/wp-content/uploads/2016/06/Be-Afraid-web.pdf.

"Canada Denies Alan Kurdi's Family Applied for Asylum." *BBC News*, September 3, 2015. www.bbc.com/news/world-us-canada-34142695.

"Canada to Turn Away Single Men as Part of Syrian Refugee Resettlement Plan." *The Guardian*, November 23, 2015. www.theguardian.com/world/2015/nov/23/canada-syrian-refugee-resettlement-plan-no-single-men.

Carpenter, R. Charli. "Recognizing Gender-Based Violence against Civilian Men and Boys in Conflict Situations." *Security Dialogue* 37, no. 1 (March 2006): 83–103. http://journals.sagepub.com/doi/abs/10.1177/0967010606064139.

Cervantes, Eren Arruna. "Mothers, Brainwashed Wives and Tomboys: Muslim Women in Armed Conflict." Muslimah Media Watch, June 27, 2013. www.patheos.com/blogs/mmw/2013/06/mothers-brainwashed-wives-and-tomboys-muslim-women-in-armed-conflict/.

Chappellet-Lanier, Tajha. "What's Next for Migrants After Paris?" *The Atlantic*, November 14, 2015. www.theatlantic.com/international/archive/2015/11/migrant-crisis-paris-attacks/416067/.

Connell, Raewyn W. *Masculinities*. Berkeley: University of California Press, 1995.

The Convention Relating to the Status of Refugees. July 28, 1951. 189 U.N.T.S. 2545.

Crenshaw, Kimberle W. "Mapping the Margins: Intersectionality, Identity Politics, and Violence against Women of Color." *Stanford Law Review* 43 (1991): 1241.

Diamond, Jeremy. "Donald Trump: Ban all Muslim Travel to U.S." *CNN*, December 8, 2015. www.cnn.com/2015/12/07/politics/donald-trump-muslim-ban-immigration/index.html.

Dockery, Wesley. "Two Years Since Germany Opened Its Borders to Refugees: A Chronology." *Deutsche Welle*, April 9, 2017. http://dw.com/en/two-years-since-germany-opened-its-borders-to-refugees-a-chronology/a-40327634.

Faloyin, Dipo. "Canada Will Welcome 25,000 Refugees, but No Single Straight Men." *Newsweek*, November 14, 2015. www.newsweek.com/canada-will-welcome-25000-refugees-no-single-straight-men-398045.

Fantz, Ashley, and Ben Brumfield. "More Than Half the Nation's Governors Say Syrian Refugees Not Welcome." *CNN*, November 19, 2015. http://edition.cnn.com/2015/11/16/world/paris-attacks-syrian-refugees-backlash/.

Freedman, Jane. *Gendering the International Asylum and Refugee Debate*. Second Edition. London: Palgrave Macmillan, 2015.

Freison, Joe. "Syrian Exodus to Canada: One Year Later, a Look at Who the Refugees Are and Where They Went." *The Globe and Mail*, December 1, 2016. www.theglobeandmail.com/news/national/syrian-refugees-in-canada-by-the-numbers/article33120934/.

Gaucher, Megan, and Alexa DeGagne. "Guilty until Proven Prosecuted: The Canadian State's Assessment of Sexual Minority Refugee Claimants and the Invisibility of the non-Western Sexual Non-Citizen." *Social Politics: International Studies in Gender, State and Society* 23, no. 3 (Fall 2016): 459–481.

Goldenziel, Jill I. "The Curse of the Nation-State: Refugees, Migration, and Security in International Law." *Arizona State Law Journal* 48 (2016): 579–636. https://ssrn.com/abstract=2684903.

Gomez, Valeria, and Karla Mari McKanders. "Refugee Reception and Perception: U.S. Detention Camps and German Welcome Centers." *Fordham International Law Journal* 40, no. 2 (2017): 523–560.

Government of Canada. "Admissions of Syrian Refugees by Province/Territory of Intended Destination, Family Status and Immigration Category." Accessed March 13, 2018. http://open.canada.ca/data/en/dataset/01c85d28-2a81-4295-9c06-4af792a7c209?_ga=2.89053395.995677009.1494444890-1096638679.1492789911.

———. "Resettled Refugees—Monthly IRCC Updates." Accessed March 13, 2018. http://open.canada.ca/data/en/dataset/4a1b260a-7ac4-4985-80a0-603bfe4aec11?_ga=2.187603808.995677009.1494444890-1096638679.1492789911.

Goyette, Jared. "It's Now Clear that Most of the Syrian Refugees Coming to the United States are Women and Children." *Public Radio International*, August 8, 2016. www.pri.org/stories/2016-08-08/it-s-now-clear-most-syrian-refugees-coming-united-states-are-women-and-children.

Greussing, Esther, and Hajo G. Boomgaarden. "Shifting the Refugee Narrative? An Automated Frame Analysis of Europe's 2015 Refugee Crisis." *Journal of Ethnic and Migration Studies* 43, no. 11 (2017): 1749–1774. https://doi.org/10.1080/1369183X.2017.1282813.

Grote, Janne, Maria Bitterwolf, and Tatjana Baraulina. "Resettlement and Humanitarian Admission Programmes in Germany: Focus-Study by the German National Contact Point for the European Migration Network (EMN)." *Federal Office for Migration and Refugees*. October 10, 2016. www.bamf.de/SharedDocs/Anlagen/EN/Publikationen/EMN/Studien/wp68-emn-resettlement-humanitaere-aufnahme.pdf?__blob=publicationFile.

Hathaway, James C. "A Reconsideration of the Underlying Premise of Refugee Law." *Harvard International Law Journal* 31, no. 1 (Winter 1990): 129–184. www.taylorfrancis.com/books/9781351562218/chapters/10.4324%2F9781315092478-12.

———. "The Evolution of Refugee Status in International Law: 1920–1950." *The International and Comparative Quarterly* 33, no. 2 (April 1984): 348–380. www.jstor.org/stable/759064.

———. "The Michigan Guidelines on the Exclusion of International Criminals." *Michigan Journal of International Law* 35, no. 1 (Fall 2013): 3–13. https://repository.law.umich.edu/cgi/viewcontent.cgi?referer=https://www.google.com/&httpsredir=1&article=1024&context=mjil.

Hathaway, James C., and R. Alexander Neve. "Making International Refugee Law Relevant Again: A Proposal for Collectivized and Solution-Oriented Protection." *Harvard Human Rights Journal* 10 (1997): 115–211. https://repository.law.umich.edu/cgi/viewcontent.cgi?referer=https://www.google.com/&httpsredir=1&article=2621&context=articles.

Horowitz, Sari, and Adam Goldman. "FBI Director: Number of Americans Traveling to Fight in Syria Increasing." *Washington Post*, May 2, 2014. www.washingtonpost.com/world/national-security/fbi-director-number-of-americans-traveling-to-fight-in-syria increasing/2014/05/02/6fa3d84e-d222-11e3-937f-d3026234b51c_story.html.

Howson, Richard. "Re-Thinking Aspiration and Hegemonic Masculinity in Transnational Context." *Masculinities and Social Change* 3, no. 1 (February 2014): 18–35. http://ro.uow.edu.au/lhapapers/1346/.

Hudson, Valerie. "Europe's Man Problem." *Politico*, January 5, 2016. www.politico.com/magazine/story/2016/01/europe-refugees-migrant-crisis-men-213500.

"Human Security Report 2005." *Liu Institute for Global Issues*, October 17, 2005. https://liu.arts.ubc.ca/research/2005-human-security-report-war-peace-21st-century/.

Inter-Agency Standing Committee. "Policy Statement for the Integration of a Gender Perspective in Humanitarian Assistance." May 31, 1999. https://interagency standingcommittee.org/gender-and-humanitarian-action-0/documents-public/policy-statement-integration-gender-perspective.

International Covenant on Civil and Political Rights. Dec. 16, 1966. 999 U.N.T.S. 171.

Lindsey, Charlotte. *Women Facing War*. Geneva: International Committee of the Red Cross, 2001.

Manjoo, Rashida. "Report of the Special Rapporteur on Violence against Women, Its Causes and Consequences." *United Nations General Assembly Human Rights Council*, May 2, 2011. www2.ohchr.org/english/bodies/hrcouncil/docs/17session/A-HRC-17-26.pdf.

Markey, Taylor. "Westernized Women: The Construction of Muslim Women's Dissent in U.S. Asylum Law." *UCLA Law Review* 64 (2017): 1302–1327. www.uclalawreview.org/wp-content/uploads/securepdfs/2017/09/Markey-Article-64-5.pdf.

McKanders, Karla. "America's Disposable Youth: Undocumented Delinquent Juveniles." *Howard Law Journal* 59, no. 1 (2015): 201–224. http://dx.doi.org/10.2139/ssrn.2725561.

———. "The Subnational Response: Local Intervention in Immigration Policy and Enforcement." *Compassionate Migration and Regional Policy in the Americas*, edited by Steven W. Bender and William F. Arrocha. London: Palgrave Macmillan, 2017. https://doi.org/10.1057/978-1-137-55074-3_4.

Musalo, Karen, Jennifer Moore, and Richard A. Boswell. *Refugee Law and Policy: A Comparative and International Approach*. Fourth Edition. North Carolina: Carolina Academic Press, 2011.

Nowrasteh, Alex. "Guide to Trump's Executive Order to Limit Migration for 'National Security' Reasons." *Cato at Liberty*, January 26, 2017. www.cato.org/blog/guide-trumps-executive-order-limit-migration-national-security-reasons.

Obama White House. "Statement by National Security Advisor Susan E. Rice on Syrian Refugee Admissions." Office of the Press Secretary. August 29, 2016. https://obamawhitehouse.archives.gov/the-press-office/2016/08/29/statement-national-security-advisor-susan-e-rice-syrian-refugee.

President Trump Exec. Order No. 13,769, 82 Fed. Reg. 8,977 (January 25, 2017), Border Security and Immigration Enforcement Improvements.

———. No. 13,769, 82 Fed. Reg. 8,977 (January 27, 2017), Protecting the Nation from Foreign Terrorist Entry into the United States.

———. No. 13,780, 82 Fed. Reg. 13,209 (March 6, 2017), Protecting the Nation from Foreign Terrorist Entry into the United States.

Puar, Jasbir K. *Terrorist Assemblages: Homonationalism in Queer Times*. Durham, NC: Duke University Press, December 2017. Razack, Sherene H. Casting Out: *The Eviction of Muslims from Western Law & Politics*. Toronto: University of Toronto Press. 2008.

Refugee Processing Center. "Demographical Profile of Refugee Arrivals Fiscal Year Syria as of 31-December 2016." http://ireports.wrapsnet.org/InteractiveReporting/EnumType/Report?ItemPath=/rpt_WebArrivalsReports/MX%20-%20Arrivals%20for%20a%20Demographic%20Profile.

Rhodan, Maya. "Are the Syrian Refugees All 'Young, Strong, Men'?" *Time*, November 20, 2015. http://time.com/4122186/syrian-refugees-donald-trump-young-men/.

Rich, Anna-Katharina. "First-time Asylum Applicants in Germany in 2015: Social Structure, Level of Qualifications and Employment, 3rd ed." *Federal Office for Migration and Refugees*, May 2016. www.bamf.de/SharedDocs/Anlagen/EN/Publikationen/Kurzanalysen/kurzanalyse3_sozial-komponenten.pdf?__blob=publicationFile.

Richard, Anne C., Leon Rodriguez, and Robert Carey. "Transcript of USCIS-DOS-HHS Press Call on Syrian Refugee Processing [Moderated by Shin Inouye]." *U.S. Citizenship and Immigration Services*, August 5, 2016. www.uscis.gov/news/news-releases/transcript-uscis-dos-hhs-press-call-syrian-refugee-processing.

Rodgers, Lucy, David Gritten, James Offer, and Patrick Asare. "Syria: The Story of the Conflict." *BBC News*, March 11, 2016. www.bbc.com/news/world-middle-east-26116868.

Sageman, Marc. *Misunderstanding Terrorism*. Philadelphia: University of Pennsylvania Press, 2017.

Schoenholtz, Andrew. "The New Refugees and the Old Treaty: Persecutors and Persecuted in the Twenty First Century." *Chicago International Law Journal* 16 (Summer 2015): 81–126.

Selod, Saher. "Citizenship Denied: The Racialization of Muslim American Men and Women Post-9/11." *Critical Sociology* (2014): 8.

Smith, Megan Denise. "Rethinking Gender in the International Refugee Regime." *Forced Migration Review* 53 (October 2016): 65–66. www.fmreview.org/community-protection/smith.html.

Texas Health & Human Servs. Comm'n v. United States, 166 F. Supp. 3d 706 (N.D. Tex. 2016).

Trump v. Hawaii, No. 17-965, 2018 WL 3116337 (U.S. June 26, 2018).

Turner, Lewis. "Who Will Resettle Single Syrian Men?" *Forced Migration Review* 54 (February 2017): 29–31. www.fmreview.org/sites/fmr/files/FMRdownloads/en/resettlement/turner.pdf.

United Nations High Commissioner for Refugees. "Canada." In *UNHCR Resettlement Handbook*. Last modified October 2016. www.unhcr.org/3c5e55594.html.

———. Chart on Refugee Resettlement Tools, March. Accessed May 16, 2018. www.unhcr.org/en-us/resettlement-data.html.

———. "Figures at a Glance." Accessed March 13, 2018. www.unhcr.org/en-us/figures-at-a-glance.html.

———. "Germany." In *UNHCR Resettlement Handbook*. Last modified April 2016. www.unhcr.org/5162b3bc9.html.

———. "Global Trends Forced Displacement in 2015." Accessed March 13, 2018. www.unhcr.org/576408cd7.pdf.

———. "Guidelines on International Protection: Application of the Exclusion Clauses: Article 1F of the 1951 Convention Relating to the Status of Refugees." Published September 4, 2003. www.refworld.org/pdfid/3f5857684.pdf.

———. "Islam and Refugees." Published December 13, 2012. www.unhcr.org/50ab90399.pdf.

———. "Resettlement Data." Accessed March 13, 2018. www.unhcr.org/en-us/resettlement-data.html.

———. "Resettlement Data Finder: Syria." Accessed March 13, 2018. http://rsq.unhcr.org/en/#zeF0.

———. "Resettlement. Solutions." Accessed March 13, 2018. www.unhcr.org/en-us/resettlement.html.

———. "UNHCR Resettlement Submission Categories." In *Resettlement Handbook and Country Chapters*, December 2016. www.unhcr.org/en-us/protection/resettlement/4a2ccf4c6/unhcr-resettlement-handbook-country-chapters.html.

United States of America, Immigration and Nationality Act, 8 United States Code § 1157 (2018).

U.S. Citizenship and Immigration Services. "The United States Refugee Admissions Program (USRAP) Consultation & Worldwide Processing Priorities." Last modified May 5, 2016. www.uscis.gov/humanitarian/refugees-asylum/refugees/united-states-refugee-admissions-program-usrap-consultation-worldwide-processing-priorities.

U.S. Department of State. "Addressing Gender-Based Violence in Emergencies." Accessed March 13, 2018. www.state.gov/j/prm/policyissues/issues/c62377.htm.

Vick, Karl. "The Syrian Refugee Crisis Shows Far More Young People Want to Flee War Than Fight It." *Time*, September 22, 2015. http://time.com/4042813/syria-refugee-civil-war-isis/.

Volpp, Leti. "Feminism versus Multiculturalism." *Columbia Law Review* 101, no. 5 (June 2001): 1181–1218.

———. "The Citizen and the Terrorist." *UCLA LAW REVIEW* 49, (2002): 1575–1600.

Weis, Paul. "The Development of Refugee Law." *Michigan Yearbook of International Legal Studies* 3, no. 1 (1982): 27–42. https://repository.law.umich.edu/cgi/viewcontent.cgi?article=1860&context=mjil.

Welle, Deutsche. Angela Merkel knew of problems at BAMF refugee agency: report, June 3, 2018. Accessed June 6, 2018. www.dw.com/en/angela-merkel-knew-of-problems-at-bamf-refugee-agency-report/a-44057515.

White House. "Presidential Proclamation Enhancing Vetting Capabilities and Processes for Detecting Attempted Entry Into the United States by Terrorists or Other Public-Safety Threats." *National Security and Defense*, September 24, 2017. www.whitehouse.gov/presidential-actions/presidential-proclamation-enhancing-vetting-capabilities-processes-detecting-attempted-entry-united-states-terrorists-public-safety-threats/.

Zard, Monette. "Exclusion, Terrorism and the Refugee Convention." *Forced Migration Review* 13 (2002): 32–34. www.fmreview.org/sites/fmr/files/FMRdownloads/en/FMRpdfs/FMR13/fmr13.11.pdf.

Zong, Jie, and Jeanne Batalova. "Syrian Refugees in the United States." *Migration Policy Institute*, January 12, 2017. www.migrationpolicy.org/article/syrian-refugees-united-states.

7 Moroccan women migrants in Europe

A transformative experience

Moha Ennaji

Introduction

Moroccan women migrants fight with all their energy in Morocco and in Europe and manage to introduce considerable changes in traditional society; they blow up the harem metaphor and what the negative aspects it entails such as resignation, servility, and fatality. The story of Moroccan women and migration is an interesting one. Today, for many Moroccan women in Europe, migration is a transformative experience. Once they have discovered a new degree of freedom, they refuse to return to the restrictive social environment of their native land.[1] In Europe, their participation in economic development is remarkable and has an impact on family relations and gender roles. It contributes to their emancipation, empowerment, and to the rupture of traditional gender relations in the family structure. When Moroccan Muslim women migrants participate in public life and in economic and social development, they transgress and subvert gender roles.

In the 1960s, Moroccan women rarely participated in migration; today, they constitute a large component of Moroccans living in Europe, North America, and the Arab Gulf (illegal migration notwithstanding, which is also becoming increasingly feminine). In statistical terms, of the more than three million Moroccan migrants in Europe, 900,000 (37%) are women.[2]

Migration is currently affected by the complexities of globalization, global ideologies, international feminism, education, employment, and women's rights. The traditional pattern of migration from Morocco to Europe, which was once male dominated, short term, and short distance, is increasingly becoming feminized, younger, long term and long distance. Migration is not only feminized but young. Seventy percent of the Moroccan community abroad is less than forty-five years old.[3]

In addition to the fact that women actively participate in migration as a family survival strategy, more and more professional women migrate independently in search of paid work to fulfill their own economic needs and not to simply join a husband or other family members. Many women are taking advantage of better pay packages in Europe and North America to accumulate enough savings to survive harsh economic conditions at home.

Morocco is indeed experiencing a substantial gendered "brain drain," which was previously underestimated in official migration statistics. Yet, there is uncertainty regarding why some women leave while others stay, whether people who leave do so permanently, and whether the brain drain will accelerate in the future.[4]

This chapter examines the transformative impact of Moroccan women's migration to Europe. It is based on the fieldwork I undertook between September 2008 and December 2013 to elicit the attitudes and achievements of Moroccan migrants in Europe.[5] The analysis of my study aims to fill the gap in literature regarding numerous questions relating to Moroccan women's status, contributions, and challenges, all of which deserve more research and more attention from migration policymakers and civil society.

During my study, I conducted interviews with forty-seven female participants who were students, salaried or independent workers, entrepreneurs, members of associations, unemployed, homemakers, and mothers of first- and second-generation immigrants; their ages varied between seventeen and seventy-six. Although many of these interviews were face-to-face, some were conducted over the telephone. I also used both casual and arranged conversations to elicit respondents' attitudes and ideas about migration. Several first-, second-, and third-generation individuals were interviewed both in their host countries and in Morocco during the summer holidays. My goal was to have a group of respondents who were representative of Moroccan migrants abroad. Other data were collected through readings of the literature on migration, documentary research, official statistics, mass media products, diaries, letters, and government reports, in addition to historical and contemporary records.

This chapter proceeds in three sections. Section "Understanding and analyzing root causes of Moroccan women's migration to Europe" describes the history and demographics of Moroccan women's migration to Europe. Section "Migration as a transformative experience for women" analyzes the results of the interviews, which determined that because Moroccan women migrants are considered less threatening than individuals from other Muslim countries, they are regarded as responsible, peaceful, and hardworking. This has changed the overall image of the Muslim woman, and of the Moroccan woman in particular, who was previously considered passive and submissive.[6] Entrepreneurship has allowed Moroccan women to "get rid of the old mentality of the Harem and has opened all doors for women to be creative, innovative, and productive."[7] Section "Gender, intersectionality, and migration" relies on the theoretical framework of intersectionality theory, which underscores the interconnection of fields of domination, such as social class, political power, gender, religion, language, ethnicity, education, and media, in order to understand the results of the fieldwork.[8] Following the work of sociologists Drs. Collins, Crenshaw, and Belleau, who demonstrate the intersectionality of ethnicity and gender, I argue that Moroccan women in Europe defy multifaceted discrimination as North Africans, as Muslims, as migrants, and as women. In this section, I compare the case of Moroccan migrant women to African and African-American women in the United States, who suffer from similar forms of oppression and are caught between their identity as women belonging to a minority group. The chapter concludes that women's emancipation through migration has undermined existing patriarchal authority that has subjugated women and confined them to domestic work. Migration for women represents a new type of feminism, which contributes to the subversion of old gender roles, gender equity, the culture of sharing and dialogue, and social development.

Understanding and analyzing root causes of Moroccan women's migration to Europe

History of Moroccan women's migration to Europe

There are three distinguishable phases in the history of Moroccan women's migration to Europe. The first occurred in the 1970s, within the context of family reunification; the second phase (the 1980s–1990s) occurred within the framework of family formation; and the third phase (the 2000s) is characterized by the feminization of migration.[9]

In the 1970s, more than 300,000 Moroccan workers left for European countries, particularly France, followed by Belgium, the Netherlands, and Germany. France created "l'Office National d'Immigration Français," (National Office of French Immigration) which operated in Casablanca until 1974. Belgium had representatives of "la Fédération des Charbonnages Belges" (The Federation of Belgium Carbon), and the Netherlands had offices of recruitment of immigrants until 1973. In 1973, the Moroccan migrant population in Europe totaled half a million people.[10]

It was assumed by the host countries' decision makers that the immigrant workers would return to their home country once they were no longer needed. However, most of them ended up settling in Europe and subsequently brought their families. According to sociologist Dr. El Manar Laalami, by the year 1999, about 1.2 million Moroccans had legal residence in one of the fifteen countries of the European Union (EU).[11]

From 1980 to 1990, successive droughts in Morocco led to crises in the agriculture and trade sectors, which created more unemployment among women—educated and noneducated alike. During the drought, wheat and barley production was at its lowest level in a decade. Dry weather across the country became yet another financial headache for Morocco, just as it sought to spur more economic growth and cut public spending. Soon after, rising food import costs came at a delicate time, as Morocco faced protests over austerity measures.[12]

Drought has a huge impact across the region because it weakens the trade balance and staunches efforts to overhaul the agriculture sector. Drought has become a structural problem that requires a long-term policy to ensure stable growth regardless of the state of the harvest, which has a negative impact on women's farming activities, income, and health. Female and male labor migration often increases during drought seasons, which can lead to permanent migration.[13] During droughts, however, women are more vulnerable than men.

For example, during droughts, there are documented increases in prostitution in urban areas, forced marriages, and increases in women's general workload.[14] Droughts have a significant impact on securing household water, food, and fuel—activities that are usually the responsibility of women and girls. In times of drought and erratic rainfall, women and girls must walk farther and spend more of their time collecting water and fuel. Girls must often drop out of school to help their mothers. Even the act of securing food for the family can turn deadly. For example, due to fear of a looming drought, on November 19, 2017, fifteen women were killed and at least forty more were injured in a stampede during a charity food distribution in Sidi Boulaalam, a village southwest of Casablanca.[15] Likewise, the liberalization of the economy and privatization pushed many women to seek work in the agriculture, textile, and trade sectors.

During the early 2000s, however, the Gulf War negatively affected the Moroccan economy with the rise of oil prices and the global financial crisis. For example, according to the Moroccan High Commission for Statistics, 33.2% of women between ages fifteen and twenty-four were unemployed in 2009. Today, women suffer more than men from unemployment in Morocco—regardless of their degrees—because of gender discrimination.[16] This shift has pushed women to migrate in order to alleviate financial hardships. As a result, the number of Moroccan women in Europe has been increasing for the past two decades. Female migration from Morocco to Europe is both economically motivated (25%) and related to family reunification or family formation (75%).[17] All of these factors: drought, the Gulf War, and women's increased vulnerability during crisis contribute to why women migrate.

Since the 2000s, more and more women have migrated as economically autonomous individuals—that is, independent from male migrants. This new generation of female migrants are young and work in various economic fields. They are a part of the third phase of migration, which is characterized by the feminization of migration. Family reunification is considered the main reason for their mobility, but what has come to be termed "the feminization" of the labor market has also accelerated the rate of female migrants for economic reasons. For a long time, female migration has been considered a mere consequence of male migration, mainly because of family reunification, which began in the seventies and caused subsequent family formation outside Morocco. However, today, it constitutes an independent phenomenon with its own specificities and issues.[18]

The demographics of Moroccan migrant women

Moroccan migrant women are not a homogeneous group. There is wide variation among their circumstances and living conditions across many different European countries. Migrant Moroccan women have their own economic, political, cultural, and legal specificities. They may be single, married, divorced, or widows. They may be housewives, mothers, students, workers, career women, unemployed, or businesswomen. They may also be highly educated; semi-educated; illiterate; from working-, middle-, or upper-class families; and monolingual, bilingual, or multilingual. They may have rural or urban roots. They are Arab, Berber, Muslim, Jewish, Christian, and secular. They may have dual citizenship, permanent residence, or visas.[19]

There are also two additional categories of women migrants. First, there are women of rural origin who have continued their traditional lifestyles—that is, they continue to work as housewives taking care of their households and children, while their husbands serve as the providers. The second category is that of women who work outside the home, either out of necessity or under the influence of the lifestyle in their host country.

Even so, a great number of these women are illiterate, or without any employment, especially women who migrated for family reunification. Educated women are usually younger second-generation migrants, individuals who have recently migrated, or those who have finished their studies abroad and have opted to stay in their host countries. They often come from modest social backgrounds.

Indeed, the integration of Moroccan migrant women in the job market depends on their status and qualifications. Migrant women with citizenship in their host countries fair better than those who are in irregular situations, and those with the highest degrees are in a much better position than those with poor credentials or no qualifications. Most female economic migrants are merely in search of stable jobs and decent lives. More than a third of them are university graduates who simply could not find jobs in Morocco.[20]

All these factors have contributed to the birth of a culture of migration which has become deeply rooted, even among school children. According to a survey of school children led by the Moroccan Association for Studies and Research on Migration (AMERM) in 1995,[21] young children were often favorable to migration, and 13% of young girls stated that they would migrate in the future if necessary.[22] Thus, it seems that there is a psychological tendency of young people to migrate outside Morocco, either legally or illegally.[23] Although less than 10% of women claimed that they had migrated to pursue their training and education, for the clear majority, migration was the only solution to flee poverty and to financially support an extended family left behind in Morocco.[24] In Morocco, women are usually vulnerable, as they suffer from a high rate of illiteracy—reaching 67.1% in rural areas according to the 2015 United Nations Children survey[25]—and are often unemployed at a 22.4% rate,[26] occupy low-skilled level jobs, and/or work numerous hours for little pay.[27] Their work is typically arduous, and they perform labor-intensive tasks. These jobs often provide few legal protections, which makes these women defenseless against unemployment and poverty.[28]

Migration as a transformative experience for women

Although some Moroccan migrant women still struggle to secure employment, ensure their financial independence, and integrate in European society, for many of them, migration is a transformative experience. Once they have discovered a new degree of freedom after migrating, they refuse to return to the restrictive social environment of their native land.[29]

When Moroccan women migrate, their participation in economic development is often remarkable and has an impact on family relations and gender roles. It contributes to their emancipation, empowerment, and to the transgression of the conservative image of women, thus rupturing traditional gender relations. Both women left behind by male migrants and women migrants themselves subvert gender roles because they participate in public life and in economic and social development.

Social norms affecting treatment of Moroccan migrant women

Many of the women I interviewed stated that migration was an opportunity for their self-development and emancipation, and most of them yearned to become more economically independent because they "felt subordinated and subjugated by their husbands and male relatives." For example, after moving to Europe a decade ago, Fayza[30] (a thirty-seven-year-old French teacher in Belgium) decided to divorce her Moroccan husband first and then sue him, because "he was a drunkard and violent."[31] She had been trained as a teacher in Morocco and taught French in a Rabat high school before migrating. In order to make ends meet in Belgium, she had to teach extra private lessons to educate her two sons, while spending the rest of her free time learning English.[32]

Interestingly, most of the women interviewees mentioned that they were less discriminated against than their migrant male counterparts. They felt that Europeans viewed their identity as women before identifying as Muslims or migrants. They associated this identification with the gallantry of European men. This perception is confirmed by sociologist Caitlin Killian, who explained, "This was particularly true of women who played the game, 'doing' gender according to French norms, and thus [getting] more aid from French people."[33] Another interviewee, Ghita, a forty-five-year-old pharmacist in France, explained that her primary association with her gender was also perhaps because women are considered less of a threat in the street, and they are seen as responsible, peaceful, and hardworking. According to Ghita, "French men in particular are more courteous with us than with North African men."[34]

Economic transformation

The integration of women in the job market has had positive effects on their families and households. For many migrant women, work enabled them to acquire a new status (as the breadwinner or the economic agent), which helped them to integrate into society and partake in active lives. This also led them to achieve independence and improved lifestyles. Salaried women, for instance, no longer depended on their husbands' income, and contributed to family budgets, savings, and the management of their own households.

In addition, women who are breadwinners make important decisions concerning their children's education and contribute to the growth of the family. It is actually the financial and economic needs of the household that push many

Moroccan husbands to allow their wives to work outside their homes, which is, for many of these men, a revolutionary step that leads to the relaxing of family and social constraints on women. This autonomous status is strong among career and entrepreneur women, as we shall see below.

Many migrant Moroccan women believe that work gives them economic independence and freedom, which reinforces their need for entrepreneurship. Migrant women recognize that there are imperative factors that control their economic freedom: they earn less, save less, and suffer more. Nevertheless, migrant women believe that their freedom is inextricably tied to their economic security and independence, which will significantly improve their chances of not becoming victims of gender-related violence in their homes, at work, and on the streets. Economic security refers to an assured and stable standard of living that provides individuals and families with the necessary level of resources to participate economically, politically, socially, culturally, and with dignity in their communities. The collective efforts of individuals, communities, businesses, and governments directed to women's economic independence and security can speed up the pace of gender equality.

Thus, entrepreneurship becomes the means through which Moroccan migrant women began to alleviate the difficult socioeconomic contexts in which they live. This is, in many ways, liberating and transformative. Some women have created their own businesses after long, unsuccessful job searches. For them, creating businesses allowed them to determine their own employment and be responsible, since running one's enterprise is not an easy task, and requires skills and hard work. It also requires the support of their families, which is crucial for entrepreneurial success. Saida, a thirty-nine-year-old young woman running her own restaurant in France, told me,

> Having my own business provides me with the opportunity to be free of constraints imposed by a boss or an administrator. I work for myself and my family, and I have created a few jobs, thus contributing to my self-development and to society.[35]

Numerous nongovernmental organizations (NGOs) and government organizations in Europe have put in place programs for training migrant women and others from diverse cultures and backgrounds to become successful entrepreneurs. Europe's Institute for Training and Research Development's (IFRED) entrepreneur program has trained and advised over 3,000 women migrants at different stages of their businesses.

From my study, it became evident that being female, migrant, and entrepreneur at the same time required three types of strategies to negotiate identities with different constituencies. One strategy is to mainly adhere to conventional images of femininity. A second one is to denounce femininity and/or ethnicity in situations, and the third is to resist the masculine connotation of entrepreneurship by disconnecting it from masculinity. This is crucial in Moroccan women's entrepreneurship which transforms gender roles and subverts traditional gender relations. In addition, migrant women entrepreneurs have expertise, strong social and cultural capital, and this can lead them to seek transnational entrepreneurship opportunities. An essential signal for the Moroccan government is to create favorable conditions in order to attract this profile of potential entrepreneurs and professionals. This kind of transnational activity is potentially good for Morocco but also for the host country and the social mobility of migrants is key for achieving a better society.

Most of the Moroccan migrant women's businesses are related to the service sector (hotels, restaurants, cafés, salons, shops, food stores, etc.). Indeed, most Moroccan women in Europe insist on rendering their migratory experience as part of the process of empowerment. Many women have opted for self-employment as a means of partaking in lucrative ethnic businesses in the fashion and food industries.[36] While others have even created small businesses in partnership with their husbands or relatives. Their entrepreneurial success has resulted in Moroccan migrant women investing in both Morocco and the host country. Their economic power has contributed to their ability to integrate into their host countries. For instance, in the Netherlands, 12% of the Moroccan entrepreneurs are female.[37] Moroccan entrepreneurial women represent 22% of Moroccan entrepreneurship in France.[38]

Likewise, in Belgium, Moroccan women migrants comprise a higher number of entrepreneurs in comparison to other migrant communities. Approximately 9% of Moroccan women in Belgium are entrepreneurs or independent workers.[39] In Spain, self-employed women represent 3% of the Moroccan female workers. These figures do not, however, mean that a female middle class is emerging. These women are, in fact, part of the elite who have received higher education and sophisticated training, and have accumulated the required experience. They are particularly active in the field of commerce, and they are often women with bachelor's or master's degrees who have been living in Europe for a long time or who originate from families of entrepreneurs or other tradespeople.

Thus, Moroccan women entrepreneurs are active and often successful. They have become visible in European public life, and most of them are no longer restricted to traditional tasks of housework and child rearing. As a consequence, they enjoy more freedom, autonomy, and emancipation. Nadia, a forty-seven-year-old woman with a clothing business in Spain, said, "I want to be my own director." Naima, forty-one, and an entrepreneur in Belgium, states that she wants "to show people what she is capable of after her husband left her."[40] A third woman, Souad (thirty-six, who owns a restaurant in France), asserts that she is "proud to be her own boss and to be responsible for her family."[41]

Migration has contributed to the emergence of a generation of responsible and enterprising Moroccan women at the economic level as much as at the sociocultural and political levels; they are symbolic figures, who, while integrated in their host societies, continue to participate in the human development of their country of origin. A survey by economist Dr. Anthias[42] reveals that these businesswomen have acquired experience, capital, and family support, and are involved in networks that enable them to start and succeed in their projects.[43]

The cultural hurdles are, thus, less important than hard regulations and gender-based discrimination.

Public engagement of Moroccan migrant women

Moreover, some Moroccan women have reached top decision-making positions. In France, Rachida Dati is the former Minister of Justice,[44] and Najat Belkacem is the former Minister of Women's Rights.[45] In Italy, Souad Sbai is a member of Parliament, and in Belgium, Nadia Sminate is currently serving as the first Moroccan mayor.[46] As a lawyer and active member of the Socialist Party, Najat Vallaud-Belkacem leads actions to strengthen local democracy, the fight against discrimination, defend the promotion of citizens' rights, and access to employment and housing. As a woman deeply involved in women's issues of her generation, she believes in gender justice and equal opportunity, which is often lacking in French society, and has led to the impoverishment of the female migrant population in particular.

Rachida Dati was Nicolas Sarkozy's spokeswoman during the 2007 French presidential election.[47] In March 2008, she was elected mayor of the Seventh Arrondissement of Paris[48] and currently serves as a member of the European Parliament.[49] She is also a self-made daughter of immigrants, who triumphantly joined President Sarkosy's bid to make France appreciate its diversity. Since her rapid political rise, Rachida Dati has been perceived as a symbol of both Sarkozyism and diversity. She is indeed the first woman of North African descent to occupy a ministry as important as that of the Justice in France. Thanks to her hard work, she rose from poverty to sublime power against all odds of French discrimination.[50]

Souad Sbai, a Moroccan-born member of Silvio Berlusconi's conservative Freedom People Party, sponsored the Italian law banning the burqa.[51] She stated that she wanted to help Muslim women better integrate into Italian society by banning them from wearing veils covering their faces in public. As a result of Sbai's advocacy, on August 2, 2011, the constitutional affairs commission passed a law that prohibits women from going in public wearing a burqa, niqab, or any other garment that covers the face.[52]

After serving as a municipal counselor in 2006, Nadia Sminate was also elected as a member of the Belgian parliament in 2010 and served as a deputy mayor of budget and finance.[53] Born in Belgium to a Moroccan father and a Flemish mother, Nadia obtained a Degree in Roman Philology at the Flemish University of Brussels. She is currently a Member of Parliament in the House of Representatives of Belgium. In the Flanders regions, which are Dutch or German speaking, there is a general reluctance to elect immigrants or their descendants to decision-making positions. However, this unfavorable attitude did not prevent her from developing a brilliant political career.

The success stories of these female politicians of Moroccan origin do not imply that all Moroccan women are visible in European public life. Their leadership, however, evinces that Moroccan migrant women enjoy more freedom, autonomy, and emancipation, thanks to their participation in the job market. This has changed the image of the Muslim woman in general and of the Moroccan woman in particular. Many Moroccan women have transformed gender relations and transgressed old family traditions and rules of conduct. They have become independent individuals with a self-adopted responsibility to contribute to the development of their host and home countries, as well as to the well-being of their families.

Female migration has also had a positive impact on families left behind in Morocco; for instance, the remittances sent back home contribute to the improved housing conditions and health and socioeconomic statuses of their families, and especially to educational opportunities for children back home.[54] The amount of remittances ($2.9 billion annually) sent by migrant women to their families back in Morocco is roughly the same as for male migrants.[55] However, studies suggest that the share of income repatriated by Moroccan women is more important than in the case of Moroccan men.[56] Women's remittances are more regular and extend over a longer period of time, and are most often sent to other women who have custody of their children.

Sociocultural implications

One key implication of the finding that women have increasing migrating potential is that this is likely to act as a significant "push" factor on skilled migration of both genders. In practical terms, most migration is undertaken collectively rather than individually. For men with permanent partners and family dependents, the opinions of those people will perhaps be the single most important factor in determining whether their own migration potential is turned into reality. Women's reluctance to return to Morocco therefore serves to keep both women and men in Europe.[57]

Intuitively, one of the policy implications of this finding might be that affirmative action on gender grounds could be an effective strategy for reducing Morocco's brain drain. However, if such affirmative action led to real or perceived disadvantaging of men, the strategy might prove counterproductive, thus encouraging skilled males to migrate, taking their female partners with them.[58]

Another flaw in any simplistic gender-based strategy to reduce the brain drain is that the gender differences identified in the survey may have been caused by factors other than gender alone. Further analysis of the survey data and, indeed, further surveys that allow more thorough demographic analysis, are required in order to investigate the cross-cutting of variables such as age, marital status, level of education, and occupation, along with gender in determining migration attitudes and behavior.

Reducing the threat of poverty and seeking better life conditions are the most important factors that motivate Moroccan women to migrate. The lesson from a gender analysis of the brain drain is that it is in the social spheres of job security, education, and health care that the solution to the loss of core skills to the economy must be sought.

The relatively new phenomenon of female migration and the female impact on the nature and duration of male migration constitutes an important change in gender roles for Morocco, thus creating new challenges for public policy. This emergence of migrant females as breadwinners puts pressure on traditional gender roles within the Moroccan family.

Moroccan migrants are increasingly becoming part of a gendered African diaspora, which is attracting international attention. Indeed, this diaspora includes a patrimony of intelligence, made up of intellectuals, professional men and women, and university students who could be put to the service of the development of Morocco and *other* African nations. This new vision is shared by all—by the African states, representatives of the diaspora, and the international community. With respect to the states, they have, at times, taken a hostile attitude toward women migrants and toward expatriate nationals in general. Nevertheless, today, it appears that these same states are beginning to realize the important potential represented by the diaspora in the economic development of their countries.[59]

Gender, intersectionality, and migration

Moroccan women migrants in Europe and Afro-American women: a comparison

There are a few significant similarities between Moroccan women migrants in Europe and African-American women in the United States. Like African-American women, Moroccan women migrants in Europe continue to suffer from steep poverty and unemployment rates that are 42% higher than white women—they find themselves in marginalization positions within society.[60] The concept of intersectionality, which grew out of the black feminist movement,[61] helps us understand the ways in which both African-American and Moroccan migrant women are marginalized and provides a lens through which to examine both of their lived experiences. The intersectionality paradigm analyzes marginalized and oppressed women combining their multiple identities, including social class, ethnic identity, migration status, gender, and power. The paradigm posits that it is the combination of the multiple identities, that cannot be analyzed in isolation, that contributes to the unique lived experiences of a particular group.

Thus far, this chapter has applied a descriptive approach to examining the impact of intersectionality on marginalized women's lives—examining the history of why Moroccan women have migrated to Europe and how their migration results in a transformative experience for the women and the communities in which they reside. From this description, my readings, and my data analysis, three salient themes emerge and connect with intersectionality. The first, self-sacrifice, depicts how these women's actions and behavior reflect a historical tendency of altruistic giving, sharing, and caring for their families, friends, and entourage. Women are often relegated to gendered roles where they are categorized as caregivers. In these overly gendered roles, both African-American and Moroccan women migrants are expected to act in self-sacrificing ways where their own needs are subjugated to the needs of their communities. Similarly, African-American women were kept in "the roles of provider, nurturer, and protector, which were necessary for the survival of the Black family unit in a White, male-dominant society."[62] For Moroccan migrant women, this phenomenon is displayed in their work, sharing of remittances, and even in the leadership positions in which they obtain in becoming the voice to speak for migrant women, Muslim women, and women in the Maghreb. The self-sacrificing role acknowledges that Moroccan migrant women cannot be seen solely in their roles as a woman, migrant, Moroccan, or Muslim. It is at the intersection of these identities in which the Moroccan migrant woman subsumes herself to constantly place the family and communities' needs above her own. Like African-American women, the strength and adaptability of Moroccan migrant women have proved critical to maintaining the family unit in the community. They have often undertaken the responsibility of heads-of-household while living with limited resources.

The second theme, marginalization, describes how both African-American and Moroccan migrant women are relegated to the margins of society. Intersectionality unpacks how African-American women and Moroccan migrant women have endured life at the margins at the intersection. Marginalization can only be understood as a concept in that it expounds on how societal factors such as discrimination, oppression, and power relations combine to shape the lives and experiences of these marginalized women. When examined disjointedly, the consequences of segregation, repression, and domination have proven to have a harmful effect on their social lives and psychological and physiological health.[63] Other researchers have elucidated that the nervous tension of life at the margins when coupled with racism and xenophobia leads to physical ailments and curtails life expectancy.[64]

The third theme, invisibility, illustrates how these women remain invisible individuals, in spite of their productivity. It is my argument that, like African-American women, Moroccan women migrants in Europe have multiple identities and individual factors that intersect to contribute to their remaining at the margins—unemployed and poor. However, there are negative results of female migration for women. Like African-American women in the United States, many Moroccan female migrants complain that they lack access to resources that would provide them with support during periods of unemployment, emotional crisis, or health problems. There are many unhelpful stereotypes about Muslim women as oppressed and passive human beings with no power whatsoever to make any changes in their lives.[65] Although a few of the participants attended associations, activities, and group meetings, they often felt out of place or did not think European people could understand their migration situations. The lack of suitable resources to deal with their socioeconomic and cultural challenges served to further marginalize these women and may have contributed to job loss, low income, or identity crises. The overwhelming majority of these women are largely assigned the least prestigious jobs, such as services, domestic work, and clothing industries. Because their skills are not always acknowledged, they are compelled to work in areas that have little to do with the training they have received. Given the increasing rate of racial and gender-based discrimination, a significant number of women have resorted to self-employment in pursuit of economic and social welfare.

The descriptive findings within the research demonstrate that even though Moroccan women migrants live on the edge of the margins, they are overcoming through submission of remittances back to Morocco and taking on unprecedented leadership roles in their host countries. These three themes raise multiple implications for future research as a result which include a community-based research project to unravel the economic, social and psychological effects of discrimination, establishing culturally sensitive research tools that quantify marginalization, and implementing interdisciplinary methods that study gender, ethnic discrimination and social disparities.[66]

Conclusion

This chapter corroborates recent research that Moroccan women regard migration as an opportunity to build new lives.[67] Women's emancipation through migration undermines the patriarchal authority that traditionally subjugates women and confines them to the home and the rearing of children. This is one of the main reasons why the clear majority of women believe that migration is irreversible and is a survival strategy that helps them focus on building a better future in their new country. Thus, they represent a new type of feminism, which contributes to the subversion of old gender roles, gender equity, the culture of sharing and dialogue, and social development.

Across Europe, female Moroccan immigrants have contributed and partaken in various fields, which, by and large, have helped advance their host countries and their own society. At home and in Europe, they have developed strategies for resisting social injustice, discrimination, and other forms of oppression. Through their hard work, they have created a broad, North African identity, providing their communities with a sense of participation in European public life. They have learned skills and adapted their customs and beliefs to European lifestyles. They have equally established positive attitudes and practices to affect their own communities, even though hegemonic European powers could interfere at will. These kinds of sociocultural and political contributions by Moroccan Muslim immigrants have evolved in unique ways. The participation of Moroccan women migrants in economic development is often significant and affects their environment as well as their gender roles. It fosters empowerment and contributes to the transgression of patriarchal gender relations.

Their contributions have affected the transformations taking place in twenty-first century Europe, which, according to many researchers, could foster migrants' integration and the strengthening of Europe's relations with North African States. This encounter could equally contribute to consolidating the dialogue between Muslims and Westerners and to developing economic, social, and cultural exchanges between Europe and North Africa. Similarly, intersectionality helps us better understand social disparities among migrant women and is manifested in the consciousness of the participants as discrimination, marginalization, existential invisibility, and resistance.

Notes

1 Caitlin Killian, *North African Women in France: Gender, Culture, and Identity* (Stanford, CA: Stanford University Press, 2006).
2 Fatima Sadiqi, "Muslim North African Women and Migration in the Context of Globalization," in *New Horizons of Muslim Diaspora in Europe and North America*, edited by Moha Ennaji (New York: Palgrave Macmillan, 2016), 163–175; see also *Bureau des Statistiques* (Rabat: 2004, 2009); *UNESCO Report, 1998*; *Consideration of Reports Submitted by States Parties Under Article 73 of the Convention: International Convention on the Protection of the Rights of All Migrant Workers and Members of Their Families: Initial Reports of States Parties due in 2004: Morocco*, https://digitallibrary.un.org/record/743795/files/CMW_C_MAR_1-EN.pdf.
3 Moha Ennaji, *Muslim Moroccan Migrants in Europe: Transnational Migration in Its Multiplicity* (New York: Palgrave 2014), see chap. 2, "How Moroccans Live in Europe."
4 Mara A. Leichtman, "Transforming Brain Drain into Capital Gain: Morocco's Changing Relationship with Migration and Remittances," *The Journal of North African Studies* 7, no. 1 (2002): 109–137.
5 Ennaji, *Muslim Moroccan Migrants in Europe*, see chap. 2, "How Moroccans Live in Europe."
6 André Lebon, "Europe and International Migration: The Situation in 1983," *Studi Emigrazione: International Journal of Migration Studies* 21, no. 73 (March 1984): 1–42.
7 Fatima Mernissi, *The Harem Within: Tales of a Moroccan Girlhood*, reprint ed. (New York: Bantam, 1995), 5.
8 Patricia Hill Collins, *Black Feminist Thought: Knowledge, Consciousness, and the Politics of Empowerment* (New York: Routledge, 2008); Marie Claire Belleau, "Intersectionality: Feminisms in a Divided World; Québec-Canada," in *Feminist Politics: Identity, Difference, and Agency*, edited by Deborah Orr et al. (Lanham, MD: Rowman and Littlefield Publishers), 51–59; Kimberlé W. Crenshaw, "Demarginalizing the Intersection of Race and Sex: A Black Feminist Critique of Antidiscrimination Doctrine, Feminist Theory and Antiracist Politics," *University of Chicago Legal Forum* 1989, no. 1 (1989): 139–167.
9 Abdelkrim Belguendouz, *Le Maroc coupable d'emigration et de transit vers l'Europe* (Unknown Binding, 2000).
10 Moha Ennaji and Fatima Sadiqi, *Migration and Gender in Morocco: The Impact of Migration on the Women Left Behind* (Trenton, NJ: Red Sea Press, 2008): 82–84.
11 Mohamed Bachir Hamdouch, *Les Marocains Résidant à L'étranger: Une Enquête Socio-économique* (Rabat: Fondation Hassan II pour les MRE; FNUAP; INSEA, 2000).
12 Lamine Ghanmi, "Analysis—Drought Highlights Morocco's Need for Farm Reform," *Reuters*, May 24, 2007, www.reuters.com/article/idUSL2471235220070524.
13 Wilfred Tichagwa, "The Effects of Drought on the Condition of Women," *Gender and Development* 2, no. 1 (1994): 20–25, doi:10.1080/09682869308520019.
14 Fatima Sadiqi and Moha Ennaji, "The Impact of Male Migration from Morocco to Europe on Women," *Finisterra* 39, no. 77 (2004): 59–76.
15 For more information, see Moha Ennaji, "Poverty Still a Major Cause for Concern in Morocco," *Morocco World News*, December 19, 2017, www.moroccoworldnews.com/2017/12/236710/poverty-morocco-essaouira-stampede-illiteracy/#respond;

see also Alexis Palmer, "Fatal Stampede for Food Aid Follows Drought in Rural Morocco," *Northeastern University Global Institute*, December 4, 2017, accessed on January 26, 2018, https://globalresilience.northeastern.edu/2017/12/fatal-stampede-for-food-aid-follows-drought-in-rural-morocco/.

16 Ennaji and Sadiqi, *Migration and Gender in Morocco*; Touria Khannous, "Moroccan Women Contrabandists: Interferences in Public Space," in *Women in the Middle East, Agents of Change*, edited by Fatima Sadiqi and Moha Ennaji (London: Routledge, 2010), 324–338.

17 See Mohamed Khachani, *L'Emigration au Féminin: Tendances Récentes au Maroc*, Budapest: Robert Schuman Institute, 2009, http://cadmus.eui.eu/bitstream/handle/1814/11613/CARIM_AS&N_2009_26.pdf?sequence=1.

18 Mohamed Khachani, *La Femme Maghrébine Immigrée dans L'Espace Economique des Pays d'Accueil, Quelques Repères*, 2001, accessed on February 21, 2017, www.archive-iussp.org/Brazil2001/s20/S27_P08_Kachani.pdf; Zineb Daoud, ed., "Basic Skills for the Vocational Integration of Moroccan Women and Girls," in *Immigrant Women and Migration* (Strasbourg: Council of Europe Press, 1995), 71–78.

19 Sadiqi and Ennaji, *Migration and Gender in Morocco*, 82–84.

20 *Ibid.*

21 Moroccan Association for Studies and Research on Migration (AMERM), ed., *La Migration Clandestine Enjeux et Perspectives* [Rabat: Publication of L'Association Marocaine d'Etudes et de Recherches sur les Migrations (AMERM); Faculté des Droit, 2000].

22 *Ibid.*

23 Sadiqi and Ennaji, *Migration and Gender in Morocco*, 82–84.

24 *Ibid.*, see chap. 3.

25 United Nations International Children's Emergency Fund, At a Glance: Morocco, accessed on May 25, 2018, www.unicef.org/infobycountry/morocco_statistics.html?p=printme.

26 Hajare El Khaldi, Women's Unemployment Hampers Economic Progress in Morocco, Morocco World News, April 4, 2018 accessed on May 25, 2018, www.moroccoworldnews.com/2018/04/243751/womens-unemployment-hampers-economic-progress-morocco/.

27 Aida Alami, "Underpaid and Unskilled, Moroccan Women Behind in the Workplace," *Financial Times*, November 23, 2015, accessed on May 25, 2018, www.ft.com/content/4c90dc22-6e97-11e5-8171-ba1968cf791a.

28 Moha Ennaji, "Violence against Women in Morocco," in *Gender and Violence in the Middle East*, edited by Moha Ennaji and Fatima Sadiqi (New York: Routledge, 2011), 200–218.

29 Killian, *North African Women in France*, 36.

30 The names present in the study are fictional in order to respect the privacy of the individuals. Ennaji, *Muslim Moroccan Migrants in Europe*.

31 *Ibid.*

32 *Ibid.*

33 *Ibid.*

34 *Ibid.*

35 *Ibid.*

36 Parvati Raghuram and Irene Hardill, "Negotiating a Market: A Case Study of an Asian Woman in Business," *Women's Studies International Forum*, 21, no. 5 (1998): 475–483.

37 Caroline Essers, "Entrepreneurship on the Public-Private Divide: Businesswomen of Turkish and Moroccan Descent Playing Family Ties," Paper presented at Reconnecting Diversity to Critical Organization and Gender Studies Critical Management

Studies Conference, Manchester, July 11–13, 2007, accessed on December 21, 2017, www.mngt.waikato.ac.nz/ejrot/cmsconference/2007/proceedings/reconnecting diversity/essers.pdf.

38 Ennaji, "Migration, Development, and Gender in Morocco," in *Migration et Diversité Culturelle*, edited by Moha Ennaji (Mohammedia: Fedala Press, 2007), 69–85; Khachani, *La Femme Maghrébine Immigrée dans L'Espace Economique des Pays d'Accueil, Quelques Repères*, 2001.

39 See Muriel Laurent et al., "Etude : L'entrepreneuriat Féminin En Région de Bruxelles-Capitale|AGENCEBRUXELLOISE,"September1,2013,https://www.abe-bao.be/fr/documents/etude-lentrepreneuriat-feminin-en-region-de-bruxelles-capitale.

40 Ennaji, *Muslim Moroccan Migrants in Europe.*

41 Ennaji, *Muslim Moroccan Migrants in Europe. Cf.* Khachani, *Les Marocains d'ailleurs* and Kacem Basfao and Hinde Taarji, *L'annuaire de l'émigration: Maroc* (Afrique-Orient, 1994), 228.

42 Floya Anthias, et al., eds., *Paradoxes of Integration: Female Migrants in Europe* (New York: Springer. 2013).

43 *Ibid.*

44 Angelique Chrisafis, The Rise and Fall of Rachida Dati, The Guardian, November 19, 2008, accessed May 25, 2018, www.theguardian.com/world/2008/nov/20/rachida-dati-france-sarkozy-pregnant.

45 May Bulman, Najat Vallaud-Belkacem: France's First Female Education Minister is Making Her Mark, *Independent*, August 30, 2016, accessed on May 25, 2018, www.independent.co.uk/news/people/najat-vallaud-belkacem-france-politics-burkini-a7214456.html.

46 See Ennaji, *Muslim Moroccan Migrants in Europe.*

47 Henry Samuel, Sarkozy Choses Left-Wingers for Cabinet, *Telegraph*, May 14, 2007, accessed on May 25, 2018, www.telegraph.co.uk/news/uknews/1551506/Sarkozy-choses-left-wingers-for-cabinet.html.

48 Elaine Sciolino, French Cabinet Position Not Enough? Then Try Mayor, *New York Times*, January 13, 2008, accessed on May 25, 2018, www.nytimes.com/2008/01/13/world/europe/13france.html.

49 Member of the European Parliament Webpage for Rachida Dati, accessed on May 25, 2018, www.rachida-dati.eu/parlement-europeen.

50 Henry Samuel, Sarkozy Choses Left-Wingers for Cabinet.

51 *Burqa* is a long, loose dress covering the whole female body from head to feet, worn in public by women in several Gulf and Asian Muslim countries.

52 *Niqab* is a veil that covers the head and face except for the eyes, and is worn by some Islamic women in public.

53 Karla Dieseldorff, Belgo-Moroccan Nadia Sminate Becomes Mayor of Londerzeel, *Morocco World News*, January 3, 2016, accessed on May 25, 2018, www.moroccoworldnews.com/2016/01/176602/belgo-moroccan-nadia-sminate-becomes-mayor-of-londerzeel/.

54 Ennaji and Sadiqi, *Migration and Gender in Morocco*, see chap. 9.

55 See Abdelkrim Belguendouz, *La Communauté Marocaine à L'étranger et la Nouvelle Marche Marocaine* (Kenitra: Elboukili, 1999); Ennaji, *Muslim Moroccan Migrants in Europe*, chap. 5.

56 Myriam Cherti, *Paradoxes of Social Capital: A Multi-Generational Study of Moroccans in the UK* (Amsterdam: Amsterdam University Press, IMISCOE Dissertations, 2008), 21.

57 Ennaji, "Moroccan Migrants in Europe and Islamophobia," *Comparative Studies of South Asia, Africa and the Middle East* 30, no. 1 (2010): 14–20.

58 Leichtman, "Transforming Brain Drain into Capital Gain."

59 Ennaji, *Muslim Moroccan Migrants in Europe.*

60 Teri D. Armour Burton, "The Lived Experience of Intersectionality among African American Women with Breast Cancer" (Doctoral dissertation, University of San Diego, 2017), 90; Ennaji, *Muslim Moroccan Migrants in Europe*; Leo Lucassen, *The Immigrant Threat* (Urbana and Chicago, IL: University of Illinois Press, 2005).
61 Crenshaw, "Demarginalizing the Intersection of Race and Sex," 139–167.
62 Armour Burton, "The Lived Experience of Intersectionality among African American Women with Breast Cancer," 90.
63 Alex L. Pieterse, et al., "Racism-Related Stress, General Life Stress, and Psychological Functioning Among Black American Women," *Journal of Multicultural Counseling and Development* 41, no. 1 (2013): 36–46, doi:10.1002/j.2161-1912.2013.00025.x; Sarah L. Szanton et al., "Racial Discrimination is Associated With a Measure of Red Blood Cell Oxidative Stress: A Potential Pathway for Racial Health Disparities," *International Society of Behavioral Medicine* 19 (2012): 489–495, doi:10.1007/s12529-011-9188-z.
64 Jessica L. Harding et al., "Psychological Stress is Positively Associated With Body Mass Index Gain Over 5 Years: Evidence from the Longitudinal AusDiab Study," *Obesity Journal* 22 (2014): 277–286, doi:10.1002/oby.20423; Robert P. Juster, et al., "Allostatic Load Biomarkers of Chronic Stress and Impact on Health and Cognition," *Neuro Science and Biobehavioral Reviews* 35, no. 1 (2010): 2–16, doi:10.1016/j.neubiorev.2009.10.002.
65 John R. Bowen, *Why the French Don't Like Headscarves: Islam, the State, and Public Space* (Princeton, NJ: Princeton University Press, 2007).
66 Crenshaw, "Demarginalizing the Intersection of Race and Sex," 139–167; Armour Burton, "The Lived Experience of Intersectionality among African American Women with Breast Cancer," 90.
67 Killian, *North African Women in France.*

Bibliography

Alami, Aida. "Underpaid and Unskilled, Moroccan Women Behind in the Workplace." *Financial Times*, November 23, 2015. Accessed May 25, 2018. www.ft.com/content/4c90dc22-6e97-11e5-8171-ba1968cf791a.

Anthias, Floya, Maria Kontos, and Mirjana Morokvasic-Müller, eds. *Paradoxes of Integration: Female Migrants in Europe.* New York: Springer, 2013.

Armour Burton, Teri D. "The Lived Experience of Intersectionality among African American Women with Breast Cancer." Doctoral dissertation, University of San Diego, 2017.

Basfao, Kacem and Hinde Taarji. *L'annuaire de l'émigration: Maroc.* Casablanca: Afrique-Orient, 1994.

Belguendouz, Abdelkrim. *Le Maroc coupable d'emigration et de transit vers l'Europe.* Unknown Binding, 2000.

Belleau, Marie Claire. "Intersectionality: Feminisms in a Divided World; Québec-Canada." In *Feminist Politics: Identity, Difference, and Agency*, edited by Deborah Orr, Dianna Taylor, Eileen Kahl, Kathleen Earle, Christa Rainwater, and Linda Lopez McAlister, 51–59. Lanham, MD: Rowman and Littlefield Publishers, 2007.

Ben Jelloun, Tahar. *Islam Explained.* New York: The New Press, 2002.

Bowen, John R. *Why the French Don't Like Headscarves: Islam, the State, and Public Space.* Princeton, NJ: Princeton University, 2007.

Bulman, May. "Najat Vallaud-Belkacem: France's First Female Education Minister is Making Her Mark." *Independent.* August 30, 2016. Accessed May 25, 2018.

www.independent.co.uk/news/people/najat-vallaud-belkacem-france-politics-burkini-a7214456.html.

Cherti, Myriam. *Paradoxes of Social Capital: A Multi-Generational Study of Moroccans in the UK*. Amsterdam: Amsterdam University Press, IMISCOE dissertations, 2008.

Chrisafis, Angelique. "The Rise and Fall of Rachida Dati." *The Guardian*, November 19, 2008. Accessed May 25, 2018. www.theguardian.com/world/2008/nov/20/rachida-dati-france-sarkozy-pregnant.

Collins, Patricia Hill. *Black Feminist Thought: Knowledge, Consciousness, and the Politics of Empowerment*. New York: Routledge, 2008.

Crenshaw, Kimberlé W. "Demarginalizing the Intersection of Race and Sex: A Black Feminist Critique of Antidiscrimination Doctrine, Feminist Theory and Antiracist Politics." *University of Chicago Legal Forum* 1989, no. 1 (1989): 139–167.

Daoud, Zineb, ed. "Basic Skills for the Vocational Integration of Moroccan Women and Girls." In *Immigrant Women and Migration*, 71–78. Strasbourg: Council of Europe Press, 1995.

Dieseldorff, Karla. "Belgo-Moroccan Nadia Sminate Becomes Mayor of Londerzeel." *Morocco World News*, January 3, 2016. Accessed May 25, 2018. www.moroccoworldnews.com/2016/01/176602/belgo-moroccan-nadia-sminate-becomes-mayor-of-londerzeel/.

El Khaldi, Hajare. "Women's Unemployment Hampers Economic Progress in Morocco." *Morocco World News*, April 4, 2018. Accessed May 25, 2018, www.moroccoworldnews.com/2018/04/243751/womens-unemployment-hampers-economic-progress-morocco/.

El Manar Laalami, Mohamed. "Attitudes et opinions." In *Les Marocains Résidant à L'étranger*, edited by Abdullah Berrada, Mohammad El Manar Laalami, Bachir Hamdouch, Mehdi Lahlou, and Mohammad Mahmoudi, 73–92. Rabat: INSEA Publications, 2000.

Ennaji, Moha. *Migration and Gender in Morocco: The Impact of Migration on the Women Left Behind*. Trenton, NJ: Red Sea Press, 2008.

———. "Migration, Development, and Gender in Morocco." In *Migration et Diversité Culturelle*, edited by Moha Ennaji, 69–85. Mohammedia: Fedala Press, 2007.

———. "Moroccan Migrants in Europe and Islamophobia." *Comparative Studies of South Asia, Africa and the Middle East* 30, no. 1 (2010): 14–20.

———. "Poverty Still a Major Cause for Concern in Morocco." *Morocco World News*, December 19, 2017. www.moroccoworldnews.com/2017/12/236710/poverty-morocco-essaouira-stampede-illiteracy/#respond.

———. "Violence against Women in Morocco." In *Gender and Violence in the Middle East*, edited by Moha Ennaji and Fatima Sadiqi, 200–218. New York: Routledge, 2011.

Ennaji, Moha, and Fatima Sadiqi, eds. *Gender and Violence in the Middle East*. New York: Routledge, 2011.

Essers, Caroline. "Entrepreneurship on the Public-Private Divide: Businesswomen of Turkish and Moroccan Descent Playing Family Ties." Paper presented at Reconnecting Diversity to Critical Organization and Gender Studies Critical Management Studies Conference, Manchester, July 11–13, 2007. Accessed December 21, 2017. www.mngt.waikato.ac.nz/ejrot/cmsconference/2007/proceedings/reconnectingdiversity/essers.pdf.

Ferrié, Jean-Noël, ed. *Annuaire de l'Afrique du Nord* 19 (1999). Accessed October 21, 2017. http://aan.mmsh.univ-aix.fr/volumes/1999/Pages/default.aspx.

Bachir Hamdouch, Abdallah Berrada, Medhdi Lahlou, Mohamed El Manar Laalami & Mohamed Mahmoudi. *Les Marocains Résidant à L'étranger: Une Enquête Socio-économique.*: Fondation Hassan II pour les MRE; FNUAP; INSEA, 2000.

Harding, Jessica L., Kathryn Backholer, Emily D. Williams, Anna Peeters, Adrian J. Cameron, Matthew J. L., Hare, Jonathan E. Shaw, and Dianna J. Magliano. "Psychological Stress is Positively Associated with Body Mass Index Gain over 5 Years: Evidence from the Longitudinal Aus Diab Study." *Obesity Journal* 22 (2014): 277–286. doi:10.1002/oby.20423.

Juster, Robert P., Bruce S. McEwen, and Sonia J. Lupien, "Allostatic Load Biomarkers of Chronic Stress and Impact on Health and Cognition." *NeuroScience and Biobehavioral Reviews* 35, no. 1 (2010): 2–16. doi:10.1016/j.neubiorev.2009.10.002.

Khachani, Mohamed. *L'Emigration au Féminin: Tendances Récentes au Maroc.* Budapest: Robert Schuman Institute, 2009. Accessed May 19, 2018. http://cadmus.eui.eu/bitstream/handle/1814/11613/CARIM_AS&N_2009_26.pdf?sequence=1.

———. *La Femme Maghrébine Immigrée dans L'Espace Economique des Pays d'Accueil, Quelques Repères,* 2001. Accessed February 21, 2017. www.archive-iussp.org/Brazil2001/s20/S27_P08_Kachani.pdf.

———. *Les Marocains d'ailleurs.* Rabat: Imprimerie Al-karama, 2004.

Khannous, Touria. "Moroccan Women Contrabandists: Interferences in Public Space." In *Women in the Middle East, Agents of Change,* edited by Fatima Sadiqi and Moha Ennaji, 324–338. London: Routledge, 2010.

Killian, Caitlin. *North African Women in France: Gender, Culture, and Identity.* Stanford, CA: Stanford University Press, 2006.

La Communauté Marocaine à L'étranger et la Nouvelle Marche Marocaine. Kenitra: El-boukili, 1999.

Ghanmi, Lamine. "ANALYSIS-Drought Highlights Morocco's Need for Farm Reform." *Reuters,* May 24, 2017. https://www.reuters.com/article/idUSL2471235220070524.

Laurent, Muriel, Pierre Herfurth, Sofia Moussourakis, and Khadija Senhadji. "Etude : L'entrepreneuriat Féminin En Région de Bruxelles-Capitale | AGENCE BRUXELLOISE," September 1, 2013. https://www.abe-bao.be/fr/documents/etude-lentrepreneuriat-feminin-en-region-de-bruxelles-capitale.

Lebon, André. "Europe and International Migration: The Situation in 1983." *Studi Emigrazione: International Journal of Migration Studies* 21, no. 73 (March 1984): 1–42.

Leichtman, Mara A. "Transforming Brain Drain into Capital Gain: Morocco's Changing Relationship with Migration and Remittances." *The Journal of North African Studies* 7, no. 1 (2002): 109–137.

Lucassen, Leo. *The Immigrant Threat.* Urbana and Chicago, IL: University of Illinois Press, 2005.

Member of the European Parliament Webpage for Rachida DATI. Accessed May 25, 2018. www.rachida-dati.eu/parlement-europeen.

Mernissi, Fatima. *The Harem Within: Tales of a Moroccan Girlhood.* Reprint edition. New York: Bantam, 1995.

Moroccan Association for Studies and Research on Migration (AMERM), ed. *La Migration Clandestine En jeux et Perspectives.* Rabat: Publication of l'Association Marocaine d'Etudes et de Recherches sur les Migrations (AMERM); Faculté des Droit, 2000.

Palmer, Alexis. "Fatal Stampede for Food Aid Follows Drought in Rural Morocco." *Northeastern University Global Institute,* December 4, 2017. Accessed January 26, 2018. https://globalresilience.northeastern.edu/2017/12/fatal-stampede-for-food-aid-follows-drought-in-rural-morocco/.

Phaneuf, Victoria M. "Negotiating Culture, Performing Identities: North African and Pied-Noir Associations in France." *The Journal of North African Studies* 17, no. 4 (2012): 671–686.

Pieterse, Alex L., Robert T. Carter, and Kilynda V. Ray. "Racism-Related Stress, General Life Stress, and Psychological Functioning Among Black American Women." *Journal of Multicultural Counseling and Development* 41, no. 1 (2013): 36–46. doi:10.1002/j.2161-1912.2013.00025.x.

Raghuram, Parvati, and Irene Hardill. "Negotiating a Market: A Case Study of an Asian Woman in Business." *Women's Studies International Forum* 21, no. 5 (1998): 475–483.

Sadiqi, Fatima. "Muslim North African Women and Migration in the Context of Globalization." In *New Horizons of Muslim Diaspora in Europe and North America*, edited by Moha Ennaji. New York, UNITED STATES: Palgrave Macmillan, 2016.

Sadiqi, Fatima, and Moha Ennaji. "The Impact of Male Migration from Morocco to Europe on Women." *Finisterra* 39, no. 77 (2004): 59–76.

Samuel, Henry. "Sarkozy Choses Left-Wingers for Cabinet." *Telegraph*, May 14, 2007. Accessed May 25, 2018. www.telegraph.co.uk/news/uknews/1551506/Sarkozy-choses-left-wingers-for-cabinet.html.

Sciolino, Elaine. "French Cabinet Position Not Enough? Then Try Mayor." *New York Times*, January 13, 2008. Accessed May 25, 2018. www.nytimes.com/2008/01/13/world/europe/13france.html.

Szanton, Sarah L., Joseph M. Rifkind, Joy G. Mohanty, Edgar R. Miller III, Roland J. Thorpe, Eneka Nagababu, Elissa S. Epel, Alan B. Zonderman, and Michele K. Evans. "Racial Discrimination is Associated with a Measure of Red Blood Cell Oxidative Stress: A Potential Pathway for Racial Health Disparities." *International Society of Behavioral Medicine* 19 (2012): 489–495. doi:10.1007/s12529-011-9188-z. 2012.

Tichagwa, Wilfred. "The Effects of Drought on the Condition of Women." *Gender and Development* 2, no. 1 (1994): 20–25. doi:10.1080/09682869308520019.

United Nations International Children's Emergency Fund. At a Glance: Morocco. Accessed May 25, 2018. www.unicef.org/infobycountry/morocco_statistics.html?p=printme.

Bibliography

Connell, R. W. Masculinities (Cambridge, UK: Polity Press, 1995).

Cordesman, Anthony H. "The [New-Old] Crises and Instability in the Middle East and North Africa in 2016," January 4, 2016. www.csis.org/analysis/new-old-crises-and-instability-middle-east-and-north-africa-2016.

Crenshaw, Kimberlé W. "Demarginalizing the Intersection of Race and Sex: A Black Feminist Critique of Antidiscrimination Doctrine, Feminist Theory and Antiracist Politics." *University of Chicago Legal Forum* 1989, no. 1 (1989): 139–167.

Crenshaw, Kimberle W. "Mapping the Margins: Intersectionality, Identity Politics, and Violence against Women of Color." *Stanford Law Review* 43, no. 6 (1991): 1241–1299.

Dowd, Nancy E. *Masculinities and Feminist Legal Theory. Vol. 1 Masculinities and the Law.* New York and London: New York University Press, 2009.

Epstein, Cynthia Fuchs. "The Difference Model: Enforcement and Reinforcement of Women's Roles in the Law." In *Social Roles and Societal Institutions*, edited by Judith R. Blau and Norman Goodman. Piscataway, NJ: Transaction Publishers, 1995: 53–72.

Korpi, Walter. "Faces of Inequality: Gender, Class, and Patterns of Inequalities in Different Types of Welfare States." *Journal of Social Politics Oxford* 7, no. 2 (July 1, 2000). https://medicine.gu.se/digitalAssets/1453/1453386_127.full.pdf.

Manjoo, Rashida. "Report of the Special Rapporteur on Violence against Women, Its Causes and Consequences." United Nations, General Assembly, Human Rights Council, May 2, 2011. http://undocs.org/en/S/RES/2106 (2011).

Vojdik, Valorie. "Gender Outlaws: Challenging Masculinity in Traditionally Male Institutions." *Berkeley Women's Law Journal* 17 (2002): 68.

United Nations Security Council Resolution 2106. Adopted by the Security Council at Its 6984th Meeting on June 24, 2013. http://undocs.org/en/S/RES/2106, 2013.

Index

Note: page numbers followed by 'n' refer to end notes.

Abbas, Mahmoud 40, 100
Abbas, Sara 104n32
Abrams, Jamie R. 150n147
Abu-Lughod, Lila 21n19
Abu Zaida, Sufian 105n53
ACLU *see* American Civil Liberties Union (ACLU)
active women 102n2
Afghanistan 8; American intervention in 138; invasion of 8
African-American women 168
age of marriage 30–1
Ahmad, Muneer 139, 151n162
Alami, Aida 172n28
Alazzeh, Ala 101
Algeria 30
"aliens" 6
Al-Masri, Hani 105n56
Alsaafin, Linah 103n23
Alsafin, Deema 104n38
Al-Saji, Alia 8, 20n23
Amended Basic Law 27
Amended Palestinian Basic Law 28
American Civil Liberties Union (ACLU) 6, 19n16
Ansari, Ansari, 20n49
anti-Islamic sentiment 10
anti-Muslim hate crimes 15–16
anti-Muslim sentiments 4, 6
Arab 72
Arabic language 28
Arab–Muslim patriarchy 70
Arab Spring 75
Arab tribalism 65, 73
Arab Uprisings 91–2, 95–6, 97–100
Arafat, Yasser 27, 103n17, 103n18
Armour Burton, Teri D. 174n61
asylum law 113, 115, 119
asylum seekers 132
attarin (spice vendors) 66
Ayalon, Hanna 78
Aziz, Jean 105n52
Aziz, Sahar F. 151n160, 151n161

Bar Associations 44
Barnett, Laura 146n45
Belgium, Moroccan workers left for 160
Belkacem, Najat 166
Berber dynasties 66
Berber tribalism 63–5, 65–6, 73, 84n38
Berber *Tuareg* societies 67
Biribonwoha, Pius 46n10
Blanchard, Eric M. 150n144
Blau, Peter M. 59, 83n11
Blitz, Brad 140, 151n166
Boomgaarden, Hajo G. 145n37
Boswell, Richard A. 145n42
Bourdieu, Pierre 64, 77, 83n28, 84n33, 87n99
Bowen, John R. 174n66
Brophy, Jere E. 87n104
Brumfield, Ben 144n23
Bulman, May 173n46
Bush Administration 8
Bush, George 138

Cainkar, Louise xix, 20n37, 20n40, 20n48, 21n51
Canada 130, 132–4, 141; denied Kurdi family's asylum application, 128; homonationalism theory and 141–2; refugee resettlement 132–4, 141; refugee vulnerability 127, 130
Canadian Women-at-Risk Program 134

Carby, Hazel V. 7
Carpenter, Michael J. 105n54
Carpenter, R. Charli 139, 140, 150n149
CATO institute 141
CEDAW *see* Convention on the Elimination of All Forms of Discrimination against Women (CEDAW)
cephalousness 63
Chafik, Mohamed 85n68
Chappellet-Lanier, Tajha 144n17
charismatic authority 58–9
Cherti, Myriam 173n57
Chicago metropolitan area 11
Child Law 31
Children and Adolescents at Risk 133
Chrisafis, Angelique 173n45
Christians 32
citizenship 42–4
Clarricoates, Katherine 78, 87n103
Code of Cannon Law 31
Collins, Patricia Hill 171n8
Collins, Randall 60, 83n12
color experience racism 7–8
Comey, James 140
conflict-related sexual violence against men 118
Connell, R. W. 8, 19n1, 149n29
Convention against Torture 117, 145n30
Convention on the Elimination of All Forms of Discrimination against Women (CEDAW) 17, 25, 26, 29–34, 36, 37, 39–45
Convention on the Nationality of Married Women 43
Cordesman, Anthony H. xvin1
Coser, Lewis A. 59, 83n10
court of justice 82
Crenshaw, Kimberlé W. 150n154
criminal law 29
cultural policing 7
cultural racism 8
cultural sniping 10–13

dabbaghin (leather workers) 66
Daly, Mary 8
dar al-Islam (the house of Islam) 66
Dati, Rachida 166
Declaration on the Elimination of Violence 17
DeGagne, Alexa 152n179
Diamond, Jeremy 144n24
Dieseldorff, Karla 173n54
disability 43
discriminatory laws: citizenship 42–4; labor law and social security 41–2; penal laws 39–41; residence 44; travel 44
divorce 35–7
Diwan (legislative bureau) 28
Dockery, Wesley 144n16
Dubai School of Government 96

economic level 71
economic security 164
education 60
egalitarianism 63
Egyptian law 26
election cycle 10
election law 29
El Khaldi, Hajare 172n27
emphasized femininity 5
Ennaji, Moha xix, 87n105, 171n3, 171n5, 171n10, 171n14, 171n15, 172n16, 172n29, 173n39, 173n58
equality 43; of inheritance 38
Essers, Caroline 172n38
Europe 5, 7, 8, 66; *see also* Moroccan women migrants
extended family structure 76

Faloyin, Dipo 144n19
family hierarchy 76
family laws in Palestine 29–30; age of marriage 30–1; divorce 35–7; guardians approval of marriage 31–2; inheritance 37–9; interreligion marriages 32–3; polygamy 33–5
Family Reunification 133
family structure in Morocco 75–7
Fantz, Ashley 144n23
Fatah 28
fatwa (religious decision) 58
Federal Foreign Office 134
Federal Office for Migration and Refugees (BAMF) 134
female migration 167
female victimization 8
femininity : conventional images of 164; emphasized 5; hegemonic xii, xiii, 3–17; norms 137; pariah 6; racism and 18
feminism 7–8
Feminist Theory: From Margin to Center (bell hook) 7
Fez 66, 68, 79
Fi at-Tufula (In Childhood) 79
financial obligations 38

First Intifada 94, 95
Fleischman, Ellen L. 103n4
foregoing laws 43
Foucault, Michel 82n2
fqih's (religious man) 58
Freedman, Jane 146n58
Freison, Joe 148n95
French colonization 68–9
French Penal Code of 1810 40

Gaucher, Megan 152n179
Gaza 26, 27, 35, 37, 41, 46n14
gender 58; interfaces 137; and Palestinian legal system 26–9; performance 8–9; policing 3–5, 9, 15, 16, 18; politics and identity xii–xiii; role assignment and perception 78
gender-based violence xiii, 3–5, 16, 17, 136, 139, 140
gender policing 5–7, 9
gender-related persecution 112–15
gender segregation 66, 69, 73, 77
genuine reform 34
Germany 127, 128, 130, 132; Moroccan workers left for 160; refugee vulnerability in 134–5
Ghanmi, Lamine 171n12
Government of Canada 148n92, 148n94
Graiouid, Said 79, 87n106
Greussing, Esther 145n37
guardians approval of marriage 31–2
Gyn/ecology (Daly) 8

Hamas 27, 28
Hammami, Rema 105n48
hammams (public baths) 67
Hampanda, Karen 122n51, 123n75
Hanieh, Akram 105n47
harassment 13–15
Hardill, Irene 172n37
hate crimes 15–16
Hathaway, James C. 131, 145n40, 146n54
Hebron 26
hegemonic femininity 5–7
hegemonic masculinity 3–5, 137, 139, 149n129
heteronormativity 5
hierarchies of power 9
hierarchy of masculinities 9
hijab 3–18, 77, 139
Hindus 71
homonationalism theory 141–2
honor killings 40
Howson, Richard 150n146
Hudson, Valerie 152n177
Hughes, Michael 61
Humanitarian-protected Persons Abroad Class (HPC) 133
humanity 59, 71, 112
Human Rights Watch (HRW) 117

Ibn Khaldun 62, 83n24
Idriss II, Moulay 66
IFRED *see* Institute for Training and Research Development (IFRED)
Ijtihad 82, 88n116
Imam (male leader of mixed prayers) 77
Immigration and Naturalization Act (INA) 111, 112, 135
Immigration and Naturalization Service (INS) 115
inheritance 37–9
Institute for Social Policy and Understanding 10
Institute for Training and Research Development (IFRED) 164
institution of monarchy 74–5
International Gay and Lesbian Human Rights Commission 16
international human rights 17–18
International Women's Peace Service 105n44
Inter-Parliamentary Union 46n9
interreligion marriages 32–3
intra-gender policing 4
Islamic gender oppression 7
Islamic High Judicial Council 39
Islamic jurisprudence 38
Islamic law 67
Islamic Maghrib 62–3
Islamic patriarchal system 67
Islamophobia 10, 137, 140–2
Israel 26–7
Israeli-Palestinian Interim Agreement 103n16

Jad, Islah 93, 94, 101, 103n5, 103n8
Japanese monarchy 86n90
Johnson, Allan 61
Jordan 4
Jordanian-enacted code 39
Judeo-Christian religious traditions 130

Kandiyoti, Deniz 84n48
Kandiyotis characterization 66
Kassam 39

Kazi, Hamida 103n14
Keddie, Nikki 73
Kelly, Nancy 115
Khachani, Mohamed 172n18
Khaldi, Fatima 105n45
Killian, Caitlin 163, 171n1
kinship 63
knowledge and appreciation 60
Korpi, Walter xvin3
Kozma, Liat 85n67
Kuran 35, 37, 38
Kuttab, Eileen 103n21

labor law and social security 41–2
Lack of Foreseeable Alternative Durable Solutions 133
lahkam (physical and symbolic authority) 75, 82
Laroui, Abdallah 60
law of divorce 36
Law of the Transfer of Immovable Property 37
laws 44
League of Nations 131
Lebon, André 171n6
Lee, Tori 105n46
Lefebvre, Henri 87n110
Legal and Physical Protection Needs 132
legal Islam 72–3
legal-rational authority 59
legislative drafters 28
legislative function 28
legislative positions 28
legislative process 27
legislature 44
legitimacy 58
Leichtman, Mara A. 171n4
Lerner, Gerda 61
Lesbian, Gay, Bisexual, Transgender, and Queer ("LGBTQ") 3
liberal secularism 3
liberal secularism and modes 3
Lorde, Audre 8

McKanders, Karla M. xix–xx, 121n16, 144n8, 149n132
Macmillan, Chrystal 51n144
Maddy-Weitzman, Bruce 73
Madhabs 73
Maghrebi urban street 80
Maghrib 62–3
Majalle 46n15, 47n26
Makhzen 60, 75, 81
Maliki Madhab 73
Maliki School 59, 72–3
Manjoo, Rashida 149n28, xvin11
Manna, Adel 50n108
Mansour, Mohamed 72–3
marriage: age of 30–1; contracts 34–5; guardians approval of 31–2; interreligion 32–3; officials 34
masculinity and femininity 6
material prison 7
medersas (religious schools) 67
Medical Needs 133
medina 66–7, 85n49
MENA region *see* Middle East and North African (MENA) region
Merkel, Angela 128
Mernissi, Fatima 77, 171n7
Merry, Sally 5, 6
Middle East and North African (MENA) 128, xi; asylum jurisprudence 112; sexual violence against men in *see* sexual violence against men
Milstein, Mati 92, 98, 104n36, 104n40
mission civilisatrice (civilizing mission) 68
monarchy, institution of 74–5
monogamy 67
Morar, Iltizam 99
More, Jennifer 145n42
Moroccan Association for Studies and Research on Migration (AMERM) 162
Moroccan High Commission for Statistics 161
Moroccan monarchy 74–5, 86n93
Moroccan Parliament 81
Moroccan street 78–80
Moroccan women migrants 158; demographics of 161–2; economic transformation 163–6; in Europe and African-American women 168–70; history of 160–1; public engagement of 166–7; social norms affecting treatment of 163; sociocultural implications 167–8; transformative impact of 159, 162–3; *see also* patriarchy in Morocco
mosque 77
Mother Jones 10
Musa Ibn Nusayr 62
Musalo, Karen 113, 121n15, 145n42
Musleh, Maath 104n37
Muslim family laws 35
Muslim Family Status Law of 1954 32
Muslim-majority countries 126, 127, 130, 136, 143n3; islamophobia, terrorism and vulnerability 140–2; victimless male refugees from 137–40

Muslim women 138; in hijab 3–12, 15–18; marriage of 32; Moroccan 158; refugee womens and 126; threats to 127, 137; as victims 139
Muwatin 45n8

Nakba 94
Nansen passports 131
Nansen refugee 127, 130
The Nation and Its "New" Women (Fleischmann) 93
neopatriarchy 69–70
Netherlands, Moroccan workers left for 160
New York 16
NGO-ization 101–2
9/11 attacks 4, 9–11, 13, 140
nnajarin (carpenters) 66
nongovernmental organizations (NGOs) 94, 135, 164
nonviolent Palestinian 100–1
Nowrasteh, Alex 151n171
nuclear family structure 76

Obama, Barack 10, 128
Occupied Palestinian Territory 96
O'Neill, Katherine Jane 104n33
Onyango, Monica Adhiambo 122n51, 123n75
oppression 8
Oslo Peace Accords 94, 100, 101
Ottoman Civil Code 46n15
Ottoman Empire 26, 37
Ottoman Penal Code of 1858 40

PA *see* Palestinian Authority (PA)
Palestine Liberation Organization (PLO) 27
Palestines accession 25–6; age of marriage 30–1; discriminatory laws 39–44; divorce 35–7; gender and 26–9; guardians approval of marriage 31–2; inheritance 37–9; interreligion marriages 32–3; polygamy 33–5; *see also* discriminatory laws; family laws in Palestine
Palestinian Authority (PA) 27, 33, 91–3, 95, 100–2
Palestinian Gandhis 97
Palestinian Labor Law 41
Palestinian laws 26
Palestinian legal system, gender and 26–9
Palestinian Legislative Council (PLC) 27
Palestinian legislators 32, 34, 36–7, 38, 39
Palestinian Liberation Organization (PLO) 94, 95
Palestinian National Council 95
Palestinian society 39
Palestinian women 25–6
Palestinian women, media representations of: Arab Uprisings 91–2, 95–6, 97–100; movement 93–5; NGO-ization 101–2; nonviolent Palestinian 100–1; in popular resistance 96–7; shared video, on Facebook 91
pariah femininity 6
parliament 81
patriarchy in Morocco 61–2; authority 57–60; Berber tribalism 63–5; family 75–7; French colonization 68–9; *Ijtihad* 82; institution of monarchy 74–5; Islamic Maghrib 62–3; *lahkam* 82; *Makhzen* 81, 82; mosque 77; parliament 81; postcolonialism 69–70; precolonial era 65–7; religion 71–4; school 77–8; street 78–80; workplace 80–1
Penal Code 39–41
penal laws 39–41
penal provisions 31
Personal Status Law of 1976 32, 33, 34, 36
PLO *see* Palestinian Liberation Organization (PLO)
polygamy 33–5
Popular Resistance in Palestine (Qumsiyeh) 102n3
Popular Struggle Coordination Committee 100
Population, Refugees, and Migration (PRM) 135, 136
postcolonialism 69–70
potential terrorists 9
power 58
Power, Carla 104n34
precolonial era 65–7
pregnant women 41
primary sources 60; institution of monarchy 74–5; religion 71–4
Private Sponsors Refugee Program 133
PRM *see* Population, Refugees, and Migration (PRM)
Puar, Jasbir K. 141, 142, 152n182

Qafisheh, Mutaz M. xx, 45n5, 49n81, 50n123, 51n147
Qumsiyeh, Mazin B. 102n3
Qur'an 59, 72, 73

race and women 7–8
racialization 8, 18

racism 18
Raghuram, Parvati 172n37
Razack, Sherene H. 7, 20n22, 143n1
Refugee Act (1980) 128
Refugee Admissions Program 135
Refugee Convention (1951) 111–14, 119, 126, 130, 143n2
refugee convention, as migration control 127–30
refugee law 113, 120n3, 131
Refugee Processing Center 149n124, 149n125
Refugee Resettlement Program 129
refugee status determination (RSD) process 132
refugee vulnerability: in Canada 133–4; in Germany 134–5; resettlement process 132–3; state-centric refugee regimes 130–1; in United States 135–6
religion 71–4
Resettlement Support Center (RSC) 135
residence 44
Residence Act 134
retirement rights 42
Rhodan, Maya 144n25
Rich, Anna-Katharina 148n97
Richter-Devroe, Sophie 104n43
Riesebrodt, Martin 83n5
Rogers, Phil 21n55
Romero, Octavio 6
RSC *see* Resettlement Support Center (RSC)
RSD process *see* refugee status determination (RSD) process
Russian Revolution 131

Sadiqi, Fatima xx–xxi, 83n13, 84n42, 84n44, 85n69, 171n2, 171n10, 171n14, 172n16
Sageman, Marc 141
Samuel, Henry 173n48
Sanders, Jo 87n100
Sbai, Souad 166
Schoenholtz, Andrew 146n56
school 77–8
Sciolino, Elaine 173n49
secondary sources 60; family 75–7; *lahkam* 82; *Makhzen* 81; mosque 77; parliament 81; school 77–8; street 78–80; workplace 80–1
Second Intifada 98, 100
Security Council Resolution 2106 xiii, xvin8
Sefrioui, Ahmed 85n64
segmentarianism 63
Selod, Saher 151n156
sexual attack 40
sexual harassment 41, 80
sexual humiliation 116
sexual orientation xiii, 114, 116, 120, 138, 141
sexual violence against men: gender-related persecution 112–16; humiliation 116; Syrian conflict 116–19
Shalhoub-Kevorkian, Nadera 96, 103n22, 104n28
Shariah 30, 38
Shariah judges 33–4
Shariah Law 30
Shari'a law 75
Sharon, Ariel 100
Sherwood, Harriet 103n24
Shoaibi, Halla xxi
Simeonov, Lazar 104n35
single parent family structure 76
Sminate, Nadia 166
Smith, Megan Denise 137, 149n30
Social Security Decree Law No. 19 42
social security, labor law and 41–2
souqs (public markets) 67
Southern Poverty Law Center (SPLC) 10, 15
spatial organization 66
street 78–80
Streitmatter, Janice L. 87n102
subordination 73–4
Survivors of Torture and Violence 132
Syrian Humanitarian Admissions Program135
Syrian men, sexual violence against 116–19, 128
Syrian refugees 129

Tamari, Salim 105n48
This Bridge Called My Back (Moraga and Anzaldúa) 7
Tichagwa, Wilfred 171n13
Tillion, Germaine 86n80
Touqan, Talal 46n12
trade unions 44
traditional authority 58, 59
Traité de Fès (the Fez Treaty) 68
transmission of Islam 63
travel 44
tribalism 62–3
tribal patriarchal system 67
Trudeau, Justin 128, 141
Trump, Donald 10, 15, 129, 137, 141
Turner, Lewis 145n39

UDHR *see* Universal Declaration of Human Rights (UDHR)
Umma 73
U.N. General Assembly 17
UNHCR *see* United Nations High Commissioner for Refugees (UNHCR)
UNICEF 118
United Nations (UN) xiii
United Nations Children survey 162
United Nations (U.N.) Commission 7
United Nations High Commissioner for Refugees (UNHCR) 111, 121n25, 122n56, 122n65, 136, 146n44, 147n66; guidelines 113–17; refugee resettlement 132–3
United Nations High Commissioner for Refugees Evaluation and Policy Unit 120n2
United Nations Security Council Resolution 112
United Nations Treaty System 25
United States 8–9, 18; refugee vulnerability in 135–6
Universal Declaration of Human Rights (UDHR) 40, 143n6
university students' unions 44
Uprising of Women in the Arab World 96
Urgent Protection Program (UPP) 133
Urquhart, Conal 103n24
U.S. American culture 5
U.S. American society 15
U.S. Citizenship and Immigration Services (USCIS) 135, 149n123
U.S. Department of State 149n122
U.S. global military policies 9
U.S. Guidance 115, 116
U.S. Immigration and Naturalization Service 122n46

Vallaud-Belkacem, Najat 166
Vick, Karl 152n175
Vojdik, Valorie K. xvin4, xxi, 120n4, 121n42, 123n80
Volpp, Leti 138, 150n35

Weber, Max 58–60, 71, 82n3, 83n6
Weis, Paul 146n48
Welle, Deutsche 145n34
West Bank 26, 27, 35, 37, 41
Western Christian culture 17
Western feminist discourses 7
Western hegemony 9
Western patriarchy 70
whiteness 17
Wing, Adrien K. xxi
Women Against the Wall 99
Women and Girls at Risk 133
women and race 7–8
Women, Race and Class (Davis) 7
womens economic rights 36
Womens Refugee Project 115
womens rights 25
Womens Wall Defense Committee 99
women wearing hijab 9–10; cultural sniping 10–13; harassment 13–15; hate crimes 15–16
workplace 80–1
World War II (WWII) 131

The Year of the Elephant 69
Yemen 4
Yogev, Abraham 78
youth observations of harassment 13–15

zaouias (Islamic *fiqhic* schools) 67
Zard, Monette 140
Zayat, Iman 50n106